India
Goes Global

Its Expanding Role in the World Economy

Catriona Purfield
Jerald Schiff
Editors

INTERNATIONAL MONETARY FUND

Production: IMF Multimedia Services Division
Cover design: Massoud Etemadi and Jorge Salazar
Cover photograph: Pablo Bartholomew/Netphotograph.com
Typesetting: Bob Lunsford
Figures: Jason Soleil

Cataloging-in-Publication Data

India goes global: its expanding role in the world economy / Catriona Purfield, Jerald
   Schiff, editors—[Washington, D.C.]: International Monetary Fund, 2006.

   p. cm.

   ISBN 1-58906-568-9

   1. India—Economic conditions. 2. India—Economic policy. 3. Banks and
banking—India. 4. Fiscal policy—India. 5. Textile industry—India. I. Purfield,
Catriona. II. Schiff, Jerald Alan. III. International Monetary Fund.
HC433.I54 2006

Price: $22.00

Please send orders to:
International Monetary Fund, Publication Services
700 19th Street, N.W., Washington D.C. 20431, U.S.A.
Telephone: (202) 623-7430   Telefax: (202) 623-7201
E-mail: publications@imf.org
Internet: http://www.imf.org

recycled paper

Contents

The following conventions are used in this publication:

- In tables, a blank cell indicates "not applicable," ellipsis points (. . .) indicate "not available," and 0 or 0.0 indicates "zero" or "negligible." Minor discrepancies between sums of constituent figures and totals are due to rounding.

- An en dash (–) between years or months (for example, 2005–06 or January–June) indicates the years or months covered, including the beginning and ending years or months; a slash or virgule (/) between years or months (for example, 2005/06) indicates a fiscal or financial year, as does the abbreviation FY (for example, FY2006).

- "Billion" means a thousand million; "trillion" means a thousand billion.

- "Basis points" refer to hundredths of 1 percentage point (for example, 25 basis points are equivalent to ¼ of 1 percentage point).

As used in this publication, the term "country" does not in all cases refer to a territorial entity that is a state as understood by international law and practice. As used here, the term also covers some territorial entities that are not states but for which statistical data are maintained on a separate and independent basis.

Preface

The team at the IMF that has worked on this book has been extremely fortunate to be involved with India precisely as it emerged as a global economic power. In the last several years, India has opened itself to the global economy and become one of the world's fastest growing economies, the leading outsourcing destination, and a favorite of international investors. At the same time, India faces daunting challenges as it seeks to continue to integrate with the world economy, sustain rapid growth, and improve the well-being of all its citizens. The studies in this book document and analyze India's impressive achievements, while examining the important and difficult steps that remain to consolidate and build on these gains. It is our hope that these studies can contribute to the vibrant public debate—both within India and outside—on the direction of economic policy in India.

This book grew out of the IMF staff's ongoing policy dialog with the Indian authorities, in particular at the Ministry of Finance and the Reserve Bank of India. The focus of several chapters was suggested by officials from these agencies, while other chapters benefited from a stimulating exchange of views as well as specific comments and suggestions made by the staff of the Reserve Bank and Ministry of Finance on earlier drafts. The Office of the Executive Director for India at the International Monetary Fund, headed by B.P Misra, has been instrumental in facilitating this dialog while providing helpful input into our work. Wanda Tseng, Deputy Director of the IMF's Asia and Pacific Department, who has led the department's work on India for several years, provided critical intellectual leadership for the project. Rabin Hattari, Yuko Kobayashi, and Nong Jotikasthira provided outstanding research and administrative assistance. Esha Ray provided invaluable support in editing the book and coordinating its production.

The opinions expressed here are those of the authors and do not necessarily reflect the views of the Indian authorities, the IMF, or IMF Executive Directors.

Abbreviations

AETR	Average effective tax rate
ASEAN	Association of South East Asian Nations
ATC	Agreement on Textiles and Clothing
BPO	Business process outsourcing
CAR	Capital adequacy ratio
CIT	Corporate income tax
CPI	Consumer price index
CSO	Central Statistical Organisation
CST	Central sales tax
CV	Coefficient of variation
ECB	External commercial borrowing
EPW	*Economic and Political Weekly*
EREER	Equilibrium real effective exchange rate
ETE	Export tax equivalent
EU	European Union
FDI	Foreign direct investment
FICCI	Federation of Indian Chambers of Commerce and Industry
FII	Foreign institutional investor
FIPB	Foreign Investment Promotion Board
FRBMA	Fiscal Responsibility and Budget Management Act
FRL	Fiscal responsibility legislation
G-5	Group of Five
G-7	Group of Seven
GDP	Gross domestic product
GNI	Gross national income
GMM	Generalized method of moments
GSDP	Gross state domestic product
GST	Goods and services tax
GTAP	Global Trade Analysis Project
ICRIER	Indian Council for Research on International Economic Relations
IFS	*International Financial Statistics*
ISP	Internet service provider
IT	Information technology
LIBOR	London interbank offered rate
METR	Marginal effective tax rate

METW	Marginal effective tax wedge
MFA	Multifiber Arrangement
NBFC	Nonbank financial company
NFA	Net foreign assets
NPA	Nonperforming asset
NPL	Nonperforming loan
NSDP	Net state domestic product
NSSO	National Sample Survey Organisation
OECD	Organization for Economic Cooperation and Development
OLS	Ordinary least squares
PIT	Personal income tax
PLR	Prime lending rate
PPP	Purchasing power parity
RBI	Reserve Bank of India
REER	Real effective exchange rate
SME	Small and medium-sized enterprise
T&C	Textiles and clothing
TFC	Twelfth Finance Commission
UN	United Nations
UNCTAD	United Nations Conference on Trade and Development
VAT	Value-added tax
VECM	Vector error correction model
WDI	*World Development Indicators*
WTO	World Trade Organization

1

Opening Its Doors: India's Emergence on the Global Stage

JERALD SCHIFF

There can be little doubt that India is an emerging global economic power. India's economic growth has averaged some 8 percent over the past three years, placing it among the world's fastest growing economies. As a result of more than a decade of solid growth, India's share of world output, at purchasing-power-parity-adjusted exchange rates, has increased from 4.3 percent in 1990 to 5.9 percent in 2005. Growth has been robust in the face of shocks, including the Asian crisis of 1997–98, several below-par monsoons, and the recent sharp increases in energy prices. In line with good growth, poverty has declined dramatically, with estimates indicating a drop in the poverty rate from 41 percent in 1992–93 to less than 29 percent in 2000. The reform process that has helped make this possible—and which began in earnest in 1991—has made steady progress despite several changes in political leadership. Looking ahead, it appears that the broad path of reform—although not the pace or details—is firmly established. And success begets success. India is now more than ever a focus for international investors, who are eager to take part in a new India.

India's recent rapid development has gone hand in hand with a marked opening of its economy. Tariffs have come down dramatically in the last decade, while capital account restrictions are being gradually lifted. During 2003/04–2004/05 India's imports (including services) rose by 39 percent a year, twice as fast as in 1990–2002, buoyed by strong investment and consumer demand. Exports grew by 37 percent a year, up from 18 percent growth in 1990–2002, as India benefited from the commodity boom and

1

expanded into engineering goods, pharmaceuticals, and business services. There is also some evidence that India is increasingly tied into regional production processes, with Asia's share in Indian imports rising steadily and with Asia becoming a major destination for India's exports. Intra-industry trade with China, in particular, is rising rapidly helping plug India into global production networks. India is also integrating into global financial systems and has benefited from rapidly rising capital inflows, including into the Indian stock market.

Reflecting these developments, India is playing a more important role in the global economy. A few examples only hint at the changes:

- India contributed nearly one-fifth of Asian domestic demand growth over 2000–05. Looking forward, India is slated to be the second-largest demand driver in the region, after China.
- India accounts for almost one-quarter of the global portfolio flows to emerging market economies, nearly $12 billion in 2005.
- India is the world's leading recipient of remittances, accounting for about 20 percent of global flows.
- India is the world's leading outsourcing destination and is fast emerging as a top 10 tourism destination.
- Indian corporates are emerging as key players in their own right. Reliance owns one of the largest refineries in the world, while Tata Steel is among the most efficient producers in the world. Indian firms, in industries including steel and oil, are looking abroad to acquire assets. And Indian corporates are increasingly carrying out their own research and development. In 2004 alone, Indian pharmaceutical companies filed about 200 patents.

India's demographics underline the potential for an extended period of rapid economic growth. India is an extremely young country, and is one of the few large countries forecast to sustain a growing labor force over the next 40 years (Figure 1.1). Estimates point to between 75 million and 110 million entrants to the labor force over the next decade, with the obvious potential to raise the economic output of the country and underpin India's competitiveness. Also, because working-age people tend to have a higher propensity to save, India should benefit from a favorable saving trend that will help finance investment and fuel rapid growth.

Opportunities, but Challenges as Well

While India is poised for economic takeoff, continuing success is by no means assured. India's development path thus far has been considerably

Figure 1.1. Working Age Population
(In percent of total)

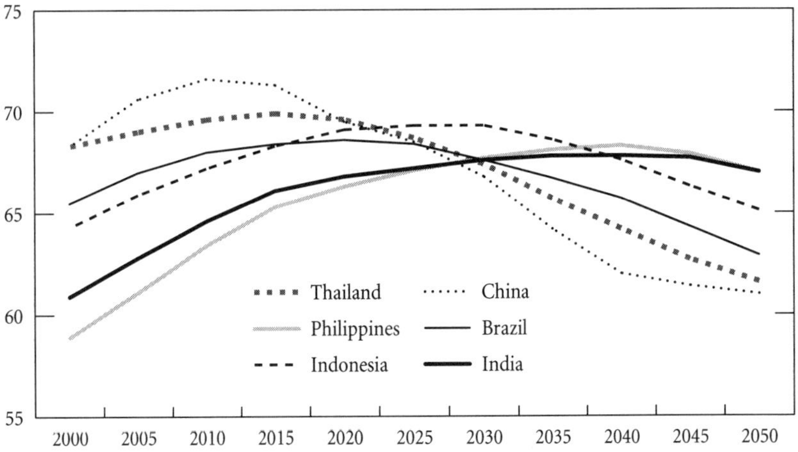

Source: United Nations, Population database.

different from those of Japan, China, Korea, and the other "Asian tigers" in previous decades. And some of these differences present unique challenges to the country as it moves forward.

Growth in India has been led by services rather than manufacturing. While India's role as an information technology (IT) provider has been well documented, and is a major growth engine for the country, more rapid development of the manufacturing sector will be needed to generate the sort of lower-skilled jobs that can serve as a ladder out of poverty for many. The current employment elasticity of growth in India implies that a 5 percent rise in real GDP leads to only a 2½ percent rise in employment, and unless this is raised substantially, the large number of new workers can become a massive problem for India rather than a boon. India has the potential to be a manufacturing giant, but needs to remove the considerable roadblocks that industry still faces—notably poor infrastructure, rigid labor laws, and relatively inhospitable business and regulatory environments. Moreover, the reliance on services growth implies a need for a large pipeline of well-trained engineers and scientists, which may not be forthcoming without significant reform of higher education.

Second, in contrast to most other Asian economies, almost two-thirds of the population still derives its income from agriculture. While this reflects in part the limited supply of manufacturing jobs, high levels of illiteracy and extreme poverty in rural areas also mean that individuals may lack information about employment opportunities or the means to move elsewhere. A large share of the population relies on subsistence agriculture, and farming remains heavily rain-dependent, with irrigation lacking in many areas. The high correlation between agricultural growth and rainfall in India (about 0.65), illustrates the dependence of growth on rainfall. For India to achieve and sustain the sort of high growth it is targeting—in the range of 8–10 percent a year—productivity in agriculture needs to be raised, but agricultural workers also need to be provided with the basic tools and opportunities to move to new jobs in manufacturing.

Third, India's fiscal deficit and debt remain large, constraining its ability to act in key areas. With general government deficits still in excess of 7 percent of GDP and government debt above 85 percent of GDP, the government's ability to meet the many urgent needs of its population—notably in rural and urban infrastructure, education, and health care—will depend on its success in raising additional revenues without choking off economic growth and limiting inefficient and low-priority spending. The infrastructure gap remains large with inadequate roads, ports, airports, and power increasingly constraining India's potential growth (Figure 1.2).

Finally, India remains—despite its ongoing reforms—a relatively closed economy. Even though India has received much attention for its role as an outsourcing destination, trade linkages remain comparatively weak. Trade is low when compared to that of other Asian countries that pursued more export-driven growth strategies. India still only accounted for about 1½ percent of the global trade in goods and services in 2005. Although trade with other emerging countries in Asia has expanded rapidly, India's participation in global production chains, while growing, is in its infancy. While the share of intra-industry trade in East Asia trade rose to 75 percent in 1996–2000 from 42½ percent in 1986–90 (Zebregs, 2004), it only rose to 18 percent from 12 percent between 1992 and 2001 in India (Cerra, Rivera, and Saxena, 2005). As emphasized throughout this volume, the authorities will need to continue to open the economy to take full advantage of globalization and ensure that India reaches its full growth potential.

The Indian authorities are well aware of the challenges they face and are moving to address them. For example, trade tariffs have been coming down for a decade—most recently in the context of the 2006/07 budget—and there are plans to bring these down further to levels of member countries of the Association of South East Asian Nations (ASEAN)—around 8 percent on average—by 2009. India is also active in bilateral and regional trade liberalization, with the South Asia Free Trade Agreement to begin in 2007, and with ongoing discussions with Mercosur, ASEAN, and China, among others. In addition, capital controls on foreign direct investment (FDI) in India and external commercial borrowing by domestic firms are

Figure 1.2. Measures of Infrastructure Access

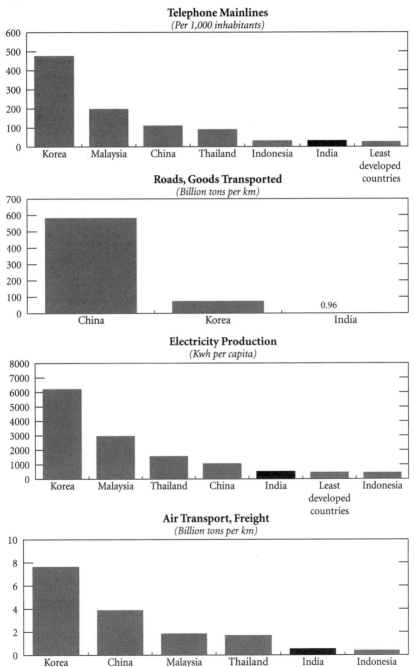

Source: World Bank, World Development Indicators database.

being eased, while the emergence of world-class Indian corporates is being encouraged by the progressive lifting of controls on outward investments. In addition, India has made improving its infrastructure its top priority. A start has been made in creating the fiscal space for greater public investment, and creating a favorable regulatory environment for private infrastructure investment, but the process has only just begun.

In other areas, progress is proving more difficult. The typical political constellation in India—a coalition government at the center and powerful governments pursuing their own agendas at the state level—has made it particularly difficult to overcome vested interests and introduce difficult structural reforms. For instance, privatization of state-owned commercial enterprises has stalled in recent years, forgoing large potential improvements in productivity. Broad labor reforms have faced strong opposition, limiting employment gains. And the inability to fundamentally reform food, fertilizer, and petroleum subsidies has meant that fiscal space for high-priority spending remains limited and incentives for farmers to diversify production and raise exports are muted.

But why quibble with what, by any measure, has been impressive success in recent years? Well, there are actually several reasons.

- *The consequences for India of a move from good growth to one of very rapid sustained growth is potentially enormous.* At 6 percent annual growth, average incomes will double in about 12 years, while at 10 percent it would take just 7 years. The impact of such a development on the living standards of the average Indian would be dramatic. By 2018, an estimated 191 million people would be pulled out of poverty under the high-growth scenario, nearly double that under the lower-growth outcome, and millions of additional people would be pulled into the burgeoning middle class.

- *It is critical that the current optimism in and about India does not morph into complacency.* It is important to remember that India has experienced previous rounds of rapid growth—the mid-1990s come immediately to mind—which were not sustained. The current economic renaissance is a reflection of 15 years of reforms, and continued strong growth will need to be infused by more such reforms. Macroeconomic sustainability—while not currently a major worry—also remains an issue. A period of robust growth in the 1980s was brought to a halt in large part by high fiscal deficits and macroeconomic imbalances and with fiscal deficits still high, India cannot be considered out of the woods in this regard.

- *Policies need to ensure that reform and growth are politically and socially sustainable.* As the 2003 national elections underscored, reforms leading to rapid growth—but which are not seen as promoting equitable sharing of the benefits from that growth—may not receive the public support necessary to ensure their completion. The reform process thus far has not eliminated the sense that there are two Indias. Poverty remains high—almost one-third of Indians live on less than a dollar a day—regional disparities are growing, and the rapidly expanding working population will need jobs. While high-tech centers generate worldwide notice and have contributed to the growth of the middle class, they remain a small enclave. It is critical that poverty reduction, already proceeding at a rapid rate, be accelerated and that poor states and regions be brought on board.

This book, then, appears at an opportune time. Are we seeing the first years of a "Golden Age" for India? Or is this another period of strong, but ultimately unsustainable, growth. Prime Minister Singh put the choice clearly in a speech in 2005, "We must think big and bold. We must move away from the paradigm of incremental growth to a paradigm of exponential growth and growth into uncharted territory." He stressed that success stories from both the public and private sectors should be replicated so that more and more Indian firms can "go global." In this book, we look more closely at that paradigm of exponential growth and at what an India that goes more fully global would like look.

A Global India: The Policy Agenda

Perhaps the best way to begin a discussion of India's economic policies in a new globalized environment is to look at what has worked thus far. In this regard, India's states—with a wide range of demographic characteristics and economic policies and outcomes—can serve as a useful "laboratory." Chapter 2 examines the determinants of the disparate economic outcomes across states, both to draw implications for policy and to assess whether poor states are catching up or being left behind. Among the key findings: the gap between rich and poor states is widening, with richer and faster growing states also more effective at generating jobs and reducing poverty. Much of this difference reflects policy choices. In particular, states that encourage private investment, limit the size of government, and focus on improving institutions see a large payoff.

With India embarked on a seemingly irreversible opening to the global economy, it is presented with important new opportunities. Policies must be directed at ensuring that India—and the broad cross-section of Indian citizens—grasps these opportunities. Chapter 3 focuses on one aspect of this effort to maximize gains from globalization: the nexus between India's increased openness to trade and the opening of its capital account. Trade and capital account liberalization have been gradual processes in India, with beneficial effects on productivity, growth, and inflation. The chapter finds, moreover, that the opening to trade and capital have been mutually reinforcing. For instance, FDI has brought with it imports from the home country as well as technological know-how and an increased capacity to export, while easing restrictions on external borrowing has raised trade by lowering borrowing costs for Indian corporates. Increased trade, in turn, has raised the demand for the hedging opportunities and financial deepening that capital account liberalization can bring. With a good deal still to accomplish to complete India's integration with the world economy, sequencing of remaining steps will need to be closely considered to maximize these synergies.

With lowered barriers to trade, it will be increasingly important that policies aim at enhancing competitiveness. In this context, Chapter 4 looks closely at the state of India's competitiveness, noting that India's export performance has been solid and that India has made significant inroads in gaining market share, both in Asia and in new markets, such as Africa. However, export performance would be greatly enhanced with improved infrastructure, lower tariffs, and a more friendly business environment. An important finding is that the exchange rate is not a bar to competitiveness, with no evidence that the rupee is fundamentally misaligned. Continued exchange rate flexibility would, then, be a key to ensuring that India can continue to enhance its global competitiveness.

Capital account liberalization has allowed India to attract large portfolio flows, but reforms are needed to raise FDI, which remains a disappointment. FDI can bring with it—in addition to increased capital—cutting-edge technology and managerial know-how. But India is not fully reaping these benefits. In 2003, the stock of FDI to India totaled just 5 percent of GDP compared, for example, to 31 percent for Thailand and 35 percent for China. But the most striking fact is that, at the same time that FDI lags, surveys consistently point to India as one of the top two or three destinations for FDI in the coming years. So, the opportunity is there for the taking. In this context, Chapter 5 examines the reasons behind India's relatively poor performance in attracting FDI. The analysis suggests that while sectoral restrictions on FDI have played some role, India's FDI regime is not overly restrictive by international standards. Rather, what is mainly holding back FDI is broader difficulties of doing business. A few statistics serve to define the problem: to start a business in Korea takes 22 days and in China 41. But in India, it takes 89 days. And enforcing a contract takes 425 days in India, more than five times longer than Korea and nearly double that in China. Addressing such bottlenecks—along with closing India's infrastructure gap—should make India one of the primary FDI destinations in the world in the coming years.

In opening itself to the global economy, a healthy and vibrant financial sector is becoming a pillar of India's development. Recent growth in India has been accompanied by increased lending and, while rapid credit growth poses some potential risks, the financial sector has become increasingly healthy. With this sound base, the authorities are now looking for ways to continue to deepen financial intermediation. Chapter 6 addresses these issues, examining how India can develop a world-class financial sector. The chapter notes that, despite recent rapid growth, the credit-to-GDP ratio and the public's access to banking services remain low and the banking system is dominated by less efficient public sector banks. Development could be spurred by allowing more private ownership in the banking system—domestic as well as foreign—eliminating structural constraints to lending to small enterprises and agriculture, and continuing to strengthen prudential oversight.

Fiscal reform—a long-standing concern—becomes all the more important in a global India. Despite recent progress, India's high fiscal deficits and heavy debt burden remain a barrier to more rapid sustained growth. Tax and expenditure reform will be needed to create space for infrastructure investment and social spending, and facilitate private investment. It is estimated that infrastructure spending needs to rise by some 3 percent of GDP a year for India to maintain its current growth performance. Also, the government aims to double spending on health and education over the medium term, a potential rise of another 3–4 percent of GDP. Moreover, with private investment on the rise, crowding out is increasingly a concern, as corporate and small business borrowers come face-to-face with the government's still large financing needs.

As discussed in Chapter 7, India's federal system has tended to complicate efforts at fiscal adjustment. India's states undertake more than half of general government expenditure and account for roughly half of the general government deficit that stands—even after several years of adjustment—in excess of 7 percent of GDP. Moreover, India's states have been more reliant on resources transferred from the center and have faced less stringent borrowing constraints than state-level governments in many other countries, contributing to fiscal indiscipline. With the 2005/06 budget, the central government has sought to address these issues. As the chapter points out, the reforms—including harder budget constraints on states and more conditionality on transfers—move in the right direction. But more needs to be done—a number of states will likely remain in a vulnerable position for some time to come, making it difficult for them to meet their objectives for higher spending on infrastructure, health care, and education.

As the government's overall spending needs are unlikely to decline for some time, tax reform, examined in Chapters 8 and 9, will be a key to addressing fiscal issues. Chapter 8 finds that, while India's tax collections are broadly in line with countries at a similar stage of development, they lag well behind those of more advanced emerging market economies. The chapter lays out a strategy for reform that could generate revenues equal to about 4 percentage points of GDP, solely via base broadening. Chapter 9 analyzes the scope for such base broadening to stimulate growth by generating efficiency gains in investment. Combined, the two chapters deliver the message that fiscal adjustment in India can, if done right, be very much pro-growth and pro-poor.

Cases in Point: Services and Textiles

India's booming services sector provides eloquent testimony to its ability to thrive with globalization. Chapter 10 examines the rapid growth in services, finding that liberalization has been a driving factor behind this growth. The ability of India to compete on the global stage is amply illustrated by the boom in IT. While a rising home-grown demand is playing some role in the IT sector's growth, the story is overwhelmingly one of India competing—and winning—in the globalized economy. The exports of the Indian IT sector grew by an estimated 32 percent in 2005/06 following similar robust growth the previous year. With Indian firms exporting services ranging from call centers to medical diagnostics to tutoring of American high school students, India's position of world leadership in IT is well known. And the IT success story is largely one of private sector initiative, with the government stepping back and focusing on providing an enabling environment.

If the growth of the IT sector underlines India's potential, the experience of the textile industry also points to the unfinished nature of the reform process. Chapter 11 examines the likely impact of the recent lifting of quotas on textiles and clothing, which provides an excellent example of the opportunities and challenges facing India. India has a centuries-old tradition of producing textiles admired around the world. Also, Indian exports were constrained by quotas before 2005, pointing to the potential for large gains with their elimination. However, performance in the textile industry in the past year has been decidedly mixed—India has gained market share, in particular in the key U.S. market, but has done so to a much lesser degree than China. And even these gains may be at risk once China's voluntary quota agreements with the United States and the European Union lapse. As the chapter makes clear, both improved infrastructure and removal of a number of structural barriers—including rigid labor laws—will be needed for India to repeat the success it has achieved in services.

Epilogue: An Engine for Global Growth?

With India seeking to strengthen global linkages, it should begin playing a significantly bigger role in the world economy. India's role as an engine for global growth has been limited by the still relatively closed nature of its economy. Even so, given its sheer size, a sustained takeoff in India can have a substantial impact in Asia and the rest of the world. More to the point, over the next five years, Indian exports are expected to more than double while imports will nearly triple. Moreover, with a rising working-age population over the next 40 years, long-term growth prospects should receive a further boost. Should India succeed as expected, new and improved Indian firms as well as a huge new middle class of several hundred million consumers will be unleashed on the global economy, with a major impact on world trade, prices, and growth. As India's manufacturing sector and exports become more competitive, it will present a major challenge for its neighbors. But a prosperous and outward-looking India would present even more opportunities for Asia and the world.

References

Cerra, Valerie, Sandra A. Rivera, and Sweta Chaman Saxena, 2005, "Crouching Tiger, Hidden Dragon: What Are the Consequences of China's WTO Entry for India's Trade?" IMF Working Paper No. 05/101 (Washington: International Monetary Fund).

Zebregs, Harm, 2004, "Intraregional Trade in Emerging Asia," IMF Policy Discussion Paper No. 04/1 (Washington: International Monetary Fund).

2

Is Economic Growth Leaving Some States Behind?

CATRIONA PURFIELD

Despite India's recent strong economic performance there is a growing concern that growth has benefited India's richer states, leaving the poorer states lagging further and further behind. As India's poorest states are also its most populous, one concern is that unless these states begin to share in the benefits of growth, an increasing proportion of the population will be left in poverty and subject to rising inequality, leading to social, political, and economic difficulties. Moreover, as many perceive that globalization and economic liberalization contributed to this state of affairs, economic divergence could erode support for further economic reform and opening of the Indian economy. These concerns gain even greater traction when one considers that about 60 percent of the forecast 620 million increase in the Indian population between now and 2051 is expected to occur in three of its poorest states: Bihar, Madhya Pradesh, and Uttar Pradesh (Visaria and Visaria, 2003).

A rich literature uses state data to test whether growth in regions within India has converged or diverged over time. However, as is often the case in such studies, the results for India are conflicting. For example, Cashin and Sahay (1996) and Aiyar (2001) find evidence of convergence after controlling for differences in initial economic conditions, but Rao, Shand, Kalirajan (1999), Bajpai and Sachs (1996), and Sinha and Sinha (2000) find divergence. Aiyar (2001) also observes that education and investment helped to reduce cross-state income divergence, while Cashin and Sahay (1996) found fiscal transfers were a significant equalizing force.

Various studies have also made opposing claims about the impact of the globalization and economic reform post-1991 on income convergence, although few have conducted rigorous statistical tests of this hypothesis. Bhattacharya and Sakthivel (2004) and Kumar (2004) assert that the reforms of the 1990s exacerbated the gap between richer and poorer states, while Ahluwalia (2002) claims that reforms in the 1990s helped reduce the gap. In light of the wide range of evidence, this chapter seeks to shed light on the debate by asking two related questions. First, have poorer states in fact fallen further behind richer states, particularly since the 1990s? Second, why have certain states performed better than others? If state-level economic policies have an impact on growth, better policies could help laggard states catch up. This chapter first presents stylized facts about growth across Indian states and then assesses empirically the question of convergence and the impact of state policy on growth and poverty before drawing conclusions.

Stylized Facts About Growth in India

The disparity in economic conditions across Indian states is large and growing (Table 2.1). Over the past three decades, the ranking of states by income into poor, medium, and rich has changed remarkably little and although poverty has declined, it has become more spatially concentrated. We highlight five key facts about the pattern of development across states.

Fact 1: The Gap Between Income Levels Across States Is Widening

The gap in per capita income between the richer and poorer states has widened over the previous three decades.[1] Rich states have also grown over three times faster than poorer states so that by March 2004, the ratio of per capita income in the richest state (Punjab) to that in the poorest state (Bihar) had risen to 4.5 from 3.4 in 1970. There is also a strong correlation between the pace of growth and initial income levels. Dividing the sample into states that grew at rates above and below the national growth rate, we find that all of the poor states plus Kerala grew more slowly than the national average over the 1970–2004 period (Table 2.2). The rapidly growing states, which included mainly the middle-income states (Andhra

---

[1]Using net state domestic product (NSDP). Gross state domestic product (GSDP) was not available for all states for this time period.

Table 2.1. Then and Now: Summary Income, Growth, and Poverty Indicators, 1970–2004

Real Per Capita Net State Domestic Product, 2000–04 (In rupees)	Real Per Capita Income (In rupees) 2003–04	Income Rank in		Real Per Capita Income of Richest to Poorest (Ratio)		Real Per Capita Income Growth (In percent) 1970–2004	Population Growth Rate (In percent) 1970–2004	Head Count of Total Poverty (In percent)		Overall Literacy Rate (In percent)	
		1970–74	1990–94	1970–74	2000–04			2000	1977–78	2001	1973
Poorest states											
14 Bihar	3,553	14	14	1.0	1.0	1.9	1.4	46.9	61.6	47.5	23.4
13 Uttar Pradesh	5,702	13	12	1.8	1.5	1.4	2.1	33.0	49.1	57.4	26.9
12 Orissa	6,487	11	13	2.1	1.6	1.4	1.7	46.3	70.1	63.6	32.4
11 Madhya Pradesh	8,284	12	11	1.8	2.1	2.6	1.3	36.8	61.8	64.1	28.2
10 Rajasthan	8,571	9	9	2.3	2.2	1.5	2.7	20.4	37.4	61.0	23.9
Middle-income states											
9 Andhra Pradesh	11,333	10	8	2.2	2.9	3.1	1.8	18.8	39.3	61.1	29.8
8 West Bengal	11,771	8	10	2.4	2.9	2.9	1.9	32.1	60.5	69.2	40.6
7 Kerala	12,109	4	7	2.9	3.1	2.5	1.3	14.5	52.2	90.9	71.9
6 Karnataka	13,141	7	6	2.4	3.4	3.2	1.9	25.6	48.8	67.0	38.5
Richest states											
5 Tamil Nadu	12,976	6	5	2.8	3.5	2.8	1.4	21.5	54.8	73.5	47.1
4 Gujarat	16,779	5	4	2.8	3.9	3.2	2.1	15.6	41.2	66.4	43.7
3 Haryana	15,721	2	2	3.2	4.0	2.8	2.5	11.8	29.6	68.6	34.0
2 Maharashtra	16,050	3	3	3.1	4.1	2.9	2.4	28.7	55.9	77.3	47.6
1 Punjab	15,800	1	1	3.6	4.2	2.6	1.9	6.0	19.3	70.0	40.4
Fourteen major states											
Weighted average	10,410	...	...	2.5	2.6	2.3	1.9	...	...	...	...
National average	13,048	...	...	2.9	3.3	2.6	2.1	28.6	51.3	65.38	...
Standard deviation	5,415	...	...	0.67	1.05	0.67	0.44	11.51	11.57	10.36	13.27
Coefficient of variation	1	...	...	0.27	0.40	0.28	0.23	0.40	0.23	0.16	...

Sources: Economic and Political Weekly States database; and IMF staff calculations.

Table 2.2. Absolute Divergence in Growth Rates

States Classified by Real Per Capita Income in 1970	Average Growth in Real Per Capita Income				
	1970–2004	1970–79	1980–89	1990–99	2000–04
Poorest states	0.46	−3.4	1.9	2.9	1.8
Middle-income states	2.74	0.8	2.2	5.6	5.0
Richest states	2.68	3.0	4.3	3.3	4.5
1970–2004					
Fastest growing states	3.07	1.9	3.8	5.5	7.7
Slowest growing states	1.43	0.6	2.6	2.6	1.8
National average	2.61	0.2	3.4	3.5	4.4

Sources: IMF staff calculations; and Economic and Political Weekly States database.

Pradesh, West Bengal, and Karnataka) and the rich states (Gujarat and Maharashtra), grew over twice as fast as the slowly growing states.

Fact 2: Richer and Faster Growing States Are Generally Better in Reducing Poverty

A state's record in reducing poverty reflects both differences in the level of growth and in the effectiveness of this growth in reducing poverty.

Overall, growth in India has reduced poverty less than proportionately and there is huge variation across states in poverty-growth elasticities (Table 2.3). Notably, not only have richer states tended to grow more rapidly, but they have been about 50 percent more effective in reducing poverty than poorer states for each percentage point of growth. [2]

To evaluate more closely the relative importance of differences in growth rates and poverty-growth elasticities, the decline in the poverty head count ratio is expressed as:

$$p_{st} = \overline{\varepsilon}\overline{g} + \overline{g}(\varepsilon_s - \overline{\varepsilon}) + \overline{\varepsilon}_s (g_s - \overline{g}),$$

where p_{st} is the reduction in the poverty rate between 1977 and 2001 in a given state, s, $\overline{\varepsilon}$ is the average India poverty-growth elasticity, $\overline{g}$ is the average India growth rate, and ε_s and g_s are the state-specific average

---

[2] For each state, we run the following regression:

$$LNPOVERTY_{st} = \alpha + \beta_s LNGDP_{st} + \varepsilon_{st},$$

where $LNPOVERTY_{st}$ is the Deaton-corrected state poverty head count ratio from the National Sample Survey, t is time (within-sample years are extrapolated), and $LNGDP$ is real per capita NSDP. β is the elasticity.

Table 2.3. Cross-State Variation in Poverty-Growth Elasticities, 1977–2001[1]

	Poverty-Growth Elasticity (B) 1977–2001	Standard Errors	Contribution to Reduction in Poverty Rate of	
			State poverty-growth elasticity relative to India average	State growth rate relative to India average
Poorest states	−0.68			
Bihar	−0.43	0.05***	−0.41	−0.18
Orissa	−1.06	0.11***	0.45	−0.87
Uttar Pradesh	−0.68	0.08***	−0.07	−0.36
Madhya Pradesh	−0.39	0.05***	−0.46	−0.02
Rajasthan	−0.82	0.05***	0.12	−0.31
Middle-income states	−0.98			
West Bengal	−0.96	0.08***	0.31	−0.07
Andhra Pradesh	−0.80	0.06***	0.09	0.23
Kerala	−1.54	0.09***	1.09	−0.04
Karnataka	−0.63	0.04***	−0.15	0.15
Richest states	−1.02			
Tamil Nadu	−1.02	0.04***	0.39	0.16
Haryana	−0.73	0.15***	0.00	−0.03
Gujarat	−1.01	0.07***	0.38	0.05
Punjab	−1.68	0.13***	1.30	−0.32
Maharashtra	−0.62	0.05***	−0.15	0.01
National average	−0.73	0.03***		
Coefficient of variation	−0.51			

Source: IMF staff calculations.

[1]Head count poverty ratio regressed on real per capita net state domestic product. White-corrected heteroskedasticity errors. All variables are in logs. *** implies significance at the 1 percent level, ** at the 5 percent level, and * at the 10 percent level.

poverty-growth elasticity and growth rates. The first term measures the average reduction in poverty, the second differences across states in the effectiveness of growth in reducing poverty, and the third differences in growth rates across states. Terms two and three can be used to classify states according to the relative importance of the pace of growth and the effectiveness of this growth in reducing poverty.

States in the upper left-hand corner of Table 2.4 have the best of both worlds: growth in these states was faster than the Indian average and was effective in reducing poverty. In contrast, states in the lower right-hand corner experienced below-average growth and its effectiveness in reducing poverty was less than average. However, Table 2.4 underscores that some fast growing states were not as effective as slower growing states in reducing poverty. The policies explored in the next section may also help explain why some states are more effective than others in reducing poverty.

Table 2.4. Ranking of States by the Sources of Poverty Reduction, 1977–2001

	High Growth[1]	Low Growth[1]
High poverty elasticity	Andhra Pradesh Gujarat Tamil Nadu	Kerala Orissa Punjab Rajasthan West Bengal
Low poverty elasticity	Karnataka Maharashtra	Bihar Haryana Madhya Pradesh Uttar Pradesh

Source: IMF staff estimates.
[1]Using gross state domestic product. Most recent poverty data available are from 2001.

Fact 3: Poor and Slower Growing States Generated Fewer Private Sector Jobs

While employment has risen across all states in the past three decades, the pace of job creation in middle- and high-income states far outstripped that of poorer states. India's poorest and most populous states where about 40 percent of the population live only account for one-quarter of organized sector employment in India, although the poor quality of employment data should be kept in mind.[3] While employment growth has in all states been driven by the public sector, the latter played a more crucial role in the poorer states where the private sector progressively shed jobs (Table 2.5).

States differ greatly in their ability to translate growth into jobs. Although puzzling for a labor-rich country, it has been well documented that growth in India has not been very job intensive—the national growth-employment elasticity for the organized sector is only 0.5. Moreover, poorer states have fared even worse than this. Notwithstanding this, Tables 2.6 and 2.7 show that high-growth states have generally been more successful in translating growth into jobs, which may also help explain why states such as Andhra Pradesh, Gujarat, and Tamil Nadu have made large inroads into poverty. However, it is also the case that some rapidly growing states (Madhya

[3]The organized or official sector comprises enterprises registered under the 1951 Industries Act and covers all enterprises that employed 100 workers or more and do not use electricity, or firms that employ 50 or more workers and use electric power. Organized employment accounts for about 10 percent of the labor force, so the analysis in this section should only be treated as indicative of broad trends in employment. However, formal sector employment may also be preferable, in a policy sense, to work in the unorganized sector, as it tends to offer higher wages.

Table 2.5. Structure of Employment in the Organized Sector[1]

	1970/71			2001/02			Annual Percentage Change			Employment Share 1970/71		Employment Share 2001/02	
	Public	Private	Total	Public	Private	Total	Public	Private	Total	Public	Private	Public	Private
	(In millions)									(In percent of total employment)			
Poorest states[2]													
14 Bihar	3.7	1.4	5.1	5.7	1.2	6.9	1.4	-0.4	1.0	74.9	25.1	83.3	16.7
13 Uttar Pradesh	0.8	0.4	1.2	1.4	0.3	1.6	1.9	-1.8	0.9	63.1	36.9	84.3	15.7
12 Orissa	1.4	0.5	1.9	1.7	0.5	2.2	0.7	-0.5	0.4	72.0	28.0	79.0	21.0
11 Madhya Pradesh	0.3	0.1	0.4	0.7	0.1	0.8	2.5	0.4	2.2	81.0	19.0	89.2	10.8
10 Rajasthan	0.8	0.2	1.0	1.0	0.2	1.1	0.8	-0.8	0.5	77.2	22.8	84.8	15.2
	0.5	0.1	0.6	1.0	0.2	1.2	2.3	2.7	2.4	81.3	18.7	79.3	20.7
Middle-income states[2]													
9 Andhra Pradesh	2.7	2.2	4.9	4.7	2.7	7.4	7.7	5.0	6.4	57.2	42.8	62.5	37.5
8 West Bengal	0.7	0.3	1.0	1.5	0.6	2.1	2.3	2.3	2.3	70.8	29.2	71.3	28.7
7 Kerala	1.1	1.2	2.3	1.5	0.7	2.3	1.1	-1.6	0.0	46.9	53.1	67.0	33.0
6 Karnataka[3]	0.3	0.4	0.7	0.6	0.6	1.2	2.3	1.2	1.8	44.2	55.8	52.8	47.2
	0.6	0.3	0.9	1.1	0.8	1.9	1.9	3.1	2.4	66.8	33.2	58.7	41.3
Richest states[2]													
5 Tamil Nadu	3.4	2.5	5.9	5.7	3.6	9.2	9.8	8.5	9.2	60.0	40.0	62.0	38.0
4 Gujarat	0.9	0.7	1.5	1.6	0.9	2.5	1.9	1.1	1.6	57.7	42.3	64.1	35.9
3 Haryana	0.5	0.5	1.0	0.8	0.7	1.6	1.6	1.5	1.5	52.3	47.7	53.6	46.4
2 Maharashtra	0.2	0.1	0.3	0.4	0.3	0.7	2.8	2.9	2.8	62.3	37.7	61.6	38.4
1 Punjab	1.5	1.2	2.6	2.2	1.4	3.6	1.3	0.6	1.0	56.1	43.9	61.4	38.6
	0.3	0.1	0.4	0.6	0.3	0.8	2.1	2.5	2.2	71.9	28.1	69.5	30.5
National average	10.7	6.7	17.5	18.8	8.4	27.2	1.8	0.7	1.4	61.1	38.4	69.0	31.0
Share of poorest states	34.6	20.7	29.1	30.3	14.4	25.4							
Share of middle-income states	25.2	32.7	28.0	25.1	31.8	27.2							
Share of richest states	31.5	37.2	33.5	30.3	42.1	34.0							

Source: Ministry of Labour.
[1]These states accounted for 90 percent of organized sector employment in 1970/71 and 86.5 percent in 2001/02.
[2]Simple average over each income group.
[3]1972/73.

Table 2.6. Cross-State Variation in Employment-Growth Elasticities, 1970/71–2001/02[1]

	Employment Growth Elasticity			Standard Errors		
	Total	Public	Private	Total	Public	Private
Poorest states[2]	0.65	0.77	0.13			
Bihar[3]	0.32	0.52	−0.46	0.06***	0.10***	0.08***
Orissa	1.41	1.62	0.18	0.20***	0.23***	0.13
Uttar Pradesh[3]	0.41	0.59	−0.16	0.08***	0.10***	0.06***
Madhya Pradesh[3]	0.28	0.31	0.10	0.09***	0.10***	0.05*
·Rajasthan	0.83	0.80	0.97	0.12***	0.11***	0.12***
Middle-income states[2]	0.44	0.51	0.37			
West Bengal	−0.10	0.22	−0.55	0.02***	0.07***	0.06***
Andhra Pradesh	0.68	0.69	0.65	0.05***	0.07***	0.04***
Kerala	0.45	0.59	0.31	0.09***	0.13***	0.06***
Karnataka	0.73	0.55	1.05	0.04***	0.06***	0.05***
Richest states[2]	0.58	0.61	0.55			
Tamil Nadu	0.49	0.55	0.39	0.05***	0.08***	0.03***
Haryana	0.78	0.84	0.69	0.07***	0.08***	0.07***
Gujarat	0.48	0.50	0.45	0.05***	0.07***	0.04***
Punjab	0.81	0.75	0.98	0.04***	0.05***	0.03***
Maharashtra	0.33	0.40	0.23	0.04***	0.05***	0.02***
National average	0.50	0.59	0.31	0.052***	0.075***	0.018***
Coefficient of variation	0.70	0.73	1.50			

Source: IMF staff calculations.
[1]Using employment in the organized sector. *** implies significance at the 1 percent level, ** at the 5 percent level, and * at the 10 percent level.
[2]Simple average across states in each income group.
[3]Regressions included a dummy variable to capture year when new state was formed.

Pradesh, Maharashtra, and West Bengal) have been less successful in generating job-intensive growth.

Fact 4: Capital and Labor Flows Do Little to Address Imbalances Across States

Economic activity is highly concentrated, and India's most populous states contribute less to output than their share in the population. The five poorest states with 40 percent of the population produce only one-quarter of total output. The richest five states, which are home to only about one-fourth of India's population, produce over 40 percent. There are also large geographical disparities in the sectoral distribution of economic activity. While about half of total agricultural value added in India is produced in the northern and central states, the coastal states of Maharashtra, Gujarat, and Tamil Nadu produced 40 percent of industrial and service

Table 2.7. Ranking of States by Sources of Employment Generation, 1970/71–2001/02

	High Growth	Low Growth
Total employment		
High employment elasticity	Andhra Pradesh	Orissa
	Haryana	Rajasthan
	Karnataka	
	Punjab	
Low employment elasticity	West Bengal	Bihar
	Gujarat	Kerala
	Madhya Pradesh	Uttar Pradesh
	Maharashtra	
	Tamil Nadu	
Private employment		
High employment elasticity	Andhra Pradesh	Rajasthan
	Gujarat	
	Haryana	
	Karnataka	
	Punjab	
	Tamil Nadu	
Low employment elasticity	Madhya Pradesh	Bihar
	Maharashtra	Kerala
	West Bengal	Orissa
		Uttar Pradesh

Source: IMF staff estimates.

sector output. Such disparities are not unusual. In fact, the concentration of economic activity observed in India is very similar to that observed by Easterly and Levine (2002) in the United States. The correlation between poverty and geographic location is also high. India's poorest states are mainly located in the central and northern regions, where the head count poverty ratios generally exceed 30 percent. Middle- and high-income states are located mainly in the coastal areas.[4]

One might expect that capital—and jobs—would tend to move to poorer states, attracted by a pool of low-paid or unemployed workers. However, the evidence shows that capital goes primarily to the richer states, exacerbating the plight of poor states. Using the stock of credit from scheduled commercial banks to proxy capital stock, we find that the five richest states received a disproportionate share of capital, about 55 percent of total stock.

---

[4]The correlation between the head count poverty rate and a dummy variable that is set equal to one if the state is located in the central and northern regions is 0.83. If the dummy variable is set to capture coastal states the correlation turns negative (–0.35).

Table 2.8. Interstate Migration, 1971–2000
(In percent)[1]

	Net Annual Migration Rate			
	1971	1981	1991	2000
Poorest states				
Bihar	–0.00112	–0.00105	–0.00030	–0.01862
Orissa	0.00036	0.00028	0.00060	0.00233
Uttar Pradesh	–0.00114	–0.00175	0.00250	–0.00458
Madhya Pradesh	0.00094	0.00028	0.00360	0.00651
Rajasthan	–0.00095	–0.00047	0.00350	–0.00351
Average	–0.00038	–0.00054	0.00198	–0.00358
Middle-income states				
West Bengal	0.00086	0.00057	0.00090	0.00623
Andhra Pradesh	–0.00035	–0.00029	0.00430	0.00035
Kerala	–0.00177	–0.00128	–0.00320	–0.00104
Karnataka	0.00035	0.00013	0.00090	–0.00434
Average	–0.00023	–0.00022	0.00073	0.00030
Richest states				
Tamil Nadu	0.00103	–0.00060	–0.00010	–0.00308
Haryana	0.00087	0.00069	–0.00040	0.03662
Gujarat	0.00034	0.00053	–0.00110	0.00857
Punjab	–0.00207	–0.00018	–0.00320	0.00827
Maharashtra	0.00181	0.00226	0.00570	0.02032
Delhi	0.02166	0.02293	. . .	. . .
Average	0.00394	0.00427	0.00018	0.01414

Sources: National Sample Survey Organisation (2001); and Cashin and Sahay (1996).
[1]Average annual net migration as a share of state population at the start of each decade.

The five poor states received only 15 percent.[5] Chapter 5 also shows that about half of total foreign direct investment (FDI) approvals in India go to five rich states.

Another possible mechanism for equilibrating incomes across states would be labor migration from poorer to richer states. In fact, labor in India does migrate to the richer states, but the overall level of labor mobility in India across state borders is very low and does little to assist the convergence process (Table 2.8). Only 6 percent of migration in rural areas and 20 percent of migration in urban areas occurred across state borders.[6] Net outward migration is highest from the northern and central states of Bihar, Uttar Pradesh, and Punjab. Delhi and the coastal states of Maharashtra and Gujarat are the prime migration destinations. India's

[5]Using the location where credit was disbursed may overstate the degree of spatial concentration if borrowers utilize the funds borrowed in financial centers, such as Mumbai, in a different state.
[6]Urban-to-urban and rural-to-urban each account for one-fifth of interstate migration.

Table 2.9. Volatility in Economic Growth

States Classified by Real Per Capita Income in 1970	Coefficient of Variation in Real Per Capita Income Growth				
	1970–2004	1970–79	1980–89	1990–99	2000–01
Poorest states	4.11	9.14	2.42	2.01	2.78
Middle-income states	2.92	7.58	1.80	1.23	0.74
Richest states	2.74	5.74	2.48	1.08	0.99
1970–2004					
Fastest growing states	3.38	7.46	2.75	1.50	1.23
Slowest growing states	1.89	4.91	1.02	0.84	0.96
National average	1.38	3.55	0.58	0.60	0.55

Sources: IMF staff calculations; and Economic and Political Weekly States database.

wealthiest states attracted about half of the total number of migrants during 1999–2000. However, limited cross-state migration is consistent with Cashin and Sahay (1996), who find that state-to-state migration in India is not very responsive to cross-state income differentials. The low level of cross-state migration may reflect language barriers and poverty, as poorer individuals may find it difficult to finance a move to a different state in the absence of family ties.

Fact 5: Growth Has Been the Most Volatile in the Poorest States

Individuals, in particular the poor, are vulnerable to large swings in income. In this context, a key fact is that growth has been the most volatile in the poorer states, and increasingly so since the early 1980s. This stands in marked contrast to the experiences of rich and middle-income states. However, Table 2.9 shows that the fastest growing states (the three middle-income and two high-income states) experienced greater volatility in growth rates than slower growing states, suggesting that despite experiencing temporary busts, on average, these states ended up with higher per capita incomes.[7]

In sum, the stylized facts in this section suggest that the income gap between richer and poorer states has widened. States differ greatly in their ability to attract investment and translate growth into more jobs and less poverty. In many ways, these findings contrast with those of the theoretical neoclassical convergence literature, which predicts that states that are

---

[7]Growth rates are averaged over five-year periods to help smooth cyclical fluctuations. The volatility in income growth between 1970 and 2004 was over three times the variation in cross-state incomes. The cross-sectional standard deviation averaged about 0.5 percentage points in the past three decades, but standard deviation over time averaged 1.6 percentage points.

initially poor should grow faster than richer ones, and that capital and labor will migrate to ensure convergence.[8] However, the concentration of economic activity across states may reflect other factors highlighted in the economic geography literature, such as locational advantages in terms of access to markets and supply sources (Redding and Venables, 2004), transport and congestion costs (Krugman, 1991), and scale economies and spillovers of knowledge and information (Fujita, Krugman, and Venables, 1999) that can lead to the agglomeration of economic activity. Moreover, the analysis also suggests that while high growth is generally associated with poverty reduction and job creation, growth alone is not enough to ensure good outcomes on these two fronts. We turn next to examine whether differences in economic policies across states affect economic performance.

Do Policies Matter?

There have been various attempts to assess econometrically whether differences in economic policies across states account for the differences in the pattern of state-level growth. Generally, states that liberalize factor markets and promote good institutions are found to have fared better than others. Besley and Burgess (2000, 2004) look at the impact of specific economic reforms on manufacturing and agricultural growth. They find that states that amended labor laws in favor of workers experienced lower growth in output, employment, investment, and productivity in the formal manufacturing sector and increases in urban poverty. In agriculture, states that amended land laws to encourage redistribution of land to laborers and the amalgamation of farms into viable units experienced higher investment, productivity, and output growth. Banerjee and Iyer (2005) use district-level data and find that areas in which proprietary land rights were historically given to landlords had significantly lower agricultural investments and productivity after independence than areas in which these rights were given to cultivators. Burgess and Pande (2004) noted that the Indian rural bank branch expansion program of 1977–90 significantly lowered rural poverty and increased nonagricultural output.[9] Kochhar and others (2006) found

[8]In a steady-state framework, per capita growth rates vary inversely with the distance a state is from its own steady-state level of growth. A poorer state with a relatively low capital-to-labor ratio should enjoy higher rates of return on capital and therefore high growth rates, as it converges to its steady state, assuming a constant returns to scale technology.

[9]Under this program, a commercial bank was granted permission by the Reserve Bank of India to open a branch in a location with one or more bank branches only if it opened four branches in locations with no bank branches.

that states with weaker institutions and poorer infrastructure experienced lower GDP and industrial growth, particularly in electricity- and infra-structure-intensive sectors. Surveys of over 2,000 business establishments across 20 states conducted by Indicus Analytics (2004) are also suggestive of a positive relationship between a state's economic policy environment and its growth performance.

To test this link more formally, we identify various time-series indicators of economic policy at the state level on the basis of the literature and the availability of data. The purpose is not to identify an exhaustive list of the determinants of growth or to rank the importance of each factor but rather to assess whether policies are linked with growth and whether they can account for the cross-state pattern of economic performance. In general, the real per capita growth rate of a state is related to two kinds of variables. The first type proxies initial economic conditions, such as the structure of a state's economy. In line with the convergence literature (Barro and Sala-i-Martin, 1999), the second group of policy variables reflects actions by the government or individuals that can have a direct effect on a state's steady-state or long-run level of per capita income. The extent of time-series data varies, but generally cover the 1973–2003 period with the exception of infrastructure where data are only available from the 1980s onward. The variables used in the analysis are described below and key correlations are illustrated in Figure 2.1.

Initial Conditions

- *Initial income.* If there is convergence, states with higher levels of income will tend to grow at a slower rate. The initial level of per capita income is measured using real NSDP and the coefficient on this variable is used to derive the rate of convergence.
- *Economic structure.* States whose economic structure is more biased toward agriculture are expected to grow more slowly reflecting the low productivity of the largely subsistence sector. The economic structure of a state is measured using the lagged ratio of agriculture and industry in a state's NSDP.

Policy Variables

- *Private investment/financial intermediation.* Absent national account data on capital stocks and investment by state, the real stock of private sector credit per capita is used as a proxy for capital investment. This variable also reflects the depth of financial intermediation. Levine,

Figure 2.1. State-Level Economic Growth and Changing Business Climate Indicators

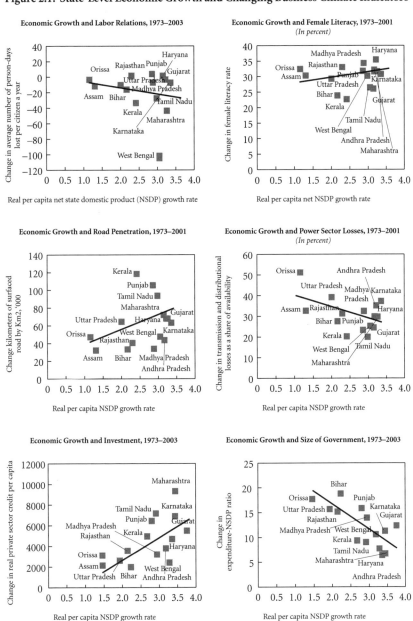

Sources: Besley and Burgess (2000 and 2004); Reserve Bank of India; Ministry of Power; Department of Road Transport and Highways; National Sample Survey Organisation; and IMF staff calculations.

Loayza, and Beck (2000) find robust evidence that financial development in general can foster faster long-run growth by ameliorating
information and transaction costs. Thus states with greater levels of
investment and/or more developed financial systems should experience a more rapid pace of growth.

- *Level and quality of human capital.* Following Barro and Sala-i-
Martin (1999), the stock of human capital is proxied using female
literacy rates.[10] Using female rather than overall literacy can also
serve as a crude proxy for the quality of education in a state, with
states that place greater emphasis on female literacy being viewed
as more progressive. Moreover, there are also numerous channels
through which female education can have an impact on the rate
of economic growth. Empirical studies show that the education of
mothers improves the education, nutrition, and health of their children. Education of women can improve the education prospects and
standards of the next generation. Thus, this variable serves both as a
control for differences in initial levels of human capital stock across
states—convergence suggests that states with initially high levels of
education would tend to experience lower growth rates—and the
dynamic impact of education on growth.

- *Size of government.* Cross-country studies of the determinants of
economic growth generally find that countries with smaller governments had better growth performance (e.g., Easterly and Levine,
2002). Here the size of government is measured using the ratio of
total state government expenditure to NSDP.

- *Industrial relations climate.* States facing fewer labor disputes are
likely to attract greater investment and this can spur growth. The
analysis uses the lagged number of person-days lost to strikes and
lockouts scaled by total organized sector employment to capture
such effects.

- *Reform of labor regulations.* State-level legislation that offers greater
protection of workers and curtails the flexibility of employers to hire,
fire, and organize their work practices may reduce productivity and
deter investment. Besley and Burgess (2004) construct a measure
that summarizes how industrial relations regulation in Indian states
changed between 1947 and 1992, and this measure is extended here
to include amendments implemented post-1992 reported in Malik
(2003). State-level amendments to the 1947 Industrial Disputes Act

---

[10]Using overall literacy rates in lieu of female literacy rates did not alter the results.

are coded so that pro-worker amendments receive a score of one, pro-employer amendments score minus one, and changes that are neutral score zero. The scores are then accumulated over time to give a continuous quantitative picture of how the labor relations environment evolved. The method classifies Andhra Pradesh, Karnataka, Kerala, Madhya Pradesh, Rajasthan, and Tamil Nadu as pro-employer states. Gujarat, Maharashtra, Orissa, and West Bengal are "pro-worker" states. India's six other large states did not implement any amendments to the Industrial Disputes Act over the period.

· *Infrastructure.* States with more extensive transport networks should be better able to facilitate economic activity and attract investors. The penetration of transport networks is measured as the number of kilometers of roads scaled by the area of the state. Likewise, states with better power networks, as measured by transmission and distributional losses of state electricity boards, should be more attractive investment locations. This variable has also been interpreted as a proxy of state reform credentials by Kochhar and others (2006), where improvements in this ratio reflect the willingness of state governments to control losses of power from their network because of theft and unwillingness to charge users.

In contrast to other studies, the use of time-series data on these variables allows the analysis to assess whether changes in policies in a given state, as well as differences in the policy environment across states, affected cross-state growth rates. Our richer database may account for differences in the findings with other studies such as Ahluwalia (2002) and Kochhar and others (2006), who rely on time-invariant or static measures of state institutions sampled at fixed points in time.

The econometric analysis utilizes a generalized method of moments (GMM) dynamic panel estimate to assess the relationship between policy and economic growth. The panel consists of data for India's 15 largest states for 1973/74–2002/03 averaged over six nonoverlapping five-year periods. The GMM estimator has the advantage that it allows past realizations of the dependent variable to affect its current level using lagged levels of the dependent and predetermined variables.[11] Time dummies are included to account for time-specific effects. Robust standard errors are reported.

The results of the analysis are summarized in Table 2.10. Specifications I and II examine the question of absolute convergence, namely whether

---

[11]Ordinary least square estimates are inconsistent in the presence of a lagged dependent variable and fixed effects.

Table 2.10. India: Determinants of State Real Per Capita Income

	Dependent Variable: Five-Year Average Real Per Capita NSDP, 1973/74–2002/03[1]				
	Absolute convergence		State policies and economic structure		
	Full sample		Full sample		Post-1990s
	I	II	III	IV	V
Constant	0.07**	0.03	0.08***	0.06***	1.18*
	(0.029)	(−0.0424)	(0.0131)	(0.0213)	(0.6965)
Initial conditions					
In initial real per capita income	0.59***	0.58***	0.42***	0.38***	0.08
	(0.218)	(0.208)	(0.160)	(0.082)	(0.088)
In initial real per capita income* post-1990s		0.02**			
		(0.009)			
In agriculture share of net state domestic product (NSDP) lagged			−0.18	−0.27***	−0.39*
			(0.069)	(0.069)	0.216
In industry share of NSDP lagged			−0.12*	−0.02**	−0.36***
			(−0.070)	(0.082)	(0.102)
Policy variables					
In investment			0.12**	0.09	0.12**
			(0.053)	(0.072)	(0.062)
In female literacy rate			−0.09	0.03	−0.09
			(0.061)	(0.059)	(0.104)
In size of government			−0.32***	−0.25***	−0.16
			(0.072)	(0.062)	(0.140)
In person-days lost to dispute per worker, lagged			−0.02*	−0.03***	0.06***
			(0.012)	(0.012)	(0.021)
Index of labor regulation, lagged			0.01***	0.01***	−0.01***
			(0.002)	(0.003)	(0.005)
Controls for state infrastructure					
Roads per km^2				0.00	
				(0.058)	
Transmission and distributional losses of electricity in percent of availability				−0.17***	
				(0.064)	
Convergence coefficient	0.01***	0.01***	0.02***	0.01***	0.16*
Half-life	49.0	112.5	44.8	61.6	4.4
Time controls	Yes	Yes	Yes	Yes	Yes
Serial correlation test (ρ value)	0.58	0.47	0.57	0.75	0.29
No. of observations	60	60	60	60	60

Source: IMF staff estimates.

[1]Robust standard errors are reported in parentheses. All variables, with the exception of the variable for labor regulation are in logs. *** implies significance at the 1 percent level, ** at the 5 percent level, and * at the 10 percent level.

poor states grow faster toward their steady state than richer states absent policy controls. Specification II interacts initial income with a post-1991 dummy variable to assess if convergence or divergence accelerated post-1991. Specifications III–V examine the relationship between growth and state-level policies. Specification III includes all those variables for which data are available from 1973/74 to 2002/03, specification IV adds indicators of infrastructure that are available over a shorter time span, while specification V assesses whether state-level policies mattered more for individual economic performance post-1991 by interacting the policy variables with the post-1991 dummy. In sum, the findings suggest the following:

- *Absolute convergence occurs very slowly.* The coefficient on lagged income in specifications I and II is significant and suggest that initially poor states grow faster than initially rich ones—so-called absolute convergence—absent controls for differences in policies and economic structure. However, the rate of convergence is only about 1½ percent a year, which implies that it takes almost 50 years to close half the gap (also known as the half-life) between any state's initial level of per capita income and its steady-state level of income. The coefficient on the interaction term for the post-1991 period suggests incomes continued to converge post-1991 but at an even slower pace than for the full period.

- *The differences observed in state incomes reflect wide gaps in their steady-state or long-run level of income.* Specifications III–V find evidence of conditional convergence. In other words, poor states grow faster than rich states once controls that proxy for differences in the policies and economic structure are held constant. But the convergence coefficient in specification III changes only marginally relative to specifications for absolute convergence and the pace of convergence is broadly in line with the findings from other international studies (see Box 2.1).[12] This suggests that differences in an individual state's steady-state or long-run income potentials—rather than specific policies—have been the main drivers of the disparities in growth performance observed in India since 1970. However, in specification V, the speed of conditional convergence increases sharply and the half-life is reduced to about 4½ years. This suggests that differences in policies implemented by states in the 1990s have became important determinants of a state's growth. This may reflect the fact that, with the move toward greater

---

[12]While the rate of convergence is close to that found by Cashin and Sahay (1996) for India in the 1960s–1980s, it is far lower than that reported by Aiyar (2001), who found convergence occurred at a rate of about 20 percent a year. The high convergence coefficient in the latter study is most likely the outcome of the fixed-effects estimator where inclusion of lagged dependent variables can result in upward bias (see Shioji, 1997, who demonstrates that fixed-effects estimates can be biased upward by between 7 percent and 15 percent; also see Islam, 1995).

Box 2.1. International Evidence on Regional Convergence

The speed of conditional convergence in incomes across Indian states mirrors that found by studies of regions in other industrial and emerging market economies. The speed of convergence across regions in developing countries or in panel data sets generally appear to be faster than that commonly found in studies of regions of industrial countries or across countries. For example, Barro and Sala-i-Martin (1991) and Sala-i-Martin (1996) show that the speed of convergence across the regions of the United States, Europe, and Japan is close to 2 percent. Islam (1995) finds that speeds of convergence across 97 countries range from 4 percent to 10 percent, depending on the method of estimation used. Canova and Marcet (1995) find that the speed of convergence across regions of Western Europe to be as high as 20 percent, whereas Caselli, Esquivel, and Lefort (1996) estimate a speed of convergence of about 13 percent a year across 97 different countries.

China. Jian, Sachs, and Warner (1996) examine convergence in incomes across China's provinces. They find only weak evidence of convergence during the central planning period (1952–65), and during the cultural revolution (1965–78) incomes across provinces diverged strongly. Convergence following the start of economic reforms in 1978 was most closely associated with rural reform, and was strong in coastal areas where trade and investment flows were liberalized. However, their study only extended to 1993 and toward the end of their sample there was some tendency toward divergence. Using a GMM estimator, Weeks and Yao (2003) show that China's provinces converged at a rate of only 0.4 percent a year in the 1953–77 period but in the postreform 1978–97 period convergence accelerated to 2.2 percent a year.

Korea. Koo, Kim, and Kim (1998) note that per capita incomes across Korea's 10 states converged between 1967 and 1992 at an annual rate of between

decentralization, a wider variety of policy approaches have been tried. Moreover, with greater openness to the global economy, good policies may be having a large potential payoff.

- *State-level policies have long-run growth effects.* Greater investment—as measured by the stock of real private credit per capita—leads to economic growth.[13] The quality of a state's infrastructure also appears to be an important determinant of growth. While specification II does not find any significant relationship between growth and road penetration, rising transmission and distributional losses in the electricity sector

---

[13]Since the GMM panel estimator controls for endogeneity, the findings suggest that the exogenous component of the relevant policy variable, take for example here investment, exerts a positive impact on economic growth.

4 percent and 6 percent. However, in two five-year subperiods between 1972 and 1982, income diverged because regions responded differently to the 1970s' oil price shocks. However, industrial policy promoted convergence during 1977–82. Migration was found to have little impact on regional convergence.

Latin America. In Brazil, Ferreira (1999) finds evidence of conditional convergence between 1939 and 1995 and estimates that by 1995 the income of a number of poor states was very close to their steady-state values, suggesting that looking forward large income disparities would remain across states. In Colombia, Cárdenas and Pontón (1995) determine a rate of convergence across Colombia's 22 departments between 1950 and 1990 of 4 percent a year without controls for initial conditions, and 5¼ percent a year if regional controls were included in the analysis. Labor migration did not play a large role in promoting convergence, except in the 1960s. Elías and Fuentes (1998) find evidence that rates of conditional convergence across regions were higher within Chile than in Argentina between 1960 and 1985. After controlling for differences in initial conditions, they estimate the rate of convergence in labor income to be 2 percent.

Spain. De la Fuente (2002) finds evidence that the speed of convergence across Spanish regions varied over time and was not necessarily fastest during periods of high national growth. Income per capita converged at an average annual rate of about 2½ percent between 1965 and 1975, slowed to about 1 percent during the crises of 1975–85, and fell to 0.4 percent between 1985 and 1995, at a time when Spain was growing faster than most industrial countries. The slowdown in the rate of convergence reflects lower employment generation and a fall in internal migration. Leonida and Montolio (2004) note that the convergence in incomes stalled in the 1980s but recommenced in the 1990s.

adversely affect a state's growth performance. On the other hand, the size of government adversely affects state-level growth suggesting that a shift in state spending from consumption to infrastructure investment could have a growth dividend. Specification V, which interacts the key policy variables with a post-1991 dummy, yields broadly similar results, although the increase in the magnitude of the coefficient on many of the policy variables suggests the policy environment of individual states became more important after 1991.

- *The impact of initial economic conditions can linger for long periods.* Specifications II–V find that states with a greater initial dependence on agriculture or industry grew more slowly.
- *It is difficult to disentangle the impact of labor market policies on growth.* Specifications III and IV suggest that, as expected, the number of

person-days lost to labor disputes in the preceding period had an adverse impact on growth. However, the result that states that enacted pro-worker legislation experienced a better growth performance is puzzling. This may be a product of the fact that legislative changes may be a poor proxy for actual labor market flexibility because some rapidly growing states have chosen to enforce loosely or even exempt firms from such provisions. In fact, the results on labor market conditions are driven by one outlier, West Bengal, a state which has been far more active than others in enacting pro-worker amendments to the Industrial Disputes Act but which has exempted many key sectors from such provisions. Once West Bengal is excluded, the coefficients on the two labor market variables become insignificant in all specifications.

- *Female literacy is not found to have a significant exogenous impact on states' growth performance.* In fact, the coefficient suggests a negative relationship with growth, a result that is shared with many other such studies in this field (see, for example, Barro and Sala-i-Martin, 1999, and Kalaitzidakis and others, 2001). Barro and Sala-i-Martin argue that female education is picking up standard conditional convergence effects whereby states with lower initial human capital grow faster given their greater distance to their steady state. Szulga (2005), on the other hand, argues that the estimate of the impact of female education on growth is biased because many educated females do not enter the labor force. Even when aggregate literacy levels are used in place of female education, human capital is again found to have a negative, albeit insignificant, effect on growth, a finding that is also confirmed by Islam (1995) in cross-country growth regressions.

In sum, the findings suggest that states can influence their relative growth performance by adopting better economic policies. A state can improve its long-run economic position by bringing about improvements in its investment, fiscal, and infrastructure policies. The results on the impact of state economic structure also point to a need in some poor performing states to diversify economic activity away from agriculture and industry and adopt policies that make these sectors more productive.

Conclusions

This chapter examined how growth and economic performance have varied across India's largest states over the past 30 years. It documented five stylized facts about their performance: (1) the gap in real per capita incomes between rich and poor states has widened over time; (2) rich and faster growing states have generally been more effective in reducing poverty; (3) poor and slower growing states have had very little success in generating private sector jobs; (4) labor and capital flows appear to do little to close the gap in incomes between poor and rich states; and (5) poor states experience the greatest volatility in economic growth.

This chapter then examined the link between state-level policies and economic growth. The econometric analysis presented evidence that state-level polices are a key factor influencing the pattern of economic growth across Indian states. Greater private sector investment, smaller governments, and better state-level institutions (as proxied by transmission and distributional losses of state electricity boards) are found to be positively associated with growth performance, but the impact of labor market policies are more difficult to discern. The historical structure of economic activity in a state also appears to matter for a state's subsequent growth performance. All this suggests that states can influence their relative growth performance and accelerate convergence through their policy choices.

Appendix. Data Description

State-level income data is derived from the Economic and Political Weekly States database and the Central Statistical Organisation. The sample of 15 states account for 95 percent of India's population and about 80 percent of its domestic product. Using these data we construct an annual series on real net state per capita incomes and the share of agriculture, industry, and services by splicing the three base year series on real NSDP to arrive at a series based in 1993/94 prices. In the absence of state-level aggregate investment or capital stock data, we utilize the stock of credit extended by scheduled commercial banks reported in the Reserve Bank of India's (RBI) Basic Statistical Tables from the banking system starting in 1973, translated into real terms using state-level NSDP deflators. Literacy rates are derived from various rounds of the National Sample Survey with intervening survey years constructed by linear extrapolation. Data on labor market regulation were provided by Tim Besley, and are available at http://sticerd.lse.ac.uk/eopp/research/indian.asp, and were updated using *Industrial Law* (Malik, 2003). Employment and labor disputes data were provided by the Ministry of Labour, as reported in the annual editions of the *Indian Labour Yearbook*. Electricity sector transmission and distribution losses as a percent of availability were derived from the

Annual Reports of State Electricity Boards available from the Ministry of Power and Planning Commission (see http://planningcommission.nic.in/reports/genrep/reportsf.htm). Data on state government spending were derived from the World Bank's States Fiscal Database and http://sticerd.lse.ac.uk/eopp/research/indian.asp, and the primary source for these data is the RBI's annual report on state finances.

References

Ahluwalia, Montek S., 2002, "State-Level Performance Under Economic Reforms in India," in *Economic Policy Reforms and the Indian Economy*, ed. by Anne O. Krueger (New Delhi: Oxford University Press).

Aiyar, Shekhar, 2001, "Growth Theory and Convergence Across Indian States: A Panel Study," in *India at the Crossroads: Sustaining Growth and Reducing Poverty*, ed. by Tim Callen, Patricia Reynolds, and Christopher Towe (Washington: International Monetary Fund).

Bajpai, Nirupam, and Jeffrey D. Sachs, 1996, "Trends in Inter-State Inequalities of Income in India," Harvard Institute for International Development, Development Discussion Paper No. 528 (Cambridge, Massachusetts: Harvard University).

Banerjee, Abhijit, and Lakshmi Iyer, 2005, "History, Institutions, and Economic Performance: The Legacy of Colonial Land Tenure Systems in India," *American Economic Review*, Vol. 95, No. 4 (September), pp. 1190–213.

Barro, Robert, and Xavier Sala-i-Martin, 1991, "Convergence Across States and Regions," *Brookings Papers on Economic Activity*: 1, pp. 107–58.

———, 1999, *Economic Growth* (Cambridge, Massachusetts: MIT Press).

Besley, Timothy, and Robin Burgess, 2000, "Land Reform, Poverty Reduction and Growth: Evidence from India," *Quarterly Journal of Economics*, Vol. 115, No. 2 (May), pp. 389–430.

———, 2004, "Can Labor Regulation Hinder Economic Performance? Evidence from India," *Quarterly Journal of Economics*, Vol. 119, No. 1 (February), pp. 91–134.

Bhattacharya, B.B., and S. Sakthivel, 2004, "Regional Growth and Disparity in India: Comparison of Pre- and Post-Reform Decades," *Economic and Political Weekly*, Vol. 39, No. 10, pp. 1071–77.

Burgess, Robin, and Rohini Pande, 2004, "Do Rural Banks Matter? Evidence from the Indian Social Banking Experiment," CEPR Discussion Paper No. 4211 (London: Centre for Economic Policy Research).

Canova, Fabio, and Albert Marcet, 1995, "The Poor Stay Poor: Non-Convergence Across Countries and Regions," Universitat Pompeu Fabra Economics Working Paper No. 137 (Barcelona).

Cárdenas, Mauricio, and Adriana Pontón, 1995, "Growth and Convergence in Colombia: 1950–1990," *Journal of Development Economics*, Vol. 47 (June), pp. 5–37.

Caselli, Francesco, Gerardo Esquivel, and Fernando Lefort, 1996, "Reopening the Convergence Debate: A New Look at Cross-Country Growth Empirics," *Journal of Economic Growth*, Vol. 1, No. 3, pp. 363–89.

Cashin, Paul, and Ratna Sahay, 1996, "Internal Migration, Center-State Grants, and Economic Growth in the States of India," *IMF Staff Papers*, Vol. 43 (March), pp. 123–71.

De la Fuente, Angel, 2002, "Regional Convergence in Spain, 1965–95," CEPR Discussion Papers No. 3137 (London: Centre for Economic Policy Research).

Easterly, William, and Ross Levine, 2002, "It's Not Factor Accumulation: Stylized Facts and Growth Models," Central Bank of Chile Working Paper No. 164 (Santiago).

Elías, V.J., and R. Fuentes, 1998, "Convergence in the Southern Cone," *Estudios de Economía*, Vol. 25, No. 2 (December), pp. 179–89.

Ferreira, Afonso Henriques Borges, 1999, "Concentração Regional e Dispersão das Rendas Per Capita Estaduais: Um Comentário," *Estudias Economicãs*, Vol. 29, No. 1 (January–March), pp. 47–63.

Fujita, Masahisa, Paul Krugman, and Anthony J. Venables, 1999, *The Spatial Economy: Cities, Regions, and International Trade* (Cambridge, Massachusetts: MIT Press).

Indicus Analytics, 2004, *Measuring Inter-State Differences in Investment Climate: A Report for the Twelfth Finance Commission* (New Delhi).

Islam, Nazrul, 1995, "Growth Empirics: A Panel Data Approach," *Quarterly Journal of Economics*, Vol. 110, No. 4 (November), pp. 1127–70.

Jian, Tianlun, Jeffery Sachs, and Andrew Warner, 1996, "Trends in Regional Inequality in China," NBER Working Paper No. 5412 (Cambridge, Massachusetts: National Bureau of Economic Research).

Kalaitzidakis, Pantelis, Theofanis P. Mamuneas, Andreas Savvides, and Thanasis Stengos, 2001, "Measure of Human Capital and Nonlinearities in Economic Growth," *Journal of Economic Growth*, Vol. 6, No. 3, pp. 229–54.

Kochhar, Kalpana, Utsav Kumar, Raghuram Rajan, Arvind Subramanian, and Ioannis Tokatlidis, 2006, "India's Pattern of Development: What Happened, What Follows?" IMF Working Paper No. 06/22 (Washington: International Monetary Fund).

Koo, Jaewoon, Young-Yong Kim, and Sangphil Kim, 1998, "Regional Income Convergence: Evidence from a Rapidly Growing Economy," *Journal of Economic Development*, Vol. 23, No. 2 (December), pp. 191–203.

Krugman, Paul, 1991, "Increasing Returns and Economic Geography," *Journal of Political Economy*, Vol. 99, No. 3, pp. 483–99.

Kumar, Sanjay, 2004, "Impact of Economic Reforms on the Indian Electorate," *Economic and Political Weekly*, Vol. 39, No. 16, pp. 1621–30.

Leonida, Leone, and Daniel Montolio, 2004, "On the Determinants of Convergence and Divergence Processes in Spain," *Investigaciones Económicas*, Vol. 28, No. 1, pp. 89–121.

Levine, Ross, Norman Loayza, and Thorsten Beck, 2000, "Financial Intermediation and Growth: Causality and Causes," *Journal of Monetary Economics*, Vol. 46, No. 1, pp. 31–77.

Malik, P.L., 2003, *Industrial Law* (Lucknow, India: Eastern Book Company).

National Sample Survey Organisation, 2001, *Migration in India, 1999–2000* (New Delhi: Ministry of Statistics and Programme Implementation).

Rao, M.G., R.T. Shand, and K.P. Kalirajan, 1999, "Convergence of Incomes across Indian States: A Divergent View," *Economic and Political Weekly*, Vol. 34, No. 13, pp. 769–78.

Redding, Stephen, and Anthony J. Venables, 2004, "Economic Geography and International Inequality," *Journal of International Economics*, Vol. 62 (January), pp. 53–82.

Sala-i-Martin, Xavier, 1996, "The Classical Approach to Convergence Analysis," *Economic Journal*, Vol. 106 (July), pp. 1019–36.

Shioji, Etsuro, 1997, "Convergence in Panel Data: Evidence from the Skipping Estimation," Yokohama National University Working Paper (Yokohama, Japan).

Sinha, Tapen, and Dipendra Sinha, 2000, "No, Virginia, States in India Are Not Converging," International Indian Economic Association Working Paper No. 2000-09-01 (September).

Szulga, Radek, 2005, "A Dynamic Model of Female Labor Force Participation and Human Capital Investment" (unpublished; University of California, Department of Economics).

Visaria, Leela, and Pravin Visaria, 2003, "Long-Term Population Projections for Major States, 1991–2101," *Economic and Political Weekly*, Vol. 38, No. 45.

Weeks, Melvyn, and James Yudong Yao, 2003, "Provincial Conditional Income Convergence in China, 1953–1997: A Panel Data Approach," *Econometric Reviews*, Vol. 22, No. 1, pp. 59–77.

3

Trade and Financial Openness

RENU KOHLI AND MICHAEL WATTLEWORTH

The Indian economy has become increasingly open over the course of the past two decades. The combined share of imports and exports in the Indian economy has doubled over the past 20 years to reach about 35 percent of GDP in 2005. Capital flows have also been on the rise—in 2005, India was the top destination in Asia for private equity funds. Most observers attribute the rise in trade and capital flows to the liberalization of the economy, particularly the reduction of trade tariffs and capital controls. This process began in the 1980s but gathered steam following the 1991 balance of payments crisis and continues today. Despite these changes, however, India still accounts for a small share of world trade in goods and services: only 1½ percent in 2005 compared, for example, to China's 6¼ percent. Its net capital inflows of 3 percent of GDP are also still small in a regional context.

The fact that India has still to make significant inroads into global trade and financial markets only serves to underscore the substantial potential for greater openness to boost growth. Both trade reforms and capital account liberalization are ongoing, and continued opening to global markets will have important benefits for India. Moreover, these two pillars of increased openness have been, and will likely continue to be, mutually reinforcing. This chapter examines more closely the linkages between trade and financial openness in India. It first reviews the international literature, which emphasizes the positive effects that financial integration can have on trade. Next, it describes the key reforms in the areas of trade and capital account liberalization in India, highlighting how they have moved in tandem over the past two decades, and explores the potential linkages between the two

37

processes. The following section conducts a more rigorous empirical analysis of the linkages between trade and financial openness in India, and the final section concludes.

The Links Between Trade and Financial Openness

Various studies across a wide range of countries find close links between trade and financial openness. Aizenman and Noy (2004) find strong bidirectional effects between the two with almost 90 percent of the feedback running from financial openness to trade. Chowdhury (2005) similarly finds financial openness to be an important driver of trade in goods and services in European countries and members of the Commonwealth of Independent States. Rose and Spiegel (2004) show that trade positively influences bilateral lending patterns, while Lane and Milesi-Ferretti (2004) demonstrate a similar positive correlation between bilateral equity holdings and trade in goods and services.

Why are financial and trade openness mutually reinforcing? The literature explores various potential reasons.

- *Foreign investment.* This is likely a key channel by which greater financial openness can affect trade. Aizenman and Noy (2005) find a two-way relationship between foreign direct investment (FDI) and trade flows, particularly in manufacturing. Swenson (2004) identifies the import stimulating effects of FDI in manufacturing for investments by member countries of the Organization for Economic Cooperation and Development (OECD) in the United States, with multinational companies importing intermediate inputs from their home country. Hanson, Mataloni, and Slaughter (2001) provide evidence that vertical FDI—defined as exports from affiliates of multinational firms to the home country—also generates higher exports of final products.
- *Reductions in the cost of capital.* Financial openness can help overcome liquidity constraints, enabling countries to specialize and exploit economies of scale, thereby raising their ability to compete internationally.[1] Moreover, the availability of trade credit can promote trade. Beck (2002) finds that financial depth (an outcome of financial openness) is associated with higher manufacturing exports and an improved trade balance in manufactured goods in a study of 65 countries over a 30-year period.

---

[1]Kletzer and Bardhan (1987).

- *Demand-side effects*. Trade increases manufacturers' exposure to fluctuations in external demand, increasing the demand for hedging instruments and/or access to external finance to help buffer these shocks. Greater trade openness can also make it harder to sustain restrictions on capital flows by providing more channels for capital flight. Svaleryd and Vlachos (2002) find that the degree of integration in international financial markets has an independent effect on openness to trade. In low-income countries, Huang and Temple (2005) note that increased goods trade typically is followed by a sustained increase in financial development.
- *Supply-side effects*. A rise in international trade in financial assets will encourage trade openness through increased risk sharing and specialization in production (Kalemli-Ozcan, Sorensen, and Yosha, 2003). Imbs (2003) shows that specialization patterns reflect openness to trade in goods and assets. Rajan and Zingales (2003) attribute the association between commercial and financial openness to political economy factors. The liberalization of cross-border trade and capital flows weaken entrenched interests of those opposed to financial development leading to a positive correlation between the two types of openness. The empirical literature on financial development and trade also finds evidence that financial and trade openness encourages financial development, which, in turn, boosts growth.[2] The growth effects of trade and financial openness increase with the level of development but taper off at higher levels of income,[3] while higher levels of financial development can facilitate greater exports.[4]

Trade and Financial Liberalization in India

The process of trade liberalization in India began in the early 1980s, but gained momentum following the 1991 balance of payments crisis. The peak tariff rate on nonagricultural goods has fallen progressively from 150 percent in 1991/92 to 12½ percent in 2006 and the share of customs revenue in GDP—about 1.8 percent of GDP in 2005/06—has halved. Nontariff barriers were also eased with licensing restrictions on raw materials and intermediate and capital goods eliminated in 1991 and a tariff line-wise

---

[2]Law and Demetriades (2004).

[3]Calderón, Loayza, and Schmidt-Hebbel (2004); Do and Levchenko (2004).

[4]Higher levels of financial development are also associated with an increase in exports; for example, exchange rate elasticities for exports are higher for countries with better finance (Becker and Greenberg, 2003).

Box 3.1. Empirical Evidence on Trade Liberalization

Empirical assessments of trade liberalization have shown the benefits of trade reforms on productivity growth and the current account, but the impact on poverty and income inequality is unclear. Trade indicators have strengthened since the 1980s, with manufacturing exports growing significantly (see table).

Manufacturing and Total Trade Indicators, 1980–2003

	Exports to GDP	Imports to GDP	Manufacturing Exports (In percent of GDP)	Services Exports (In percent of GDP)	Manufacturing Imports (In percent of GDP)	Total Trade to GDP	Manufacturing Trade (In percent of GDP)
1980s	4.4	6.8	2.6	1.4	3.6	11.2	6.3
1990s	7.5	8.9	5.6	2.1	4.6	16.4	10.2
2000–03	9.3	11.1	7.0	4.5	5.7	20.4	12.7

Sources: IMF, *Balance of Payments Statistics*; World Bank, *World Development Indicators*; and IMF staff calculations.

At the firm level, trade liberalization has been particularly beneficial to total factor productivity growth in industries close to the technological frontier (Aghion and others, 2003; Siddharthan and Lal, 2004), firms located in regions or sectors with a more flexible labor environment, and those that were privately managed (Topalova, 2004a). However, the impact on poverty and income inequality remains inconclusive (Topalova, 2004b; Mishra and Kumar, 2005).

The effect of trade reforms on macroeconomic variables has also been positive. Most studies conclude that trade liberalization resulted in a trade surplus in intermediate and capital goods, rising imports and exports (Goldar, 2002; Virmani and others, 2004), increased intra-industry trade (Veeramani, 2004), and greater diversity and resilience in the balance of payments (Virmani, 2003). As a result of the reductions in trade protection since the early 1990s, economic growth accelerated at both the national and state levels (Ahluwalia, 2000, 2002).

import policy introduced in 1996. As a result, the share of unrestricted import products in total imports has increased to more than 95 percent from under two-thirds in 1996 and the proportion of "canalized"[5] items in total imports declined from 27 percent to 19 percent between 1988/89 and 1997/98.[6] The impact of these reforms has been mostly positive (Box 3.1).

In parallel, the government began to gradually relax controls on capital inflows, particularly direct and portfolio investments from the early

---

[5] Goods that could only be imported via state-owned corporations.

[6] Quantitative restrictions are maintained on about 5 percent of tariff lines because of health, safety, moral conduct, and security reasons.

Figure 3.1. Trade and Financial Openness
(In percent of GDP)

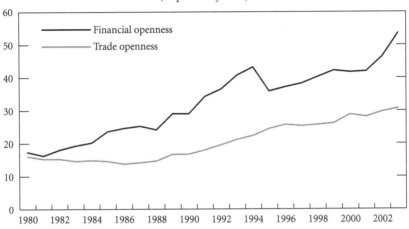

Sources: Lane and Milesi-Ferretti database on capital stocks and flows; and IMF, *International Financial Statistics*.

1990s (Box 3.2). A relatively well-developed equity market facilitated these reforms. Reforms initiated between 1991 and 1997 aimed to increase the extent of foreign investor participation in the stock market while expanding the range of sectors open to FDI. Quantitative ceilings on foreign investment through the stock exchange were steadily raised and the domestic debt market was opened to some limited foreign investment in 1997. At the same time, the government also made it easier for resident corporates to tap international financial markets, while keeping controls on resident individuals in place. Initially, access to foreign commercial borrowings by corporates was confined to infrastructure, core (industries that produce primary products as raw material inputs for other firms), and export-oriented industries, but was subsequently extended to other manufacturing firms. However, throughout the capital account liberalization process, controls have been maintained on the maturity and end-use of external borrowings, and the flow of funds into India have been controlled via quantitative ceilings to keep external debt indicators at sustainable levels thereby safeguarding India's vulnerability to external shocks.

These reforms were successful in raising India's openness to trade and financial flows (Figure 3.1).[7] The share of exports in GDP jumped from 6.2

[7]The authors are grateful to Gian Maria Milesi-Ferretti for providing data on capital stocks and flows.

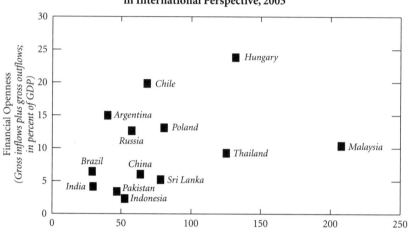

Figure 3.2. India's Financial and Trade Openness
in International Perspective, 2003

Sources: Lane and Milesi-Ferretti database on capital stocks and flows; and IMF, *International Financial Statistics*.

percent in the 1980s to 15.1 percent of GDP during 2000–05. Import shares also climbed from 8.9 percent of GDP to 17.1 percent of GDP over the same period. The pace of import growth accelerated in the 1990s and the structure of imports moved toward technology-intensive and export-oriented products, with capital and intermediate goods emerging as principal import items. (Chapter 4 also shows that Indian exports have made inroads into new markets and have broadened into the high-growth areas of iron and steel, petroleum, and pharmaceutical products.) Financial flows have multiplied, driven mainly by a surge in portfolio inflows and external commercial borrowings. Nevertheless, as Figure 3.2 shows, India still ranks low on measures of trade and financial openness compared with other emerging market economies.

Trade and financial openness appear to be complementary both over time and across countries. Measures of trade and financial openness in India are positively correlated over the 1970–2003 period and the correlation appears stronger in the post-1991 liberalization period (Figure 3.3). Gross financial flows also display a strong and positive correlation with the current account balance (net flows) in the postreform period and a bivariate regression of the change in trade and financial openness constitutes further evidence of the positive relationship between the two.

One channel through which financial liberalization may have contributed to greater trade in India is through the cost of capital. Table 3.1 shows that

**Figure 3.3. Correlation of Financial and Trade Openness:
Financial Openness and the Current Account**
(Five-year averages)

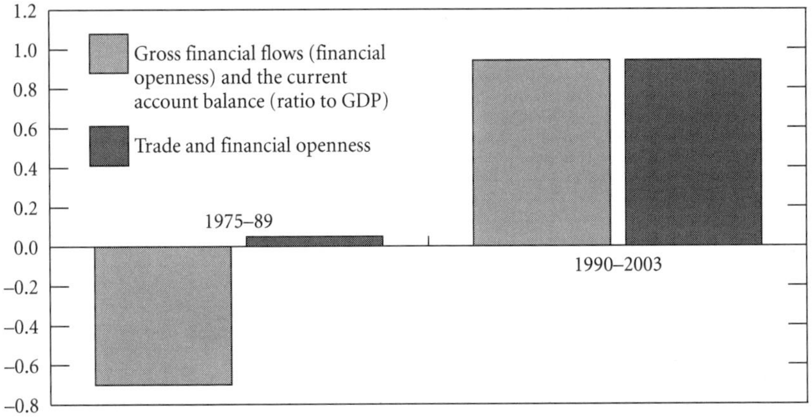

Sources: Lane and Milesi-Ferretti database on capital stocks and flows; and IMF, *International Financial Statistics*.

the cost of external capital declined sharply over the course of the 1990s, and the fact that the share of private debt in total external debt rose from 40 percent in 1995 to over 60 percent in 2004 appears to confirm that domestic firms were taking advantage of their enhanced freedom to borrow abroad. The liberalization of foreign equity inflows will also have augmented the supply of equity finance and lowered domestic borrowing costs.

FDI has not historically been a major driver of India's growing openness, in contrast to many Asian countries, but it is increasingly becoming so. FDI inflows to India have been comparatively low (see Chapter 5) and initial FDI inflows were concentrated in areas such as domestic appliances, food and dairy products, and financial sectors that sought to tap India's large domestic market rather than establish export potential. The notable exception was the information technology (IT) sector, which was identified as a thrust area for foreign investment in the early stages of liberalization.[8] In recent years, however, FDI inflows and export growth in manufacturing sectors such as chemicals, electronics, and engineering as well as services have accelerated (Figure 3.4). Moreover, the indirect effects of FDI—including technological and skill advancement, spillovers, and related externalities—are clearly visible in India.

[8]See Government of India (1993).

Figure 3.4. Exports by Sector
(In millions of U.S. dollars)

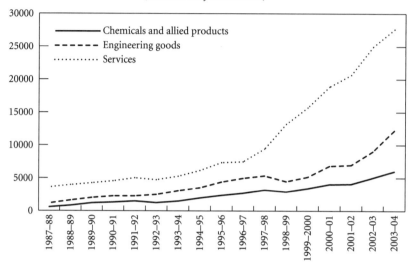

Sources: Reserve Bank of India, *Handbook of Statistics*.

Table 3.1. Domestic and Foreign Borrowing Costs, 1981–2003

	Nominal Lending Rates (1)	CPI Inflation (2)	Real Lending Rates (1 – 2)	One-Year LIBOR (3)	Exchange Rate (Percent change) (4)	Effective Cost of Foreign Loans (3 + 4)
1981	16.5	13.1	3.4	16.1	10.2	26.3
1985	16.5	5.5	11.0	9.1	8.9	18.0
1991	16.5	13.9	2.6	6.3	29.9	36.2
1992	19.0	11.8	7.2	4.2	14.0	18.2
1993	19.0	6.4	12.6	3.6	17.6	21.3
1994	15.0	10.2	4.8	5.6	2.9	8.5
1995	16.5	10.2	6.3	6.2	3.4	9.6
1996	14.5	9.0	5.5	5.8	9.3	15.0
1997	14.0	7.2	6.8	6.1	2.5	8.6
1998	14.0	13.2	0.8	5.5	13.6	19.2
1999	12.0	4.7	7.3	5.7	4.4	10.1
2000	11.5	4.0	7.5	6.8	4.4	11.2
2001	11.5	3.7	7.8	3.9	5.0	8.9
2002	10.8	4.4	6.4	2.2	3.0	5.2
2003	10.3	3.8	6.4	1.4	−4.2	−2.8

Sources: Reserve Bank of India, *Handbook of Statistics*; IMF, *International Financial Statistics*; and IMF staff calculations.

Table 3.2. Correlations Between Decomposed Financial and Trade Flows, 1991–2003[1]

	Trade Openness in Goods	Trade Openness in Services	Manufacturing Trade Openness	Manufacturing Exports (Share in GDP)	Manufacturing Imports (Share in GDP)
FDI openness (sum of FDI inflows and outflows/GDP)	0.85*	0.82*	0.87*	0.43*	0.75*
Portfolio openness (sum of portfolio inflows and outflows/GDP)	0.35	0.09	0.26*	0.02	0.05
Loans openness (sum of loans assets and liabilities/GDP)	−0.29*	−0.14*	−0.2*	0.25*	−0.44*

Sources: IMF, *Balance of Payments Statistics*; and IMF staff calculations.
[1]Sample restricted to 1991–2003 as the subcategories, FDI and portfolio, only start from 1991, after liberalization. * indicates significant at the 10 percent level.

Foreign investment is beginning to emerge as an important channel through which financial openness has an impact on trade. The bulk of FDI inflows have gone to the export-oriented sectors, which registered strong growth over the 1990s. Between 1992/93 and 2001/02 the chemical and allied products (12 percent), engineering goods (21 percent), electronics and electrical sector (9 percent), and the services sector (9 percent) accounted for the bulk of cumulative FDI inflows. IT services, the original beneficiary of many of the investment inflows, have also grown exponentially with their share of total exports rising to 21 percent in 2003/04 from a mere 3 percent in 1996/97. Openness to FDI inflows and outflows appears to have stimulated trade via increased imports, including imports of intermediate inputs from the home country by multinational firms. Indeed, correlations of subcomponents of financial flows and trade (Table 3.2) suggest that the removal of direct restrictions on foreign investment has been associated with a rise in trade. Most of this association is due to an association between manufacturing imports and FDI, with the FDI openness-exports link also positive, but less strong. Other capital flows, such as portfolio inflows and loans, are not as strongly associated with trade, with correlations that are weak or even negative.[9] The following section explores

---

[9]The negative correlation might be due to the combining of loan transactions by government, the monetary authority, banks, and the private sector.

Box 3.2. Capital Account Liberalization

Among the key steps to liberalize the capital account since the early 1990s are the following:

Inflows

Foreign direct investment (FDI). Initial liberalization of FDI inflows saw investment limits in new and existing industrial companies raised from 40 percent to 51 percent of paid-up capital, and up to 74 percent in specific industries. The technology transfer requirement was removed and the scope of FDI expanded beyond export-oriented, import-substituting industries. FDI was initially subject to approval, but the list of industries automatically approved has progressively widened so that by 2000 almost all industries were under the automatic route. (Under the automatic route, prior approval is not required; only the reporting stipulations have to be met.) In January 2004, FDI limits in several sectors, including banking and petroleum and natural gas, were raised.

Portfolio investment. Foreign institutional investors (FIIs) were first allowed to make portfolio investments in the equity market in 1993. In 1997, FIIs were allowed to invest in the Indian debt market subject to specific ceilings that have been progressively relaxed, although they remain low.

External borrowing. India's policy on external commercial borrowings (ECBs) has been dictated by the need to keep external debt at sustainable levels. As a result, controls on ECBs have limited the cost, quantity, maturity, and end-use of these inflows. Controls have been progressively relaxed. Domestic borrowers operating in the infrastructure, export, and manufacturing sectors are permitted to access international financial markets. However, long-term borrowings are favored over short-term borrowings and ECBs beyond specific ceilings require approval from the Reserve Bank of India (RBI).

Nonresident deposits. India permits nonresidents to hold deposits. However, the interest rates paid on these deposits are subject to specific ceilings that are linked to international rates.

Outflows

India's approach to the liberalization of capital outflows has been one of facilitating direct overseas investments by Indian corporates while keeping the capital account largely closed for resident individuals. Overseas investments are recognized as an important avenue for expanding Indian businesses. Accordingly, rules and procedures related to these have been liberalized significantly. Resident corporates and partnership firms can invest up to 200 percent of their net worth in overseas joint ventures or wholly owned subsidiaries. Exporters and exchange dealers are allowed to maintain foreign currency accounts and to use them for their overseas businesses. Individuals were generally unable to transfer funds from India without RBI approval until 2004 when residents were permitted to take $25,000 abroad a year without prior approval. The ability of Indian mutual funds to invest abroad has also been enhanced; in 2006, the quantitative ceiling on such investments has been revised, and the types of eligible investments broadened.

these linkages more formally, particularly the role of FDI in promoting greater trade openness.

Econometric Analysis

To test the link between financial openness and trade more formally we estimate a simple econometric model. The change in trade is modeled as a function of the one- and two-period lagged values of the change in financial openness and a set of conditioning macroeconomic explanatory variables. The latter include per capita income growth (pcy), the gross fiscal deficit to GDP ratio (percent), the log of the change in the real exchange rate index (q_t), and the domestic and the foreign rates of interest, i and i^*. A dummy for the post-1991 period is also included to test whether relationships have changed since reform took off. The reverse specification, focusing on the impact of trade openness upon future financial openness, is also estimated. To minimize the risk of simultaneity bias the macroeconomic variables are also lagged. Tables 3.3 and 3.4 use annual 1970–2003 data to model the relationship, while Tables 3.5 and 3.6 use quarterly data from 1990 to 2004.[10]

The results reveal that changes in financial openness (ΔFO) have a positive and significant impact on trade openness (ΔTO).[11] In terms of magnitudes, specification 1 of Table 3.3 indicates that a 10 percent increase in financial openness is associated with a 2.1 percent increase in trade openness two years later, a finding that is robust to the exclusion of the post-1991 liberalization dummy. Since financial openness proxies as a measure of capital account openness, our results suggest that the easing of capital controls in India has had a positive effect by encouraging trade, although at this level of aggregation, it is difficult to establish the exact channel of influence. However, the coefficient on financial openness is significantly lower than that estimated by Aizenman and Noy (2004) who, using panel data from a sample of developing economies, find a coefficient of 0.43. This suggests that the impact of lagged financial openness on contemporary trade openness in India may be below the developing country average.

---

[10]The size of the sample is constrained by the availability of the Lane and Milesi-Ferretti financial openness measure. A summary description of the variables is given in the Appendix.

[11]Both variables are first-difference stationary processes. There was also at least one cointegrating relation between the two variables, suggesting a stationary linear combination of the two in one direction.

Table 3.3. OLS Estimates: Impact of Financial Openness on Trade Openness, 1970–2003[1]

(Annual)

	ΔTO_t	ΔTO_t
	1	2
ΔFO_{t-1}	−0.073	−0.011
	1.11	0.22
ΔFO_{t-2}	0.21	0.18
	4.37***	2.22***
pcy_{t-1}		0.0002
		0.20
Δq_{t-1}		−0.08
		1.78**
$Grossfiscaldeficit_{t-1}$		−0.002
		1.63*
i_{t-1}		−0.002
		2.44***
i^*_{t-1}		−0.0009
		2.23**
π_{t-1}		0.001
		1.76**
Liberalization dummy	0.009	
	2.51***	
Adj R^2	0.24	0.40
DW	1.99	2.36
ρ	−0.55***	−0.57**
No. of observations	24	24

Source: Authors' calculations.

[1]All regressions assume an AR(1) process, ρ is the coefficient term. OLS specification with heteroskedasticity-consistent errors. ***, **, and * indicate 1 percent, 5 percent, and 10 percent significance levels, respectively.

With respect to the macroeconomic controls included in specification 2, an increase in per capita GDP, a real exchange rate depreciation, and declining domestic or global interest rates as well as a smaller budget deficit are expected to increase trade openness. All these variables enter the expanded regression in specification 2 with the expected sign, and all are significant with the exception of per capita GDP growth.

The results also show that a change in trade openness has a positive and significant impact on financial openness. A unit increase in trade openness is found to lead to a 4–6 percent increase in financial openness two years later (Table 3.4).[12] Including macroeconomic control variables in speci-

---

[12]A unit increase in trade openness in the past one period has the impact of significantly reducing contemporary financial openness by approximately 0.34, which is counterintuitive; a Wald test restricting the coefficient on this lag to be zero indicates that the restriction is statistically valid. The F-statistic is 3.28, indicating that the null hypothesis, $\Delta TO_{t-1} = 0$ cannot be rejected.

Table 3.4. OLS Estimates: Impact of Trade Openness on Financial Openness, 1970–2003[1]

(Annual)

	ΔFO_t	ΔFO_t
	1	2
ΔTO_{t-1}	−0.34	−0.11
	1.81*	1.19
ΔTO_{t-2}	0.46	0.63
	1.87*	3.52***
pcy_{t-1}		0.0005
		0.22
Δq_{t-1}		0.02
		0.44
$Grossfiscaldeficit_{t-1}$		0.004
		1.60*
$(i - i^*)_{t-1}$		0.002
		3.68***
Adj R^2	0.46	0.72
DW	1.62	2.49
ρ		−0.62***
No. of observations	24	24

Source: Authors' calculations.

[1]Regressions 1 and 2 control for an influential outlier in 1995, the coefficient values of which are −0.09*** and 0.11*** . All regressions assume an AR(1) process, ρ is the coefficient term. OLS specification with heteroskedasticity-consistent errors. ***, **, and * indicate 1 percent, 5 percent, and 10 percent significance levels, respectively.

fication 2—per capita GDP growth, a positive interest rate differential, a real exchange rate appreciation, and higher fiscal deficits—makes the coefficient on financial openness stronger.[13] While the coefficient on budget deficit/GDP ratio suggests a significant influence of increased government expenditure on financial openness, the insignificant impact of real exchange rate changes is puzzling. This regression, however, is sensitive to the 1995 outlier which reflects a sharp drop in net portfolio inflows in that year (Table 3.4).

One drawback of using aggregated trade and capital flow data in this type of analysis is that it does not yield any information about which trade and financial flows are related. We, therefore, exploit the information from the quarterly balance of payments statistics to examine this issue. Table 3.5 expresses the change in total trade openness (ΔTO) as a function of total FDI openness ($\Delta Fdiopenness$), total portfolio equity openness

[13]The finding is also robust to the inclusion of other variables such as the wholesale rate of inflation, and the exclusion of insignificant variables.

Table 3.5. Impact of FDI, Portfolio, and Loan Openness on Trade Openness[1]
(Goods, services, and business services, 1990:1–2004:1)

Dependent variable → Explanatory variables ↓	ΔTOG_t 1	ΔTOS_t 2	$\Delta TOBS_t$ 3
$\Delta Fdiopenness_{t-3}$		0.11*** 4.59	0.22*** 3.12
$\Delta Fdiopenness_{t-4}$	0.06*** 3.05		
$\Delta Portfolioopenness_{t-2}$		−0.017** 1.88	−0.001 0.06
$\Delta Portfolioopenness_{t-3}$	−0.012** 1.85		
$\Delta Loansopenness_{t-3}$		0.05*** 3.54	0.10*** 2.80
$\Delta Loansopenness_{t-4}$	0.012 1.23		
Δq_{t-1}	−0.008** 2.26		
Δq_{t-2}		−0.008*** 2.47	−0.04*** 2.69
i^*_{t-1}	0.04*** 3.30		
i^*_{t-5}		−0.012** 2.01	−0.015 1.01
Adj R^2	0.22	0.40	0.26
DW	1.92	1.94	2.06
ρ	−0.51***	−0.57***	−0.46***
No. of observations	42	48	48

Source: Authors' calculations.

[1]All regressions assume an AR(1) process, ρ is the coefficient term. OLS specification with heteroskedasticity-consistent errors. ***, **, and * indicate 1 percent, 5 percent, and 10 percent significance levels, respectively.

($\Delta Portfolioopenness$), and total loans openness ($\Delta Loansopenness$).[14] Table 3.6 simply replaces the right-hand-side variables with financial openness now defined as openness to FDI inflows ($\Delta Fdiinopenness$), portfolio inflows ($\Delta Piiopenness$), and inward loans ($\Delta Liopenness$).[15] We began with a general lag structure that included up to eight lags and progressively removed insignificant lags to arrive at a parsimonious specification.

FDI flows are found to boost trade in both the goods and services sectors (Table 3.5). The coefficients indicate that a percentage point rise in openness to FDI increases trade in goods (ΔTOG_t) by 0.6 percent and trade in services (ΔTOS_t) by 1 percent with about a one-year lag. Using business services trade ($\Delta TOBS_t$) in lieu of overall services reveals an

---

[14] Sum of each inflow and outflow as share of GDP. See the Appendix for description.
[15] FDI, portfolio, and loan inflows as share of GDP. See the Appendix for description.

Table 3.6. Impact of FDI, Portfolio, and Loan Inflows Openness on Trade Openness[1]
(Goods, services, and business services, 1990:1–2004:1)

Dependent variable → Explanatory variables ↓	ΔTOG_t	ΔTOS_t	$\Delta TOBS_t$
$\Delta Fdiinopenness_{t-3}$		0.11*** 5.07	0.24*** 3.72
$\Delta Fdiinopenness_{t-4}$	0.06*** 3.45		
$\Delta Piiopenness_{t-2}{}^2$	−0.007* 1.69	−0.017** 1.95	0.0005 0.004
$\Delta Liopenness_{t-3}{}^2$	0.02* 1.69	0.05*** 3.58	0.11** 2.92
Δq_{t-1}	−0.002 0.73		
Δq_{t-2}		−0.009*** 3.33	−0.04*** 2.82
i^*_{t-1}	0.03*** 2.80		
i^*_{t-5}		−0.012*** 2.73	−0.016 1.06
Adj R^2	0.16	0.42	0.28
DW	1.97	1.94	2.06
ρ	−0.32*	−0.58***	−0.47***
No. of observations	47	48	48

Source: Authors' calculations.

[1]All regressions assume an AR(1) process, ρ is the coefficient term. OLS specification with heteroskedasticity-consistent errors. ***, **, and * indicate 1 percent, 5 percent, and 10 percent significance levels, respectively.

[2]$\Delta Piiopenness_{t-2}$ and $\Delta Liopenness_{t-3}$ denote portfolio and loan inflows openness, respectively (see the Appendix).

even larger response of 2.4 percent. However, openness to portfolio flows is associated with a reduction in trade in goods (−0.007) and services (−0.017). The impact on business services is insignificant. Replacing net portfolio flows with portfolio inflows in Table 3.5 does not alter this finding.

Increased access to external financing also boosts trade. A percentage point rise in external borrowings has a positive impact on trade openness in services (0.5 percent). The impact of access to external loans on business services trade is twice as strong, while the impact on trade in goods is insignificant. But when aggregate loans are replaced with loan inflows in Table 3.6, the impact on goods trade becomes significant, but remains much smaller than the impact on services trade. These results suggest that increased access to external commercial borrowings as part of the capital account liberalization process has facilitated trade in goods and services by reducing the cost of capital. The differential impact of various types of financial openness highlights the productive links of FDI and loans with trade. The exception is equity flows that are more equally dispersed across domestic and external sectors and are associated with a reduction in trade openness.

Conclusions

The main contribution of this chapter is to use time-series data to examine the impact of financial openness on trade openness. The chapter finds a significant mutual impact of the two kinds of openness. Although the impact of trade openness on financial openness is not very surprising, the role of financial integration in driving trade openness is striking. FDI is found to be strongly associated with increased trade in both goods and services, suggesting that further liberalization of FDI could increase India's trade potential.

Financial liberalization stimulated trade through the foreign investment and the cost of credit channels. The findings of this chapter also provide evidence on the benefits from capital account liberalization. Restrictions on external capital account transactions can operate as both direct or indirect restrictions on trade development, and the removal or gradual elimination of these controls can help boost India's role as a global player. The results suggest that trade openness should be complemented with financial sector reforms to increase the gains from trade liberalization. The mutual impact of both kinds of openness also contributes toward building a consensus for trade and financial sector reforms.

Appendix. Data Sources and Definitions

Variable Name	Definition/Construction of Variable	Source
Trade openness	Sum of exports and imports as share of GDP.	IMF, *International Financial Statistics* (*IFS*).
Financial openness	This measure calculates gross levels of foreign direct investment (FDI), portfolio, and other assets and liabilities via accumulation of corresponding inflows and outflows, with valuation adjustments. It is thus less volatile than flow measures of financial integration and less prone to measurement error.	Lane and Milesi-Ferretti (2004).
FDI openness	Sum of FDI inflows and outflows as share of GDP.	IMF, *IFS*.
FDI inflow openness	FDI inflows as share of GDP.	IMF, *IFS*.
Portfolio openness	Sum of portfolio inflows and outflows as share of GDP.	IMF, *IFS*.
Portfolio inflow openness	Portfolio inflows as share of GDP.	IMF, *IFS*.
Loans openness	Sum of loan inflows and outflows as share of GDP.	IMF, *IFS*.
Loan inflow openness	Loan inflows as share of GDP.	IMF, *IFS*.
Manufacturing trade	Sum of manufacturing exports and manufacturing imports in percent of GDP.	World Bank, *World Development Indicators* (*WDI*).
Manufacturing exports	Manufacturing exports in percent of GDP.	World Bank, *WDI*.
Manufacturing imports	Manufacturing imports in percent of GDP.	World Bank, *WDI*.
External assistance	External aid.	Reserve Bank of India (RBI), *Handbook of Statistics*.
Foreign investment	Foreign investment.	RBI, *Handbook of Statistics*.
Private loans	Commercial borrowings.	RBI, *Handbook of Statistics*.
Sectoral percentage shares in cumulative FDI inflows	Sum of respective sectoral FDI inflows as percentage to total FDI inflows between 1992/93 and 2000/01.	Report of the Committee on FDI, Planning Commission (2002).
Services, chemicals, and engineering exports	Exports figures in millions of U.S. dollars.	RBI, *Handbook of Statistics*.
Nominal lending rate	Prime lending rate.	IMF, *IFS*.
pcy	Change in log of real per capita income.	World Bank, *WDI*.
Grossfiscaldeficit	Gross fiscal deficit as percentage of GDP.	RBI, *Handbook of Statistics*.
Δq	Change in log of real per capita income.	RBI, *Handbook of Statistics*.
$(i - i^*)$	Prime lending rate minus the six-month LIBOR.	IMF, *IFS*.
π	Change in the wholesale price index.	IMF, *IFS*.
Liberalization dummy	Dummy taking value of 0 before 1991 and 1 thereafter.	

References

Aghion, P., R. Burgess, S. Redding and F. Zilibotti, 2003, "The Unequal Effects of Liberalization: Theory & Evidence from India" (unpublished).

Ahluwalia, M.S., 2000, "Economic Performance of States in Post-Reforms Period," *Economic and Political Weekly*, Vol. 35, No. 19 (May), pp. 1637–48.

———, 2002, "Economic Reforms in India Since 1991: Has Gradualism Worked?" *Journal of Economic Perspectives*, Vol. 16, No. 3, pp. 67–88.

Aizenman, J., and I. Noy, 2004, "On the Two Way Feedback Between Financial and Trade Openness," NBER Working Paper No. 10496 (Cambridge, Massachusetts: National Bureau of Economic Research).

———, 2005, "FDI and Trade—Two Way Linkages?" East-West Center Working Papers, Economics Series No. 76 (April).

Beck, Thorsten, 2002, "Financial Development and International Trade: Is There a Link?" *Journal of International Economics*, Vol. 57 (June), pp. 107–31.

Becker, B., and D. Greenberg, 2003, "Financial Development and International Trade," paper presented at CEPR/Banca D'Italia Conference on Financial Structure, Product Market Structure and Economic Performance.

Calderón, César, Norman Loayza, and Klaus Schmidt-Hebbel, 2004, "External Conditions and Growth Performance," Central Bank of Chile Working Paper No. 292 (Santiago).

Chowdhury, A., 2005, "The Impact of Financial Openness on Economic Integration: Evidence from Europe and the CIS," paper presented at a Seminar in Helsinki, February 10–11 (Bank of Finland and Institute for Economies in Transition).

Do, Quy-Toan, and A. Levchenko, 2004, "Trade and Financial Development," paper presented at LACEA (San José, Costa Rica).

Goldar, B., 2002, "Trade Liberalization and Manufacturing Employment: The Case of India," Employment and Employment Strategy Papers, 2002/34 (Geneva: International Labor Organization).

Government of India, 1993, *Report of the High Level Committee on the Balance of Payments* (New Delhi).

Hanson, G.H., R. Mataloni, Jr., and M. J. Slaughter, 2001, "Expansion Strategies of U.S. Multinational Firms," NBER Working Paper No. 8433 (Cambridge Massachusetts: National Bureau of Economic Research).

Huang, Y., and J.W. Temple, 2005, "Does External Trade Promote Financial Development?" CEPR Discussion Paper No. 5150 (London: Centre for Economic Policy Research)

Imbs, J., 2003, "Trade, Finance, Specialization, and Synchronization," IMF Working Paper No. 03/81 (Washington: International Monetary Fund).

Kalemli-Ozcan, S., B.E. Sorensen, and O. Yosha, 2003, "Risk Sharing and Industrial Specialization: Regional and International Evidence," *American Economic Review*, Vol. 93, No. 3 (June), pp. 903–18.

Kletzer, K., and P. Bardhan, 1987, "Credit Markets and Patterns of International Trade," *Journal of Development Economics*, Vol. 27, Issues 1–2, pp. 57–70.

Lane, P.R., and G.M. Milesi-Ferretti, 2004, "International Investment Patterns," IMF Working Paper No. 04/134 (Washington: International Monetary Fund).

Law, S.H., and P. Demetriades, 2004, "Capital Inflows, Trade Openness and Financial Development in Developing Countries," Money Macro and Finance (MMF) Research Group Conference 2004, No. 38 (St. Andrews: Money Macro and Finance Research Group).

Mishra, P., and U. Kumar, 2005, "Trade Liberalization and Wage Inequality: Evidence from India," IMF Working Paper No. 05/20 (Washington: International Monetary Fund).

Rajan, R., and L. Zingales, 2003, "The Great Reversals: The Politics of Financial Development in the Twentieth Century," *Journal of Financial Economics*, Vol. 69, Issue 1 (July), pp. 5–50.

Reserve Bank of India, 2004, *Report on Currency & Finance*, No. 86 (Mumbai).

Rose, A.K., and M.M. Spiegel, 2004, "A Gravity Model of Sovereign Lending: Trade, Default, and Credit," *IMF Staff Papers*, Vol. 51 (Special Issue), pp. 50–63.

Siddharthan, N.S., and K. Lal, 2004, "Liberalization, MNE and Productivity of Indian Enterprises," *Economic and Political Weekly*, Vol. 39, No. 5, pp. 448–52.

Svaleryd, H., and J. Vlachos, 2002, "Markets for Risk and Openness to Trade: How Are They Related?" *Journal of International Economics*, Vol. 57, No. 2 (August), pp. 369–95.

Swenson, D., 2004, "Foreign Investment and the Mediation of Trade Flows," *Review of International Economics*, Vol. 12, Issue 4, pp. 609–29.

Topalova, P., 2004a, "Trade Liberalization and Firm Productivity: The Case of India," IMF Working Paper No. 04/28 (Washington: International Monetary Fund).

———, 2004b, "Factor Immobility and Regional Impacts of Trade Liberalization: Evidence on Poverty and Inequality from India" (unpublished; Cambridge, Massachusetts: Massachusetts Institute of Technology).

Veeramani, C., 2004, "Trade Liberalization, Multinational Involvement, and Intra-Industry Trade in Manufacturing," ICRIER Working Paper No. 143 (New Delhi: Indian Council for Research on International Economic Relations).

Virmani, A., 2003, "India's External Reforms—Modest Globalization, Significant Gains," *Economic and Political Weekly*, Vol. 38, No. 32, pp. 3373–90.

———, B.N. Goldar, C. Veeramani, and V. Bhatt, 2004, "Impact of Tariff Reforms on Indian Industry: Assessment Based on a Multi-Sector Econometric Model," ICRIER Working Paper No. 135 (New Delhi: Indian Council for Research on International Economic Relations).

World Bank, 2004, *Trade Policies in South Asia: An Overview*, Vol. II (Washington).

4

Maintaining Competitiveness in the Global Economy

CATRIONA PURFIELD

The appreciation of the rupee in recent years has raised concerns about India's export competitiveness. Since end-2002, the Indian rupee has appreciated by 6 percent and 8 percent against the U.S. dollar and in real effective terms, respectively. Imports have grown at rapid clip and in the course of the past year, the current account has moved from a position of surplus to one of deficit. Against this background, this chapter assesses external competitiveness, reviewing India's export performance and estimates of the "equilibrium" real effective exchange rate.

Export Performance

India has witnessed a marked acceleration in export growth in recent years (Table 4.1). Since 2000, the value of India's exports has grown three times faster than in the latter half of the 1990s. This acceleration has been led by services exports—particularly software and information technology (IT)—which continue to gain momentum with growth pushing past 100 percent in 2004/05.[1] Much less appreciated is the fact that exports of Indian goods have also performed strongly since 2000. As a result, exports

---

[1]The high rate of service export growth in 2004/05 may reflect, in part, misclassification of earnings.

Table 4.1. Indicators of Export Growth
(Annual percentage change)

	1995/96–1999/2000	2000/01–2004/05	2000/01	2001/02	2002/03	2003/04	2004/05
Export value	6.1	21.0	15.9	0.2	20.5	20.3	47.4
Goods	3.0	15.5	21.1	−1.6	20.3	20.4	24.9
Services	16.4	33.3	3.6	5.4	21.1	20.2	105.7
Export volumes	10.3	14.4	17.0	3.7	15.5	8.0	32.7
Goods	7.1	9.2	22.2	1.7	15.2	8.1	12.4
Services	21.1	26.1	4.5	9.0	16.0	7.9	85.2

Sources: Reserve Bank of India; and IMF staff estimates.

of goods and services now account for about one-fifth of Indian GDP, up from a mere 10 percent a decade ago.

India's exports have become more diverse by region. The past five years have seen India's market share of Asian goods imports nearly double. As a result, Asia has surpassed the European Union (EU) as the most important destination for Indian exports, accounting for almost one-third of total goods exports, suggesting that India may be becoming integrated into regional production chains.[2] The EU now only accounts for about one-fifth of Indian exports, down from almost 30 percent a decade ago, and the share of the United States has also fallen to 17 percent from 20 percent. With its trading partners becoming more diverse—gains in the Middle East and Africa have been even more impressive than in Asia with India now accounting for almost 4 percent of the Middle East's imports and just over 2 percent of Africa's imports—India has become less dependent on, and vulnerable to, developments in specific markets. This has helped India to sustain a rapid pace of export growth even as growth in some key industrial markets slowed in recent years.

India's export base has also broadened and become more dynamic. Looking at the composition of India's exports by commodity group and its share of world exports by commodity reveals a pattern of accelerating growth and diversification. In the mid-1990s, export growth was in single digits and narrowly based (Table 4.2). The pickup in growth since 2000 has occurred across a wide range of categories. Figure 4.1, which plots the changing world market share of India's 15 largest products (at the SITC 3-digit level) against the changing share of those products in world trade illustrates that Indian exporters are moving into some of the most dynamic

[2]For example, auto components in India are exported as inputs for Asian automobile makers.

Table 4.2. Composition of Goods Exports

	Share of World Goods Trade			Average Annual Growth Rate			Contribution to Growth		
	1990–95	1996–2000	2000–03	1990–95	1996–2000	2000–03	1990–95	1996–2000	2000–03
Food and live animals	1.0	1.2	1.2	17.0	−2.1	7.8	22.5	−4.2	8.0
Beverages and tobacco	0.3	0.3	0.3	−2.7	0.7	7.4	−0.2	0.1	0.3
Crude materials	0.9	0.9	1.1	−2.4	−4.3	22.7	−1.2	−2.6	8.1
Mineral fuel and lubricants	0.2	0.2	0.5	0.1	39.6	23.4	0.0	8.9	9.9
Animal and vegetable oils and fats	0.7	0.8	0.8	40.7	5.4	0.3	1.7	0.4	0.0
Chemicals	0.5	0.6	0.7	14.1	11.9	15.7	9.0	15.6	14.4
Manufactured goods	1.5	1.6	1.9	13.8	8.9	10.4	43.3	45.6	32.0
Machinery and transport	0.1	0.1	0.1	12.2	6.9	19.5	7.4	7.1	14.2
Miscellaneous manufactured items	1.0	1.0	1.1	11.8	10.5	8.7	19.9	28.6	14.1
Commodities, n.e.s.	0.0	0.0	0.0	−4.7	…	112.3	−2.4	…	−1.0
Total	0.6	0.6	0.7	12.2	7.6	12.2	100.0	100.0	100.0

Sources: World Integrated Trade Solution; and IMF staff calculations.

segments of world trade.[3] In areas such as petroleum products, organic chemicals, and electrical equipment, which account for a growing share of global trade, India's exports have been growing faster than the global average. Since 1990, India's share of the global petro-product export market has doubled, while its share of the chemicals and electrical equipment markets has tripled, albeit from a small base.

Despite these gains India's export performance has lagged that of Asia and its share of global exports remains low. Indian exports have grown more slowly than in the rest of Asia, and particularly China (Figure 4.2). India continues to account for a relatively small share of global goods exports. China accounts for over six times as much, and four member countries of the Association of South East Asian Nations (ASEAN)—Indonesia, Malaysia, Philippines, and Thailand—together account for almost four times as much. The picture changes little when exports of services are included with India's market share in global goods and service exports rising only to 1.3 percent.

The fact that India has not made greater inroads into world export markets is surprising given India's low wages and strong productivity growth. Indians earn only a fraction of their competitors, about $0.60 an hour.

---

[3]The size of the bubble in Figure 4.1 represents the value of each export in 2003. So for example, India's market share of global mineral manufactures—its largest manufacturing export where it accounts for 5½ percent of world trade—rose by 1.3 percentage points between 1990 and 2003 but the share of this good in global exports has fallen marginally.

Figure 4.1. World Market Position of Indian Exports, 1990–2003

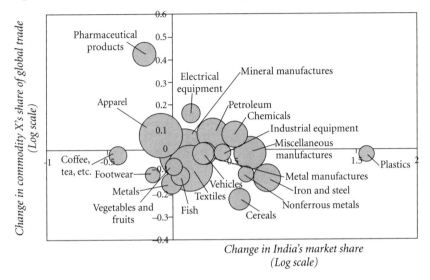

Sources: World Integrated Trade Solution; and IMF staff calculations.

While wages in certain sectors, such as IT, have been rising at rates of about 20 percent a year since 2000, a large informal sector and steady supply of new labor entrants is likely to have limited the pressure on overall wage levels. Labor has also become more productive. Rodrik and Subramanian (2005) estimate that labor productivity in India grew by over 3½ percent since the 1980s. Improvements in labor productivity have helped boost overall productivity in the manufacturing sector with estimates suggesting that total factor productivity in the official manufacturing sector rose annually by 3½ percent over the course of the 1990s and the early part of this decade.

Various surveys suggest that poor infrastructure and a high regulatory burden hinder India in making greater inroads into world markets (Figure 4.3). Poor roads and inadequate investment in ports and airports result in long delays and higher transport costs for Indian exporters. It takes 24 days for Indian exports to reach the United States compared with only 15 days from China, and 12 days from Hong Kong SAR (Winters and Mehta, 2003). In addition to facing some of the highest industrial electricity prices in the world, electricity outages cost Indian firms 8 percent of annual sales, four times higher than in China. Customs processing times are also slow. Shipments take just over 10 days to clear Indian customs compared with

Figure 4.2. India's Export Performance Relative to Other Asian Countries
(Value of country X's exports in percent of world goods exports)

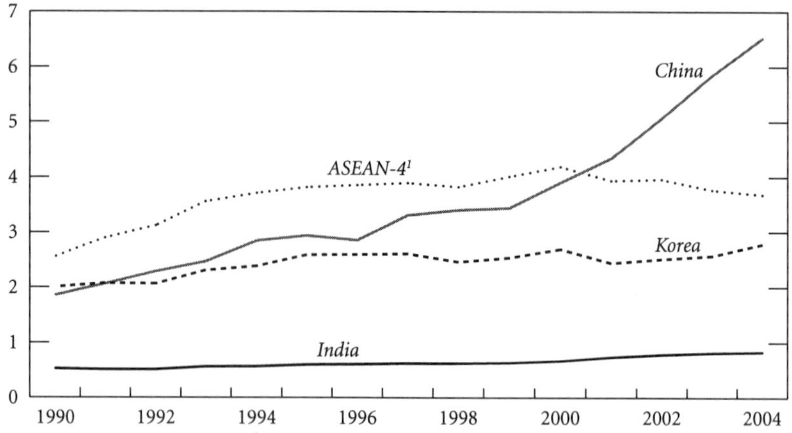

Source: IMF, *Direction of Trade Statistics.*
[1]Indonesia, Malysia, Philippines, and Thailand.

only 7 days in Korea and Thailand. Cumbersome procedures and regulations work to increase the cost of imported and domestic inputs used in producing Indian exports.

High import tariffs have also discouraged exports. In addition to raising the cost of imported intermediate imports for the export sector, import tariffs lower the price of exports relative to domestic sales, making exports less attractive. They also alter the level of wages and rates of return on capital. Despite the progress made in reducing trade tariffs in recent years—the average nonagricultural tariff declined from over 40 percent in 1997 to 17 percent in 2005—such tariffs are still about twice as high as the average of member countries of ASEAN. IMF staff estimates that India's import tariffs are equivalent to a tax on exports of about 31 percent, which is well above the simple average export-tax equivalent in developing countries of about 12.6 percent. If nontrade barriers, such as technical and safety requirements were included, the anti-export bias implied by India's tariff system would be even higher. These estimates suggest a strategy that seeks to reduce import tariffs by subjecting higher rates to deeper cuts than lower rates could boost the value of Indian exports by as much as 10 percent relative to a 2001 base. Complete elimination of import tariffs would boost their value by 45 percent.

The performance of the Indian textile sector following the removal of the quotas under the Multifiber Arrangement (MFA) regime is a case in

Figure 4.3. IMD Competitiveness Indicators, 2005

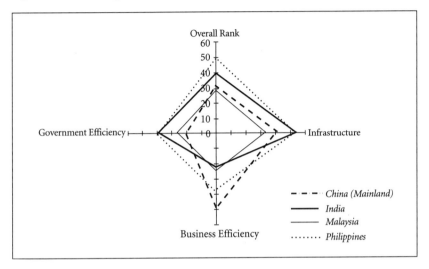

Source: International Institute for Management Development (IMD), *World Competitiveness Yearbook, 2005*.

point. In the first six months following the removal of these quotas, exports from China to the United States in liberalized tariff lines rose at rates in excess of 200 percent, while those to the EU rose by about 80 percent (Ananthakrishnan and Jain-Chandra, 2005). Through September 2005, Indian exports, in value and volume terms, to the United States grew by a more modest rate of about 20 percent, with similar rates of growth being experienced in the EU market. The fact that India has not gained larger market share in the textile sector following the removal of the quotas that bound Indian textile exports for decades reflects problems of scale economies, inflexible labor markets, low rates of investment, lack of full duty drawback, and poor infrastructure.

Exchange Rate and Competitiveness

The impact of the exchange rate on competitiveness is typically examined by estimating measures of a real "equilibrium" exchange rate. Studies on India employ one of three approaches. The extended purchasing power parity (PPP) approach assumes PPP holds in the long run but several factors interact to prevent the actual exchange rate from converging to this level in the near term. The "equilibrium" exchange rate is estimated using a single equation relating the actual real effective exchange rate (REER) to its determinants. The macroeconomic balance approach estimates the change in REER needed to bring about equilibrium in the balance of payments, where equilibrium is defined as a situation where the current account equals either the "normal" level of capital inflows, or the "structural" savings-investment balance. The third, the base approach, compares the actual REER to a base year where the REER and the current account were in "equilibrium." Each approach has drawbacks. The PPP approach assumes that perfect labor mobility links wages in the traded and nontraded sectors and that the law of one price holds continuously for the traded goods sector so that prices in this sector are given exogenously, conditions that may not hold in reality. Results are also sensitive to the variables included in the model. The macroeconomic balance approach relies heavily on researchers' judgment on what constitutes "normal" balance of payments flows. The base approach does not account for how the underlying "equilibrium" evolves over time with changes in the economy.

The various methodologies yield a wide range of estimates about the impact of the exchange rate on competitiveness. Table 4.3 summarizes the results from these various studies, including the estimates of the gap between the actual REER and its "equilibrium" level. Estimates of this difference range from –40 percent to 8 percent depending on the methodology used. The wide range of results highlights the extreme difficulty in determining an "equilibrium" exchange rate, particularly in a developing country where a multitude of factors can influence exchange rates and ongoing structural changes make underlying relationships unstable.

Developments in the Real Effective Exchange Rate

The accuracy of any assessment of the impact of the exchange rate on competitiveness hinges on an accurate measure of the REER. An outdated REER index risks giving misleading signals about competitiveness if it does not include information on how inflation and the exchange rate are evolving relative to India's most important trading partners. When assessing developments in India, most analysts have utilized the Reserve Bank of India's (RBI) five-country REER index that is based on the average bilateral trade shares of G-5 countries during the 1992/93–1996/97 period and wholesale price index inflation rates. Asian and other emerging market economies are not included in the index, despite their growing importance as trading partners. The RBI released a revised REER index in December 2005 that includes China and Hong Kong SAR. This study utilizes a revised measure of India's consumer-

Table 4.3. Estimates of Deviation from the Equilibrium Real Effective Exchange Rate

Study	Sample	Dependent Variable	Independent Variables			Assessment Year	Estimated Gap to Equilibrium
			Relative productivity	Net foreign assets	Other		
Extended PPP panel estimates							
Davoodi (2005)	133 countries; Penn World Tables, 2000	Relative price level to the U.S.	Relative per capita GDP to the U.S.	...	...	2000	−40 percent
Benassy-Quéré and others (2005)	15 countries, 1980–2001	CPI-based REER	Ratio of CPI to PPP	Cumulative current accounts scaled by GDP	...	2001	−16.4 percent
Lee and others (2005)	39 countries, 1980–2003	CPI-based REER	GDP per worker relative to trading partners	Cumulative current accounts scaled by GDP	Commodity terms of trade; output of manufactured goods	2004	−30 percent
Macroeconomic balance approach							
Union Bank of Switzerland (2003)	India	CPI-based REER	...	...	...	2005	Approx. −7 percent
Base year comparison							
JP Morgan/Deutsche Bank	India	RBI 5-country REER	...	...	...	2005	Approx. 5–10 percent

Table 4.4. Revised RBI and IMF Country Weights in REER Indices
(In percent of total)

	Old RBI 5-Country	IMF Broad 43-Country
Euro area		34.6
Germany	19.7	
France	6.3	
United States	38.7	18.8
Japan	18.7	7.1
United Kingdom	16.6	6.2
China		3.8
Other emerging Asia		13.5
Other countries		16.1

Source: Bayoumi, Lee, and Jayanthi (2005).

price-index (CPI)-based REER that utilizes updated weights (Table 4.4) using data from 46 industrial and emerging market economies derived from Bayoumi, Lee, and Jayanthi (2005). In addition to capturing the impact of changing trade patterns, the weights also reflect services, as well as goods trade, and incorporate the competition Indian exports face when they compete with goods of trading partners in third markets.

The revised index suggests that the REER fluctuated in a relatively tight band over the past decade, with some marked exceptions. Since the adoption of a managed float in 1993, pressures on the rupee to appreciate in real effective terms arising from a rising inflation differential with trading partners was contained to a large extent by nominal effective depreciation. However, the exchange rate regime afforded India ample flexibility to cope with shocks, with the slow upward appreciation of the REER punctuated by sharp depreciations in the context of the 1995 Mexican and the 1997 Asian crises when sudden stops in capital inflows triggered large depreciations in the nominal value of the rupee (Figure 4.4).

The updated REER shows that while the rupee appreciated in real effective terms over the course of 2005/06, it did so by less than suggested by older measures. While the revised REER generally tracks the RBI measure quite well, the updated index shows that the rupee appreciated in real effective terms by about 4½ percent since 1993, and by 5 percent since the start of the 2005/06 fiscal year (Figure 4.5). In contrast, the more dated five-country RBI REER index points to an appreciation of about twice this magnitude, while the RBI's revised REER index that was released late December 2005 suggests the rupee appreciated in real terms by a more modest 6.4 percent since 1993. However, comparing the current value of the REER to some fixed historical point can present a misleading picture about competitiveness as the appreciation of the exchange rate may reflect

Figure 4.4. CPI-Based Real Effective Exchange Rate and Its Components
(1993=100)

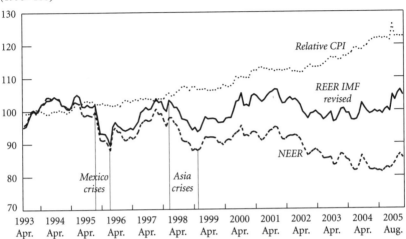

Source: IMF staff calculations.

improvements in underlying economic fundamentals that do not impair competitiveness. Deriving estimates of the underlying "equilibrium" real effective exchange rate to compare with the actual REER will provide greater insights about how the exchange rate is affecting competitiveness.

Determinants of the Real Effective Exchange Rate

An extended relative PPP approach is used to explain movements in the updated CPI-based REER. The approach is based on the premise that a country's nominal exchange rate tends to converge to its PPP-determined level, but various factors can prevent convergence in the near term. These factors are used in a single equation to estimate the REER and the latter is said to be in equilibrium when it equals the estimated exchange rate equation. The model estimated here incorporates the impact of relative productivity gains, as well as other fundamentals:

- *Relative productivity gains* proxied by GDP per worker relative to trading partners (*In_Prod*).[4] According to Balassa-Samuelson, faster productivity growth in the home country's tradable sector relative to its nontradable sector, compared to trading partners, typically pushes up wages in the tradable sector, which in turn leads to higher

---

[4]The author would like to thank Jaewoo Lee for providing this data.

Figure 4.5. RBI Five-Country REER and IMF Revised REER Measure
(1993=100)

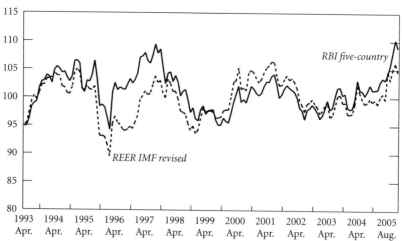

Sources: Reserve Bank of India (RBI); and IMF staff calculations.

nontradable wages and prices and an appreciation in the real exchange
rate.

- *Openness to trade* measured by the ratio of the sum of goods and
  services trade to world trade or, alternatively, Indian GDP. Trade
  liberalization usually leads to an increase in imports, deterioration in
  the current account balance, and a depreciation in the real exchange
  rate. Most studies use the ratio of goods trade to GDP. Here, we
  broaden the measure of trade to include services so that it more
  closely matches our measure of the REER. We also measure openness by scaling India's imports and exports by world trade to try to
  capture if increased openness translated into a greater share of world
  trade.
- *Net foreign assets* (NFA) of India (as calculated by Lane and Milesi-
  Ferretti, 2005) scaled by GDP. A long-run increase in the home country's NFA position (or a decline in its indebtedness) would require
  a smaller trade surplus over the medium term to match the lower
  level of debt service, which in turn requires a more appreciated real
  exchange rate.

The "equilibrium" exchange rate is estimated using cointegration tech-
niques. The long-run equilibrium (cointegrating) relationship between the
real exchange rate and the explanatory variables is derived from a vector

Table 4.5. Real Effective Exchange Rate Determinants

Variable	Specification[1]	
	1	2
Dependent Variable: *REER*		
Constant	−4.69	9.73
In_Prod	4.49	0.77
	(3.98)	(3.24)
NFA	−1.64	−0.50
	(−4.27)	(10.1023)
Open_World Trade	−7.27	
	(−4.37)	
Open_GDP		−1.86
		(11.8459)
Dummy_92–93		0.22
		(−5.13789)

Source: IMF staff estimates.

[1]*T*-statistics are reported in parentheses below coefficient estimates. All estimates are derived using a vector error correction model (VECM). The short-term dynamics derived using the VECM are available on request and include one-year lags of the dependent and explanatory variables and the coefficients are significant and of the expected sign.

error correction model using annual data from India from 1980 to 2004.[5] The results are reported in Table 4.5. Specification 1 measures openness by scaling India's trade by world trade; Specification 2 scales openness by GDP and includes a dummy variable to capture the move to a managed float in 1992–93. The coefficients of the cointegrating relationship and the realized values of the explanatory variables are used to derive the path of the "equilibrium" exchange rate to compare to the actual real exchange rate. Relative to panel-based studies, this has the advantage of deriving India-specific coefficients. However, the results derived need to be treated with caution. The relatively short time-series constrains the number of variables that can be included in the model and the series may not be sufficiently long to capture long-run structural relationships, resulting in imprecise estimates. It also limits the number of variables that could be included in the analysis.

While the results are sensitive to model specification, they suggest that the recent appreciation of the rupee has not been out of line with the estimated real "equilibrium" exchange rate. The coefficients in each model are statistically significant. Specification 1 implies that a 1 percentage point increase in India's productivity relative to its trading partners results in a

[5]Stationarity tests confirm the variables are all I(1). Johansen trace and maximum eigenvalue tests point to a single cointegration vector at the 10 percent level of significance.

Figure 4.6. Specification 1: Actual and Equilibrium REER (EREER)
(1995=100)

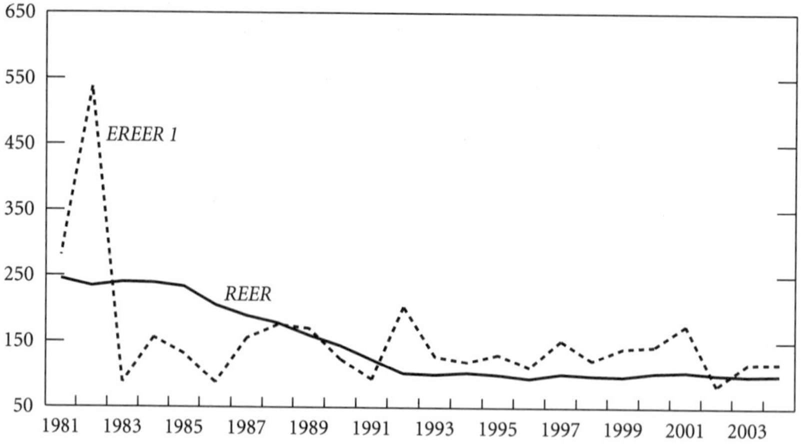

Source: IMF staff calculations.

sizable real appreciation. On the other hand, a 1 percentage point increase in the NFA position is associated with a depreciation of just over 1½ percent.[6] Comparing the estimated path of the "equilibrium" real effective exchange rate to the actual exchange rate in Figure 4.6 suggests that by end-2004 the actual real value of the rupee was about 15 percent below its "equilibrium" level. However, the coefficients in Specification 1 are large especially relative to the other studies, and Figure 4.6 also reveals long persistence in deviations in the real exchange rate from "equilibrium" and possible structural breaks in the "equilibrium" relationship[7] that call into question the reliability of the model. Thus, Specification 2 reestimates the long-run relationship including a dummy variable to capture the change in the exchange rate regime in 1992–93, and measures openness relative to GDP to avoid problems of endogeneity when scaling by world trade. The coefficients are closer in magnitude to those derived in other studies and imply that the real exchange rate was broadly in line with the real "equilibrium" exchange rate at end-2004 (Figure 4.7).

---

[6]The sign is counter to expectations. Other studies on Eastern European countries by Rahn (2003) and Alberola (2003) find a similar sign. Capital inflows may initially cause debt service to rise and the exchange rate to depreciate until such inflows translate into investment.

[7]The Gregory-Hansen test confirmed the existence of a structural break in the cointegrating relationship in 1992–93.

Figure 4.7. Specification 2: Estimates of the Equilibrium REER (EREER)
(1995=100)

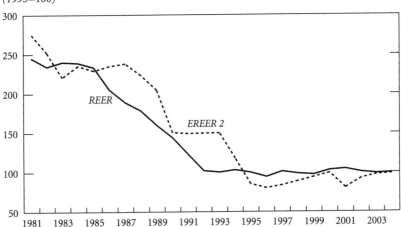

Source: IMF staff calculations.

The findings highlight the difficulty in modeling the "equilibrium" REER and the uncertainty attached to specific point estimates. Country-specific time-series studies of the type conducted here generally give smaller estimates of misalignment than studies that use a panel of countries.[8] The results are sensitive to how the fundamentals are modeled, highlighting the problems of relying on point estimates in such a framework. Moreover, the analysis excludes factors such as the terms of trade, the reduction in trade tariffs, and removal of quantitative restrictions, which in India's case would have tended to exert downward pressures on the "equilibrium" real exchange rate. Nonetheless, the econometric results and India's recent export performance suggest that at least at end-2004 the exchange rate was not contributing to competitiveness problems.

Outlook for India's Export Competitiveness

The econometric analysis suggests that various opposing forces will affect the future direction of the rupee. As agricultural workers are absorbed by the rest of the economy and structural reforms are implemented, India can expect to see continuing large gains in productivity. This implies that for

---

[8]See Égert, Halpern, and MacDonald, 2004.

Figure 4.8. Effective Exchange Rate Flexibility
(Ratio of exchange rate movements to reserve movements)

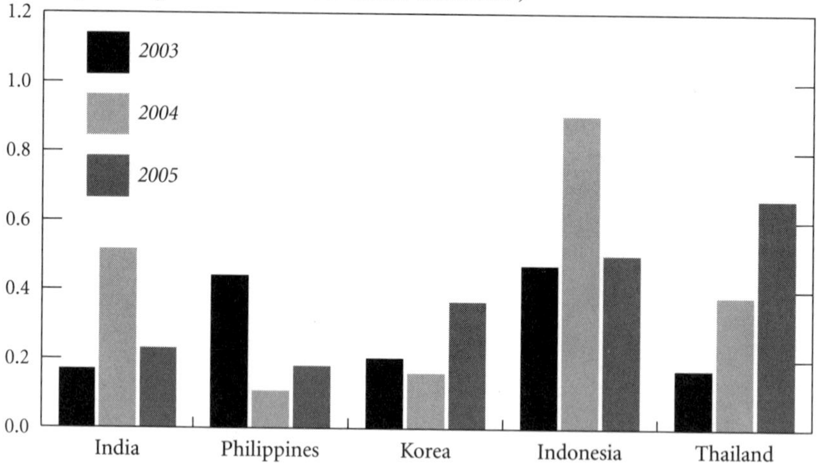

Source: IMF staff calculations.

the foreseeable future India's economy will likely grow faster than that of its trading partners. Using estimates from the model for the Balassa-Samuelson effect, assuming that India will grow in real terms by 6½ percent a year, and taking the weighted average medium-term growth rate of India's trading partners, the real exchange rate can be expected to appreciate by just over 2 percent a year in the coming years.[9] Capital inflows are likely to lead to a stronger NFA position, potentially adding to appreciation pressures. However, trade liberalization, and factors such as increased investment in import-intensive infrastructure, are likely to work against these pressures.

Going forward safeguarding India's export competitiveness will require flexibility in exchange rate management. Flexibility in the nominal exchange rate has increased, both in absolute terms and after taking into account differences across countries in the volatility in capital inflows (Figure 4.8).[10] Given the uncertainty about the future direction of the rupee it will be important to allow two-way flexibility in the exchange rate to respond to the diverging pressures, otherwise India risks experiencing inflationary (or deflationary) pressures.

---

[9]The 10-year average growth rates reported in International Monetary Fund (2005) are 2 percent a year for the EU, 3.3 percent for the United States, and 5.3 percent for emerging market and developing countries.

[10]Exchange rate flexibility is measured by comparing the volatility of the exchange rate to the volatility of reserves. The closer this ratio is to zero, the nearer the exchange rate system is to a fixed regime.

Conclusions

Despite recent gains, India remains a comparatively closed economy and the strides it has made into global markets in recent years only hint at its potential. India is making inroads into new markets and product areas, but it still has some way to go before it attains a level of market penetration that can rival its Asian neighbors. Although the real exchange rate has appreciated in recent years this does not appear to have contributed to a competitiveness problem. Looking forward, steps to lower trade tariffs and nontariff barriers and improve the investment climate, as well as flexibility in exchange rate management, will be key if India is to build on its advantages and become a leading global exporter.

References

Alberola, E., 2003, "Real Convergence, External Disequilibria and Equilibrium Exchange Rates in the EU Acceding Countries" (unpublished; Madrid: Bank of Spain).

Ananthakrishnan, Prasad, and Sonali Jain-Chandra, 2005, "The Impact on India of Trade Liberalization in the Textiles and Clothing Sector," IMF Working Paper No. 05/214 (Washington: International Monetary Fund).

Bayoumi, Tamim A., Jaewoo Lee, and Sarma Jayanthi, 2005, "New Rates from New Weights," IMF Working Paper No. 05/99 (Washington: International Monetary Fund).

Bénassy-Quéré, Agnès, Pascale Duran-Vigneron, Amina Lahrèche-Révil, and Valérie Mignon, 2005, "Real Equilibrium Exchange Rates: A G-20 Panel Cointegration Approach," in *Dollar Adjustment: How Far? Against What?* ed. by C. Fred Bergsten and John Williamson (Washington: Institute for International Economics).

Égert, Balázs, László Halpern, and Ronald MacDonald, 2004, "Equilibrium Exchange Rates in Transition Economies: Taking Stock of the Issues," CEPR Discussion Paper No. 4809 (London: Centre for Economic Policy Research).

Davoodi, Hamid, 2005, "Long-Term Prospects for the Real Value of the Tenge," in *Republic of Kazakhstan: Selected Issues*, IMF Country Report No. 05/240 (Washington: International Monetary Fund).

International Monetary Fund, 2005, *World Economic Outlook,* September, World Economic and Financial Surveys (Washington).

Lane, Philip R., and Gian Maria Milesi-Ferretti, 2005, "A Global Perspective on External Positions," IMF Working Paper No. 05/161 (Washington: International Monetary Fund).

Lee, J., G.M. Milesi-Ferretti, L. Ricci, and S. Jayanthi, 2005, "Equilibrium Real Exchange Rates: Estimates for Industrial Countries and Emerging Markets" (unpublished; Washington: International Monetary Fund).

Rahn, Jörg, 2003, "Bilateral Equilibrium Exchange Rates of EU Accession Countries Against the Euro," BOFIT Discussion Paper No. 11 (Helsinki: Bank of Finland).

Rodrik, Dani, and Arvind Subramanian, 2005, "From 'Hindu Growth' to Productivity Surge: The Mystery of the Indian Growth Transition," *IMF Staff Papers*, Vol. 52, No. 2, pp. 193–228.

Union Bank of Switzerland, 2003, *The Complete RMB Handbook, Asian Economic Perspectives*, UBS Investment Research (Hong Kong SAR).

Winters, Alan, and Pradeep S. Mehta, eds., 2003, *Bridging the Differences—Analyses of Five Issues of the WTO Agenda*, CUTS (Jaipur, India: Center for International Trade, Economics and Environment).

5

How Can India Attract More Foreign Direct Investment?

SONALI JAIN-CHANDRA

Foreign direct investment (FDI) is favored over other capital flows by emerging market countries. FDI is not debt creating, is less volatile than portfolio flows, and is relatively resistant during financial crises (Albuquerque, 2003). FDI has also been associated with positive spillovers through technology transfer and training to local industry (Blomström and Kokko, 2003), and may lead to enhanced export performance and growth (Borensztein and others, 1998).

FDI flows into India have risen since the 1990s but remain low, compared with other emerging market countries (Table 5.1).[1] Starting at similar magnitudes (relative to GDP) of inflows in the early 1990s, FDI into China has taken off, while FDI into India has trickled in. In 2004 India received FDI inflows of around 0.5 percent of GDP, whereas China received FDI worth 3.2 percent of GDP. In dollar terms, China received 16 times the FDI than India in 2004.

At the same time, investor surveys point to a strong interest in India as a destination for FDI. Investor surveys by the United Nations Conference on Trade and Development (UNCTAD) and A.T. Kearney in 2004 and 2005 place India as the second most attractive destination for FDI.[2] This

---

[1]The Indian authorities revised the FDI data to conform to international standards by including reinvested earnings. The data used here are the revised FDI data net of outflows.

[2]India is perceived as a future "hot spot" for FDI, second only to China, according to the United Nations Conference on Trade and Development (2004). This finding relies on available relevant leading macroeconomic and microeconomic indicators influencing future FDI flows, as well as the findings of the three UNCTAD global surveys.

Table 5.1. Foreign Direct Investment in Selected Countries, 2004

	Net Foreign Direct Investment	
	In percent of GDP	In billions of U.S. dollars
Chile	7.1	6.7
Vietnam	5.3	2.3
Singapore	5.0	5.4
China	3.2	53.1
Argentina	2.6	3.9
Malaysia	2.2	2.6
Mexico	2.1	14.1
Venezuela	1.7	1.9
Sri Lanka	1.5	0.3
Brazil	1.4	8.7
Pakistan	0.9	0.9
Bangladesh	0.7	0.4
India	0.5	3.4
Korea	0.5	3.4
Nepal	0.5	0.0
Indonesia	0.4	1.1
Thailand	0.4	0.7
Philippines	0.1	0.1

Source: IMF, *World Economic Outlook.*

indicates that while India is on investors' radar screens, the interest has not yet translated into actual FDI inflows. The A.T. Kearney (2005) survey finds that investors expect India's attractiveness to increase as the government maintains focus on reforms and removes the infrastructure and regulatory barriers.

This chapter studies the reasons for the underperformance of FDI in India and examines potential measures to enhance it. Utilizing panel data for a number of emerging market countries, the chapter concludes that the most important factors affecting FDI are not FDI-specific policies but, rather, broader economic policies including corporate taxes, trade openness, and other business climate issues, such as regulatory quality and burden. This chapter also looks at differences across Indian states in attracting FDI and concludes that broad business climate issues largely determine FDI location.

Foreign Direct Investment Regime in India

India's regulatory regime for FDI has been gradually liberalized since 1991, and, as a result, the regime is no longer particularly restrictive by international standards.[3] Before 1991 all FDI proposals were considered on a case-by-case basis with FDI capped at 40 percent of total equity investment. In 1991, the policy was amended to allow automatic approval of up to 51 percent ownership in 34 sectors. This list was expanded to cover 111 sectors in 1997. In 2000, the policy was altered to one using a "negative list" approach. Since then, 100 percent FDI is permitted in most sectors via the automatic route, with the requirement that the Reserve Bank of India (RBI) be notified within 30 days. There are important exceptions to this general policy for which FDI approvals are routed through the Foreign Investment Promotion Board. These exceptions include industries subject to licensing, the acquisition of an existing Indian company under certain conditions,[4] industries where the foreign investor has a presence in the same field, and industries where sectoral policies apply (Table 5.2). FDI is not permitted in retail trading, lottery business, gambling and betting, atomic energy, and agriculture and plantation.

FDI Inflows: Is India an Outlier?

As India's FDI regime is relatively unrestrictive, the key question is what other factors could explain the underperformance of FDI. Some papers emphasize macroeconomic stability and openness, while others the quality of institutions.[5] The standard determinants of FDI include labor market conditions, the quality of infrastructure, corporate taxation, inflation, trade openness, market size, corruption and administrative procedures, and bottlenecks. Existing qualitative work on India emphasizes factors limiting FDI, such as relatively high tariffs and limited scale of export processing zones, stringent labor laws, high corporate tax rates, exit barriers, a restrictive FDI regime, and the lack of transparent sectoral policies for FDI.[6] The

---

[3]India ranks 26th of 117 countries in terms of the "impact of rules on FDI" (see World Economic Forum, 2005). A lower rank is better. Most other emerging market countries fare more poorly: Thailand (39), Mexico (51), Indonesia (66), China (68), the Philippines (79), Brazil (80), and Poland (81). In the same survey, India ranks 36th of 117 countries in terms of the restrictiveness of foreign ownership. Most other emerging market countries again fare more poorly: Malaysia (37), Mexico (42), Korea (61), Thailand (66), Indonesia (69), Brazil (70), China (80), and the Philippines (107).

[4]For the acquisition of shares in an existing Indian company in the financial services sector and where the rules of the Securities and Exchange Board of India apply.

[5]For details, see Mercereau (2005), Dollar and others (2004), Hines (1996), Javorcik and Spatareanu (2004), Wei (2000), and Wheeler and Mody (1992).

[6]See Bajpai and Sachs (2000). Progress in the liberalization of the FDI regime has taken place since this paper was written.

Table 5.2. Sectoral Caps and Controls on Foreign Direct Investment in India, 2004

Sector	Cap	Controls
Private sector banking	74	Subject to Reserve Bank of India (RBI) guidelines. The cap is applicable only to private sector banks that are identified by RBI for restructuring.
Nonbanking financial companies (NBFCs)	100	Various minimum capitalization norms for fund-based NBFCs.
Insurance	26	Automatic route available, subject to obtaining license from the regulatory body. 2004/05 budget proposed raising it to 49 percent; however, this is not yet operational.
Airports	74/100	74 percent foreign direct investment (FDI) under automatic route. Government approval required for FDI beyond it.
Domestic airlines	49	Automatic route available. Foreign equity participation up to 49 percent and investment by expatriate Indians up to 100 percent. Subject to no direct or indirect equity participation by foreign airlines.
Telecommunications		Restrictions include licensing, FDI beyond 49 percent needs approval from Foreign Investment Promotion Board (FIPB), and divestiture of 26 percent in five years.
	74	For basic, cellular, value-added services, and global mobile personal communications by satellite, subject to licensing and security requirements, and a lock in period for transfer of equity.
	100	For e-mail, voice mail, Internet service providers (ISPs) not providing gateways.
	74	For ISPs with gateways, radio-paging and end-to-end bandwidth. FDI beyond 49 percent requires government approval.
Petroleum (refining)	26	Cap applies to public sector units. Automatic route not available.
	100	Cap applies to private Indian companies. Automatic route available.
Petroleum (other than refining)	100	Automatic route available. FDI of 100 percent is possible in oil exploration in small and medium-sized fields, petroleum product marketing, and natural gas/liquefied petroleum gas (approval required).
Housing and real estate	100	Automatic route available. Applies to townships, housing, built up infrastructure, and construction-based development projects.

Table 5.2 *(concluded)*

Sector	Cap	Controls
Coal and lignite	100	For most activities in this sector.
	74	For coal exploration or mining. Other restrictions apply.
Venture capital		Requires RBI approval. Subject to regulations under the Foreign Exchange Management Act.
Trading	51	Automatic route available. Meant for export activities.
Atomic minerals	74	For subsectors, mining, separation, value addition, and integrated activities.
Defense and strategic industries	26	Automatic route not available. Subject to licensing and security requirements.
Agriculture	0	No FDI is permitted.
	100	Tea, including tea plantations. Restrictions apply, including approval from government, divestiture of 26 percent in five years, and approval in case of change in land use.
Print media	100	FDI allowed in publishing and printing scientific and technical magazines, periodicals, and journals.
	26	In newspapers and periodicals dealing with current events, subject to editorial control by Indian residents.
Broadcasting	100	In television software production.
	49	In cable networks, direct to home (including both FDI and foreign institutional investors).
Mining	74	Automatic route available in the exploration and mining of diamonds and precious stones.
	100	Automatic route available in the exploration and mining of gold, silver, and other metals.
Postal services	100	FDI of 100 percent in courier services, with prior approval. No FDI allowed in the distribution of letters.
Establishment and operation of satellites	74	Automatic route not available.

Source: Ministry of Commerce and Industry, Department of Industrial Policy and Promotion.

Global Competitiveness Report 2005–06, based on investor surveys, lists key constraints to doing business in India (Figure 5.1). A.T. Kearney (2004) notes that investors favor China over India, citing as factors market size, access to export markets, government incentives, favorable cost structures,

Figure 5.1. India: The Most Problematic Factors for Doing Business[1]
(In percent of responses)

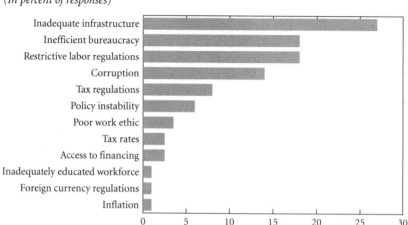

Source: World Economic Forum (2005).
[1]From a list of 14 factors, respondents were asked to select the 5 most problematic for doing business and rank them between 1 (most problematic) and 5. The bars in the figure show the responses weighted according to their rankings.

infrastructure, political stability, and the macroeconomic climate. India's potential attractiveness stems from its highly educated work force, management talent, rule of law, and transparency.[7]

Despite being one of the fastest growing economies, the investment climate in other emerging markets in Asia appears to be more conducive to attracting FDI inflows (Table 5.3). Compared to selected Asian countries, India's overall infrastructure quality ranks low (World Economic Forum, 2005). The significant burden of bureaucratic red tape and regulation in India further worsens the investment climate. For instance, it takes 89 days to start a business in India, more than double the time required to start up in China. The enforcement of contracts takes longer in India (425 days) than the average in the sample. Also, once in business, firms find it difficult to exit.[8] Labor market rigidities are especially onerous in India.

---

[7]A.T. Kearney surveys highlight the different perceptions about China and India, with China as a leading manufacturer and the fastest growing consumer market and India as the world's business process and information technology provider with longer-term market potential.

[8]Gorg (2002) examines U.S. investment in 33 countries to conclude that exit costs are more important than incentives to attract FDI.

Table 5.3. Snapshot of the Investment Climate in Selected Emerging Market Countries

	India	China	Indonesia	Korea	Malaysia	Thailand
Macroeconomic environment						
GDP per capita (constant						
2000 U.S. dollar, 2004)	538.4	1,161.5	906.2	12,742.5	4,220.6	2,399.4
GDP growth (2005 proj.)	7.4	9.0	6.0	3.8	5.5	3.5
Gross capital formation						
(current U.S. dollar, 2003)	138.3	627.0	42.0	177.9	22.2	35.8
Inflation (2005 proj.)	3.9	3.0	8.1	2.9	3.0	4.2
Openness (trade in goods as						
a percent of GDP, 2004)	32.6	79.4	57.7	66.1	221.0	124.6
Current account (percent of						
GDP, 2005 proj.)	−2.5	6.1	1.2	1.9	13.5	−2.5
International reserves (billion						
U.S. dollar, 2004)	131.2	618.6	36.3	199.0	66.7	49.8
Governance indicators (2004)[1]						
Voice and accountability	0.3	−1.5	−0.4	0.7	−0.4	0.2
Political stability	−0.8	−0.1	−1.4	0.5	0.4	−0.1
Government effectiveness	0.0	0.1	−0.4	0.9	1.0	0.4
Regulatory quality	−0.6	−0.5	−0.4	0.7	0.4	0.0
Rule of law	−0.1	−0.5	−0.9	0.7	0.5	−0.1
Control of corruption	−0.1	−0.5	−1.2	0.2	0.3	−0.3
Infrastructure						
Overall infrastructure quality						
(rank out of 117 countries)[2]	78.0	69.0	66.0	23.0	14.0	33.0
Electric power consumption						
(kwh per capita, 2002)	379.8	987.1	411.0	6,171.1	2,831.8	1,625.8
Internet users (per 1,000						
people, 2003)	17.5	63.2	37.6	609.7	344.1	110.5
Roads, paved (percent of total						
roads, 1999)	45.7	91.0	57.1	74.5	75.8	97.5
Telephone main lines (per 1,000						
people, 2003)	46.3	209.0	39.4	538.3	181.6	104.9
Bureaucratic red tape and						
corporate taxation						
Number of start-up procedures						
to register a business (2004)	11	12	12	12	9	8
Time to start a business						
(days, 2004)	89	41	151	22	30	33
Time to enforce a contract						
(days, 2004)	425	241	570	75	300	390
Time to exit a business (years, 2004)	10	2	6	2	2	3
Protection against dismissal[3]	0.9	0.3	0.7	0.3	0.0	0.3
Efficiency of legal framework						
(rank out of 117)[2,4]	30	57	73	38	16	36
Burden of government regulation						
(rank out of 117)[2]	76	30	45	14	3	11
Transparency of government						
policymaking (rank out of 102)[2,5]	41	33	64	25	14	31
Efficiency of the tax system						
(rank out of 117)[2]	55	51	35	46	8	20

Table 5.3 *(concluded)*

	India	China	Indonesia	Korea	Malaysia	Thailand
Highest marginal tax rate, corporate rate (percent, 2004)[6]	36	30	30	27	28	30
Difficulty in firing index (2004)	90	40	70	30	10	20
Hiring and firing practices (rank out of 117)[2,7]	111	26	67	41	43	38

Sources: World Bank, *World Development Indicators,* World Bank Governance Database, and World Bank Doing Business Database 2004; World Economic Forum, *Global Competitiveness Report 2005–06;* and Botero and others (2003).

[1]Higher values correspond to better outcomes.

[2]A higher rank implies a better outcome.

[3]Methodology: Among other factors, protection against dismissal is measured by taking into account whether an employer has to notify a third party before firing one worker, whether the employer needs the approval of the third party, and if the employer must provide retraining before dismissal.

[4]Defined as the legal framework for private businesses to settle disputes and challenge the legality of government actions and/or regulations.

[5]Defined as to what extent firms are usually informed clearly and transparently by the government on changes in policies and regulations.

[6]2002 data for China.

[7]Hiring and firing workers is impeded by regulations or is flexibly determined by employers.

To examine the potential obstacles to FDI more formally, we estimate the following reduced form equation using a fixed effects model:

$$FDI_{i,t} / GDP_{i,t} = \alpha_i + \beta X_{i,t} + \varepsilon_{i,t},$$

where α_i is the country-specific effect and the matrix $X_{i,t}$ contains the lagged independent variables (to alleviate the simultaneity bias), including standard determinants of FDI and institutional quality variables.[9] All indicators used in Table 5.3 cannot be included simultaneously in the panel because of insufficient data. However, the core variables included in each specification are the marginal statutory corporate tax rate, a proxy for infrastructure development (the number of telephone lines per 1,000 inhabitants), inflation, and openness (trade as a percent of GDP). Institutional quality is measured by the World Bank governance indicators (voice and accountability, political instability, government effectiveness, regulatory burden, rule of law, and corruption). As these variables are highly correlated, they are sequentially included in the regressions to avoid multicollinearity. To check for robustness, we also include alternative measures of institutional quality.

---

[9]Data sources include the World Bank's *World Development Indicators,* the IMF's *International Financial Statistics,* RBI *Annual Reports,* the FDI database of the Organization for Economic Cooperation and Development, the *World Investment Report,* the World Bank Governance Database (Kaufmann and others, 2004), and Political Risk Services (PRS) Group's *International Country Risk Guide.* The countries in the sample are the ones listed in Table 5.1. The estimation is done using an unbalanced panel from 1980 to 2002.

We find that marginal corporate tax rates, trade openness, and institutional factors, and, to some extent, the quality of infrastructure are significant determinants of FDI (Table 5.4).[10] While the results are sensitive to the specification, they are nevertheless indicative of the potential for the large response of FDI to reforms. Assuming that India's response to a policy change is the same as the average country in the sample:

- A decrease in the marginal corporate tax rate in India from the current rates to that of China would increase FDI by 1 percentage point of GDP. (For details on investor friendly tax policy, see Chapter 9.)
- An increase in trade openness in India to China's level would garner another 0.6 percentage points of GDP in FDI. The benefits from further trade liberalization are examined in detail in Chapter 3.
- Improving regulatory quality in India to the level of Thailand would add another percentage point of GDP in FDI inflows.
- If India halves the number of days needed to start a business or halves the years needed to resolve insolvency, FDI could rise by 0.7 percentage points and 1.4 percentage points of GDP, respectively.

Labor market flexibility also appears to be an important factor determining FDI, and India has a relatively inflexible labor market.[11] Protection against dismissal is stringent in India (Table 5.3) as in downturns it is exceedingly difficult to fire workers. Correlation between the labor market flexibility and FDI across countries suggests that countries with inflexible labor markets receive less FDI.[12]

How Do FDI Inflows and the Business Climate Vary Across Indian States?

FDI has been concentrated in a few Indian states. During 2000–03, 5 out of 29 rapidly growing states received 60–70 percent of FDI inflows into India: Andhra Pradesh, Delhi, Karnataka, Maharashtra, and Tamil Nadu. Even among these states, there is considerable heterogeneity. Maharashtra received more than ten times the amount of FDI per capita than

---

[10]Regressions using the between panel estimator conclude that the quality of infrastructure is a determinant of FDI.

[11]However, for emerging market countries time-series data on labor market indicators are generally not available and therefore they are not included in the regression analysis.

[12]Javorcik and Spatareanu (2004) also find that, for a sample of 25 European countries, increased labor market flexibility is associated with larger FDI inflows. For a sample of 11 emerging market countries, the correlation between FDI as a share of GDP and the World Bank's "difficulty of firing index" is −0.52.

Table 5.4. Results of the Panel Estimation of the Determinants of Foreign Direct Investment[1]

	(1)	(2)	(3)	(4)	(5)	(6)	(7)	(8)	(9)	(10)	(11)	(12)	(13)	(14)	(15)
Openness	0.022 (2.94)*	0.025 (3.60)*													
Corporate tax	−0.176 (2.27)**	−0.157 (2.22)**	−0.172 (2.07)**	−0.062 (0.88)	−0.067 (0.9)	−0.101 (1.25)	−0.082 (1.01)	−0.033 (0.43)	−0.176 (1.87)***	−0.195 (2.08)**	−0.179 (1.95)***	−0.158 (1.74)***	−0.191 (2.24)***	−0.181 (2.26)**	−0.191 (2.24)**
Inflation	−0.033 (0.88)	−0.036 (1)	0.031 (1.04)	0.027 (0.88)	0.003 (0.09)	0.03 (0.98)	0.013 (0.42)	−0.025 (0.67)	−0.03 (0.8)	−0.024 (0.64)	−0.013 (0.34)	0.018 (0.47)	−0.013 (0.34)		
Telecommunications	18.402 (1.91)***	10.805 (1.18)	6.379 (0.79)	6.067 (0.72)	6.337 (0.7)	9.307 (1.1)	9.461 (1.13)	3.293 (0.3)	6.25 (0.57)	6.056 (0.55)	7.827 (0.74)	2.506 (0.23)	2.115 (0.21)	2.506 (0.23)	
Voice and accountability			−1.096 (1.41)												
Government stability				0.521 (2.58)*											0.521 (2.58)*
Law and order					1.278 (3.55)*										
Corruption						0.786 (1.90)***									
Days to start-up							−0.015 (1.73)***								
Years to resolve insolvency								−0.25 (1.83)***							
Days to enforce a contract									−0.006 (2.12)**						
Corruption										2.016 (3.41)*					
Rule of law											1.993 (2.99)*				
Regulatory quality												1.45 (2.21)**			
Government effectiveness													2.188 (3.42)*		
Political stability														2.145 (3.98)*	
Constant	7.075 (2.90)*	5.494 (2.33)**	7.662 (2.95)**	4.413 (2.02)**	4.008 (1.68)***	5.24 (2.04)**	4.601 (1.81)***	3.519 (1.46)	8.93 (3.03)*	9.292 (3.15)*	8.896 (3.10)*	5.754 (1.85)***	4.079 (1.3)	3.787 (1.35)	4.079 (1.3)

Source: Author's calculations.

[1] Absolute value of z-statistics in parentheses. ***, **, and * indicate significance at 10 percent, 5 percent, and 1 percent levels, respectively.

Table 5.5. Approvals and Inflows of Foreign Direct Investment (FDI) into Indian States and Territories

	FDI Inflows (2000–02) (In billions of rupees)	FDI Approvals (2000–02) (In billions of rupees)	Realization Ratio	FDI/State Domestic Product		FDI/ Population 2000
				2000	2001	
Andhra Pradesh	8.8	17.0	51.9	0.2	0.3	3.3
Assam	0.1	0.0	...	0.0	0.0	0.0
Bihar	0.0	0.3	5.0	0.0	0.0	0.0
Gujarat	4.3	24.2	17.7	0.0	0.1	0.6
Haryana	0.0	6.7	0.0	0.0	0.0	0.0
Himachal Pradesh	0.0	8.1	0.0	0.0	0.0	0.0
Karnataka	27.9	42.8	65.1	0.6	1.3	11.0
Kerala	1.8	7.2	24.7	0.1	0.1	1.7
Madhya Pradesh	0.2	4.0	5.6	0.0	0.0	0.1
Maharashtra	114.4	103.0	111.0	1.7	1.2	37.0
Meghalaya	0.0	0.0	...	0.0	0.0	0.0
Orissa	0.0	2.4	0.0	0.0	0.0	0.0
Punjab	0.0	0.4	0.0	0.0	0.0	0.0
Rajasthan	0.1	5.6	1.5	0.0	0.0	0.0
Tamil Nadu	26.4	61.9	42.6	0.4	0.6	8.9
Uttar Pradesh	0.0	11.2	0.0	−0.1	0.0	−1.2
West Bengal	2.3	12.5	18.6	0.2	0.0	2.9
Chattisgarh	0.0	0.2	0.0	0.0	0.0	0.0
Chandigarh	10.1	0.5	2,003.6	4.0	0.1	181.2
Dadra and Nagar Haveli	0.0	0.0	500.0	...	...	0.9
Delhi	123.7	63.5	194.7	4.7	...	178.3
Goa	1.9	4.7	41.0	...	...	22.8
Pondicherry	3.0	8.5	35.3	0.0	8.8	0.0

Sources: Ministry of Finance; and CEIC Asia database.

Andhra Pradesh in 2000 (Table 5.5). It is also these very states that are most successful in converting FDI approvals into actual inflows.[13]

Investor surveys of business climate are consistent with the observed patterns of FDI flows. A survey of foreign investors (Federation of Indian Chambers of Commerce and Industry, 2004) puts Maharashtra in the clear lead in terms of investor perception. In the survey of investment climate of Indian states by the Confederation of Indian Industry and World Bank (2002), Maharashtra and Gujarat are classified as the best investment climate states while Kerala, West Bengal, and Uttar Pradesh are classified as poor investment climate states. While the perceptions of business climate in states are appropriately correlated with the inflows of FDI, there are outliers. For

---

[13]This analysis includes data for only a few years, and it is possible that it takes longer for approved FDI to translate into realized inflows.

**Figure 5.2. Indian States: Foreign Direct Investment (FDI)
and Infrastructure and Labor Markets**
(In percent of responses)

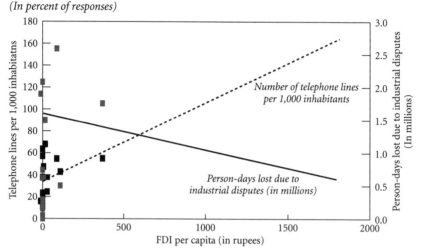

Sources: Ministry of Finance; Indiastat; CEIC Asia database.

example, Delhi gets much more FDI than would be indicated by an assessment of its business climate, probably reflecting its role as India's capital.

Differences in FDI appear to be explained by differences in the functioning of labor markets, regulatory burden, and infrastructure quality.[14] Labor market flexibility appears to be important in determining FDI as states with poor labor market indicators (such as the most person-days lost due to strikes) fare worse in terms of FDI inflows (Figure 5.2).[15] There is some evidence that infrastructure is also a determinant of FDI location. Specifically, states with a higher density of telephone lines attract more FDI (Figure 5.2). Finally, the burden of regulation also influences the location of FDI. States where it takes longer to enforce contracts and clear customs are also states with lower FDI (Figure 5.3).

State-specific policies and incentives to attract FDI are not a substitute for improving the overall business climate. The federal structure in India empowers the states to design their own investment policies to attract FDI,

---

[14]The absence of consistent time-series data for Indian states precludes a rigorous econometric investigation.

[15]While there are national labor laws, states do have the power to amend national legislation. According to an assessment of the investment climate by the World Bank (2002), Indian states with the best investment climate have on average 11.9 percent of overstaffing, while this number rises to 15.5 percent in states having a poor investment climate.

**Figure 5.3. Indian States: Foreign Direct Investment (FDI) Inflow
and the Burden of Regulation**

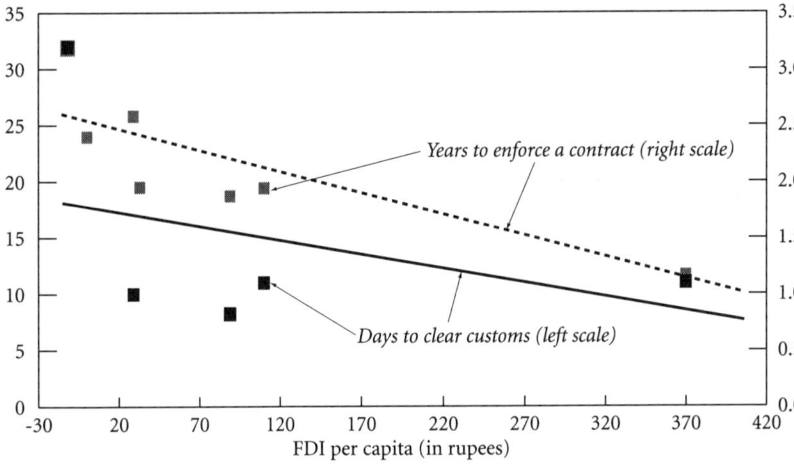

Source: IMF staff calculations.

along with instituting specific incentives for certain sectors. A one-stop clearance window is now available in most states for investors to meet all regulatory requirements and obtain all approvals. In addition, some states have offered tax concessions, capital and interest subsidies, and reductions in power tariffs. For instance, Karnataka has been aggressive in attracting FDI and has outlined a series of policies, such as investment subsidies, exemptions for export-oriented units, and refunds and fiscal incentives for specific industries such as information technology, biotechnology, and business process outsourcing. While incentives make it easier to conduct business, they are unlikely to be the main determinant of the location of FDI.[16] This is borne out by the experience of states such as Haryana, Himachal Pradesh, and West Bengal, which offer incentives, but attract little FDI.

---

[16]Most studies conclude that tax incentives neither affect significantly the amount of direct investment nor usually determine the location to which investment is drawn (Wells and Allen, 2001; Chang and Cheng, 1992; Foreign Investment Advisory Service, 1999; International Monetary Fund, 2003; Tanzi and Shome, 1992; and United Nations Conference on Trade and Development, 2004). In fact, Lim (1983) finds a negative relationship between incentives and investment, as the latter compensates for an otherwise unfavorable business climate. A survey of firms in member countries of the Association of South East Asian Nations shows that the removal of incentives will not have a great impact on investment decisions (Mirza and others, 1997).

Conclusions

The most important factors influencing FDI into India are not FDI-specific policies but, rather, broader economic policies including corporate taxes, trade openness, and other business climate issues, such as regulatory quality and burden. India has made considerable progress in liberalizing its FDI regime, which is a necessary but not a sufficient condition to attract significant FDI inflows. The differences across Indian states in attracting FDI further underscore the importance of the business climate in determining FDI rather than FDI-specific incentives. With the current international attention on India's tremendous potential for FDI, it would be an opportune time to push for rapid progress on structural reforms to drastically increase FDI inflows.

References

Albuquerque, Rui, 2003, "The Composition of International Capital Flows: Risk Sharing Through Foreign Direct Investment," *Journal of International Economics*, Vol. 61 (December), pp. 353–83.

A.T. Kearney, 2004 and 2005, "FDI Confidence Index" (Alexandria, Virginia: Global Business Policy Council).

Bajpai, Nirupam, and Jeffrey D. Sachs, 2000, "Foreign Direct Investment in India," Development Discussion Paper No. 759 (Cambridge, Massachusetts: Harvard Institute for International Development).

Blomström, Magnus, and Ari Kokko, 2003, "The Economics of Foreign Direct Investment Incentives," NBER Working Paper No. 9489 (Cambridge, Massachusetts: National Bureau of Economic Research).

Borensztein, Eduardo, Jose De Gregorio, and Jong-Wha Lee, 1998, "How Does Foreign Direct Investment Affect Economic Growth?" *Journal of International Economics*, Vol. 45, Issue 1, pp. 115–35.

Botero, Juan, Simeon Djankov, Rafael La Porta, Florencio Lopez-de-Silanes, and Andrei Shleifer, 2003, "The Regulation of Labor," NBER Working Paper No. 9756 (Cambridge, Massachusetts: National Bureau of Economic Research).

Chang, Ching-huei, and Peter W.H. Cheng, 1992, "Tax Policy and Foreign Direct Investment in Taiwan," in *The Political Economy of Tax Reform*, ed. by Takatoshi Ito and Anne O. Krueger (Chicago: University of Chicago Press).

Confederation of Indian Industry and World Bank, 2002, *Competitiveness of Indian Manufacturing: Results from a Firm-Level Survey* (New Delhi).

Dollar, David, Mary Hallward-Driemeier, and Taye Mengistae, 2004, "Investment Climate and International Integration," Policy Research Working Paper No. 3323 (Washington: World Bank).

Federation of Indian Chambers of Commerce and Industry (FICCI), 2004, *FICCI's FDI Survey 2004: The Experience of Foreign Direct Investors in India* (New Delhi).

Foreign Investment Advisory Service, 1999, "Thailand: A Review of Investment Incentives" (Washington).

Gorg, Holger, 2002, "Fancy a Stay at the Hotel California? Foreign Direct Investment, Taxation and Firing Costs" (unpublished; Bonn: Institute for the Study of Labor).

Hines, James, 1996, "Altered States: Taxes and the Location of Foreign Direct Investment in America," *American Economic Review*, Vol. 86 (December), pp. 1076–94.

International Monetary Fund, 2003, *Foreign Direct Investment in Emerging Market Countries: Report of the Working Group of the Capital Markets Consultative Group* (Washington).

Javorcik, Beata, and Mariana Spatareanu, 2004, "Do Foreign Investors Care About Labor Market Regulations?" Policy Research Working Paper No. 3275 (Washington: World Bank).

Kaufmann, Daniel, Aart Kraay, and Massimo Mastruzzi, 2004, "Governance Matters III: Governance Indicators for 1996–2002," Policy Research Working Paper No. 3106 (Washington: World Bank).

Lim, David, 1983, "Fiscal Incentives and Direct Foreign Investment in Less Developed Countries," *Journal of Development Studies*, Vol. 19 (January), pp. 207–12.

Mercereau, Benoît, 2005, "FDI Flows to Asia: Did the Dragon Crowd Out the Tigers?" IMF Working Paper No. 05/189 (Washington: International Monetary Fund).

Mirza, Hafiz, Frank Bartels, Mark Hiley, and Axèle Giroud, 1997, "The Promotion of Foreign Direct Investment into and Within ASEAN: Towards the Establishment of an ASEAN Investment Area," ASEAN Secretariat (Jakarta).

Tanzi, Vito, and Parathasarathi Shome, 1992, "The Role of Taxation in the Development of East Asian Economies," in *The Political Economy of Tax Reform*, ed. by Takatoshi Ito and Anne O. Krueger (Chicago: University of Chicago Press).

United Nations Conference on Trade and Development, 2004, *Prospects for FDI Flows, Transnational Corporation Strategies and Promotion Policies: 2004–2007* (Geneva).

Wei, Shang-Jin, 2000, "How Taxing Is Corruption on International Investors?" *Review of Economics and Statistics*, Vol. 82, No. 1, pp. 1–11.

Wells, Louis, and Nancy Allen, 2001, "Tax Holidays to Attract Foreign Direct Investment: Lessons from Two Experiences," Foreign Investment Advisory Service (Washington).

Wheeler, David, and Ashoka Mody, 1992, "International Investment Location Decisions: The Case of U.S. Firms," *Journal of International Economics*, Vol. 33, Issues 1–2 (August), pp. 57–76.

World Bank, 2002, "Improving the Investment Climate in India," *Pilot Investment Climate Assessment* (Washington).

———, 2003, *Doing Business in 2004* (Washington).

World Economic Forum, 2004, "Executive Opinion Survey," *Global Competitiveness Report* (Geneva).

———, 2005, *Global Competitiveness Report 2005–06* (Geneva).

6

On the Way to a World-Class Banking Sector

Dmitriy Rozhkov

In recent decades, the level of a country's financial development has been accepted as one of the key determinants of the country's economic growth. A positive relationship between financial development and growth has been established in the economic literature since the works of Schumpeter (1911) and Gurley and Shaw (1955), and has later been shown to exist at the cross-country, industry, and firm levels. More recently, a number of studies indicated that financial development is one of the determinants of economic growth.[1]

A developed and efficient financial (and, in particular, banking) system is important for the overall level of a country's development for two related reasons. First, it provides an incentive for households to put their savings in a formal financial system, thereby making those savings available for productive investment. Second, it helps to ensure that available financial resources are applied according to their most productive uses, thereby maximizing the returns on investments, and improving productivity in the economy. In other words, the key economic contribution of banks is their role in efficiently intermediating between borrowers and lenders.

Furthermore, a strong and efficient financial sector helps to reduce vulnerabilities, which is especially important in the presence of large and potentially volatile capital flows. While theoretical predictions are some-

---

[1]King and Levine (1993), Levine (1997), Rajan and Zingales (1998), and Favara (2003).

Figure 6.1. Indicators of Financial Depth, 1980–2005
(In percent)

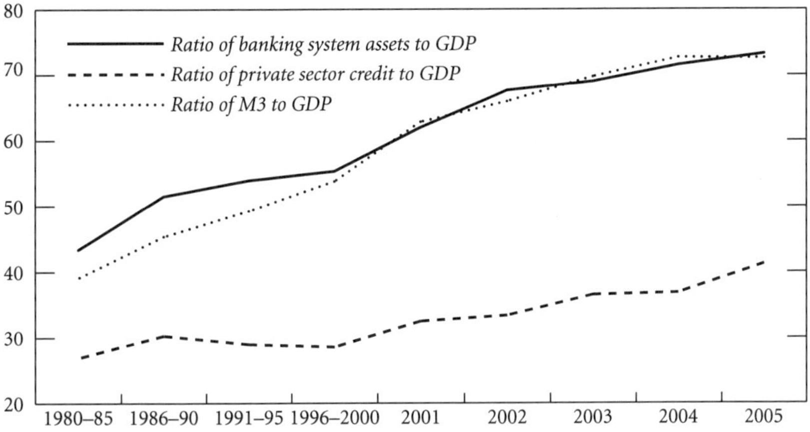

Source: Reserve Bank of India.

what ambiguous, many recent empirical studies have suggested that greater openness and competitiveness of banking systems reduce the probability of a systemic banking crisis.[2]

This chapter looks at India's progress in building a strong and efficient banking system. It reviews the recent developments in the Indian financial sector, and assesses potential risks to the banking system posed by the recent rapid credit growth. It then turns to the remaining obstacles to financial development.

Recent Developments in the Indian Financial Sector

In recent decades, India has achieved significant progress in developing and deepening its financial system. All commonly used measures of financial sector depth (such as the ratios of banking system assets, deposits, and loans, and broad money (M3) to GDP) have substantially increased (Figure 6.1).

Furthermore, in the 1990s and early 2000s, the Indian authorities have taken important steps toward deregulation of the banking sector. Interest rates have been progressively deregulated on both the deposit and lending

---

[2]Beck, Demirgüç-Kunt, and Levine (2003); Boyd and De Nicoló (2005); and Al Jalal, Boyd, and De Nicoló (forthcoming).

Figure 6.2. Growth in Total Credit and Deposits, 2000–05
(In percent)

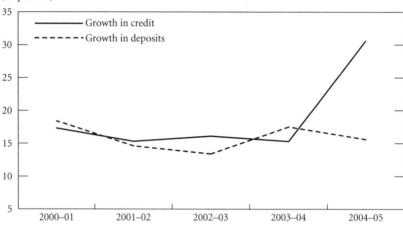

Source: Reserve Bank of India.

sides,[3] and competition has increased through entry of new private and foreign banks (Koeva, 2003). Over the same period, disclosure standards for banks have improved, and bank regulation and supervision have been steadily strengthened.

Most recently, the pace of financial development in India has accelerated. In 2004–05, annual growth of bank credit in India was 30.6 percent, compared with a growth of 15.6 percent in deposits (Figure 6.2). As a result, the credit-to-deposit ratio reached a record 66 percent in March 2005, and exceeded 100 percent when only new loans and deposits are considered. Data for April–December 2005 indicate that the growth of credit continued at an annual rate of just over 30 percent, while deposits grew by 17 percent in annualized terms over the same period.

As a result of this acceleration, in 2004 India had the fastest real rate of credit growth in Asia, followed by Indonesia (Table 6.1). However, India's experience with such high rates of credit growth was not unique. In fact, it was outpaced by several countries in emerging Europe and Central Asia, where real rates of credit growth exceeded 40 percent, driven in part by financial deepening and by the entry of foreign banks. Credit growth rates were lower among the industrial countries in Europe, but in some of

---

[3]The remaining restrictions on interest rates include a cap for small loans (under Rs 200,000) at the prime lending rate, and a floor on short-term deposit rates.

Table 6.1. Real Credit Growth in Selected Countries and Regions, 2002–04
(In percent)

	Real Growth of Credit to Private Sector[1]			Private Sector Credit to GDP			Capital to Risk-Weighted Assets	NPLs to Gross Loans	Return on Assets
	2002	2003	2004	2002	2003	2004	2004	2004	2004
India	16.5	5.7	25.3	33.5	32.9	38.3	13.4	6.6	1.2
Indonesia	5.4	13.4	18.9	18.9	20.9	23.4	20.9	13.4	2.5
Sri Lanka	4.4	9.7	12.9	28.6	29.9	31.5	10.0	16.0	...
Bangladesh	12.5	3.8	10.2	27.2	26.8	28.2	8.7	17.6	0.7
China	18.2	19.4	7.1	135.8	147.1	140.5	3.9[2]	15.6[3]	...
Emerging Asia	6.2	4.6	8.1	77.5	78.1	77.1	14.2	10.9	1.3
Emerging Europe	15.1	22.5	21.0	32.1	34.7	38.0	17.5	7.6	1.5
Western Europe	3.0	5.0	7.1	133.7	137.2	141.1	12.7	1.9	1.0
Latin America	1.6	−3.9	3.8	33.8	31.5	31.0	16.1	6.6	1.6
Middle East and Central Asia	14.6	15.8	20.5	35.1	36.0	37.6	18.3	13.6	1.7
Sub-Saharan Africa	11.5	11.8	8.3	14.1	15.2	14.7	16.9	13.3	3.1

Source: IMF, Monetary and Financial Systems Department.
[1]Deflated by end of period CPI.
[2]Not risk-weighted capital ratio.
[3]State-owned commercial banks.

them they significantly exceeded the GDP growth rates (notably in Ireland, Spain, and Greece).

In addition to financial deepening, recent credit growth in India was also partly driven by cyclical factors. Strong income growth, rapidly growing consumer demand, and decreasing borrowing costs have contributed to rising demand for credit. India is now going through an upward phase of an economic cycle, with real GDP growing at an average annual rate of about 8 percent over the last three years. IMF staff estimates using the Hodrick-Prescott filter indicate that recently credit growth has begun to outpace the cyclical upturn (Figure 6.3). In 2004, credit growth in India was 8 percent above trend, with GDP growth a much smaller 1 percent above trend.

Indian credit growth has been relatively broad based (Table 6.2). In the year ended in March 2005, nationalized banks[4] (accounting for 47 percent of total credit of the banking system) saw their credit growing fastest, at 33.6 percent, but other groups of banks were not far behind. Credit in metropolitan areas was the fastest growing (Bangalore and Mumbai witnessed the

[4]Public banks in India comprise the State Bank of India group and banks that were nationalized in the late 1970s and early 1980s.

Figure 6.3. Cyclical Components of Real Credit Growth, 1994–2004[1]

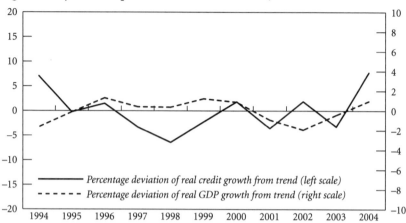

Sources: Reserve Bank of India; and IMF staff estimates.
[1]Trends are estimated using Hodrick-Prescott filter.

fastest growth of credit, 49 percent and 42 percent, respectively), but credit in rural areas (representing 9 percent of the total) also grew by 25 percent.

Priority sectors (which include agriculture and small-scale industries) were the main contributors to the growth in nonfood credit (Table 6.3). Priority sectors accounted for 40 percent of the total 28 percent growth of nonfood credit. Within the priority sectors, agriculture loans in particular were a main driver of growth with a 35 percent increase in 2004–05. This continued the trend of the last 10 years, which saw the share of industry in the total loan portfolio of commercial banks declining from 54 percent in 1995/96 to 38 percent in 2004/05.

Another important development over the same period was a reduction in Indian corporations' reliance on bank loans as a source of financing. Unlike in most developing countries, Indian companies do not rely exclusively on banks for financing. The corporate bond market is fairly active,[5] and companies have started to use the capital market and external borrowings more actively (although in the last few years this trend likely was driven by a fast appreciation of the Indian stock market). Between 2000 and 2005, the share of equity in total resource mobilization of the Indian cor-

---

[5]In 2004/05, total resources raised from the debt markets were Rs 2.051 billion (6.6 percent of GDP). The corporate sector accounted for 29 percent of that amount, with the remaining 71 percent taken by the government. About 93 percent of corporate debt in 2004/05 was raised through private placements (Sharma and Sinha, 2006).

Table 6.2. Growth of Loans and Deposits by Type of Bank and by Region

	Deposits March 2004	Deposits March 2005	Loans March 2004	Loans March 2005	Share in Total Credit March 2005
	Annual growth rates, in percent				In percent
By groups of banks					
State Bank of India group	19.7	15.7	16.1	26.0	23.1
Nationalized banks	16.2	15.9	15.6	33.6	47.4
Foreign banks	28.6	5.2	15.3	24.6	6.7
Regional rural banks	12.1	10.0	18.2	24.7	2.8
Other scheduled commercial banks	23.4	17.8	23.8	31.9	20.1
All scheduled commercial banks	18.7	15.6	17.3	30.6	100.0
By population groups					
Rural	10.7	9.4	14.0	24.9	9.2
Semiurban	11.2	10.5	19.7	28.9	11.3
Urban	14.1	13.7	24.8	24.4	16.4
Metropolitan	26.6	19.8	15.5	33.4	63.1
By major banking centers					
Mumbai	31.3	20.5	10.5	41.8	27.5
Delhi	28.6	22.3	15.9	26.6	12.2
Chennai	21.6	13.7	16.4	16.7	5.0
Bangalore	33.6	19.9	31.6	49.0	4.3
Kolkata	16.4	17.7	13.8	22.5	3.9
Hyderabad	17.8	18.4	31.3	34.7	2.6
Ahmedabad	41.4	34.3	11.6	25.9	1.6
Pune	13.6	17.5	20.0	27.7	1.2
Jaipur	12.5	19.2	40.8	35.9	1.0
Chandigarh	10.8	17.1	42.5	3.5	1.0

Source: Reserve Bank of India.

porate sector (equity and debt) increased from 4.2 percent to 26.5 percent (Sharma and Sinha, 2006). The ratio of stock market capitalization to GDP in India is significantly higher than in low-income countries and in most economies in transition, although it is still lower than in many emerging market economies in Asia and in industrial countries (Figure 6.4).

Consumer credit in India is starting from a very low base, but is growing rapidly. In 2004, total household credit (which includes mortgage loans and consumer durables credit) was lower than in most emerging market economies in Asia, when measured in percent of GDP or of total credit (Table 6.4).[6] However, mortgage loans were growing at a faster rate than in

[6]In central and southeastern Europe, which also experienced a period of rapid growth of consumer loans from a low base, consumer loans at end-2004 were equal to 12.4 percent and 11.9 percent of GDP, respectively.

Table 6.3. Credit Growth by Sector
(Percent change)

| | Percent Change | | Contribution to Credit Growth |
	2003/04	2004/05	2004/05
Priority sector	24.7	31.0	11.2
Agriculture	23.2	35.2	...
Small-scale industry	9.0	15.6	...
Others	38.3	37.0	...
Industry (medium and large)	5.1	17.4	5.9
Petroleum	−16.8	19.2	...
Infrastructure	41.6	52.3	...
Automobiles	−5.8	20.0	...
Cement	−11.5	7.4	...
Housing	42.1	44.6	3.2
Nonbanking financial companies	18.9	10.8	0.2
Wholesale trade	10.1	36.0	1.2
Export credit	17.2	14.3	1.1
Gross nonfood bank credit	17.5	27.9	27.9

Source: Reserve Bank of India.

any other emerging market Asian economy, and credit card debt was picking up as well, albeit from very low levels.

Retail banking is increasingly viewed by Indian banks as an attractive market segment. The expansion of the retail banking segment can be attributed to a growing middle class with high disposable income, wider choices of consumer durables, increased acceptance of credit cards, and increased demand for housing loans, spurred by attractive tax breaks. In addition, the Reserve Bank of India (RBI) has taken a number of initiatives to increase transparency and competition in the credit market, including the dissemination of information on lending rates of banks since 2002, and the creation of a credit registry.

Risks from the Recent Rapid Credit Growth

The rapid credit growth described in the previous section is a welcome development, since it is mostly a sign of increasing financial depth. However, credit growth at the speed that was recently experienced in India inevitably brings with it some potential risks, related to possible weaknesses in risk assessment by banks, as well as potential problems for capital adequacy and liquidity. The key task of the policymakers, therefore, is not to slow down the credit growth, but to minimize the risks associated with it, to make

Figure 6.4. Stock Market Capitalization to GDP, End-2004
(In percent)

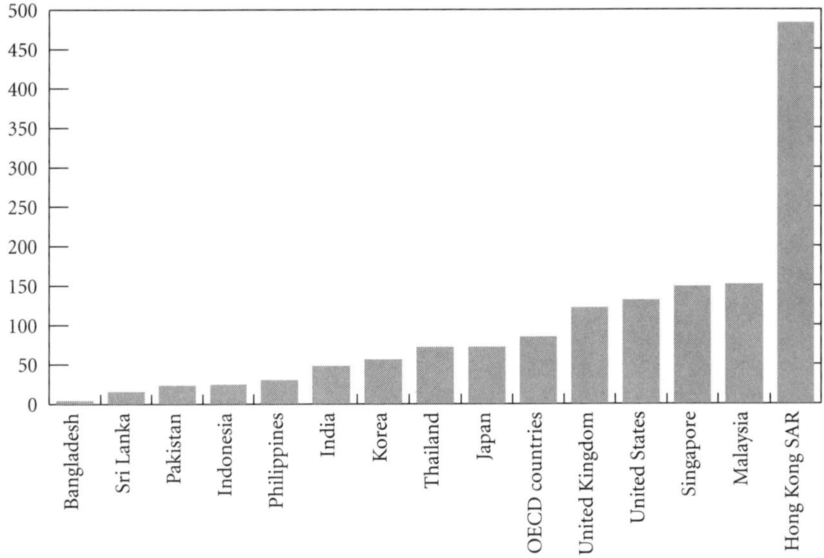

Source: Beck, Demirgüç-Kunt, and Levine (2000) database updated in January 2006.

sure the credit growth is sustainable. Moreover, there is always a question of whether market mechanisms are allowed to work to allocate credit in the most efficient way. The next two sections deal with these issues in turn. This section will look at potential risks from the rapid credit growth, and the next section will analyze the remaining obstacles to efficient allocation of credit and to the financial sector development in general.

While most lending booms do not end with a banking crisis, most significant episodes of banking distress in the last 20 years were preceded by rapid credit growth (Figure 6.5). Various empirical studies estimate the likelihood of a banking crisis following a lending boom to be as high as 20 percent.[7] Some countries that experienced a financial crisis in the last 20 years had a credit-to-GDP ratio at the time of the crisis as low as 40 percent, similar to the current Indian level.

Fast credit growth can trigger banking distress through two channels—macroeconomic imbalances and deterioration of loan quality. At present, macroeconomic risks from fast credit growth appear to be minimal in India.

---

[7]Duenwald, Gueorguiev, and Schaechter (2005); Dell'Ariccia (2006); and Kaminsky and Reinhart (1999).

Table 6.4. Consumer Credit in Asia, 2004

	Hong Kong SAR	India	Korea[1]	Malaysia	Philippines[1]	Singapore	Taiwan Province of China	Thailand
Household credit (percent of GDP)	58.9	7.2	61.0	52.4	5.4	54.1	52.5	22.6
Household credit (percent of total credit)	35.6	22.0	56.2	44.5	16.4	50.3	41.6	24.4
Mortgage loans (percent of total household credit)	83.0	47.3	55.1	56.5	38.4	61.9	59.8	65.9
Credit card debt (percent of total household credit)	6.4	3.3	35.4	37.7	16.1	35.4	31.7	26.8
Growth of mortgage loans in 2003–04	−1.9	42.0	15.5	15.4	4.1	15.9	15.5	15.6
Growth of credit card debt in 2003–04	0.7	36.0	−36.1	14.0	16.1	−0.3	31.1	29.7
Nonperforming loan (NPL) ratio for credit card debt	5.4	6.3	34.0	4.2	19.4	3.2	...	...

Sources: For India, Reserve Bank of India; for other countries, "The Growth of Consumer Credit in Asia," *Hong Kong Monetary Authority Quarterly Bulletin*, March 2005.

[1]For Korea and the Philippines, NPL ratio is for 2003.

**Figure 6.5. Average Credit to GDP Ratio in Eight Countries
That Had Financial Crisis in 1987–97[1]**

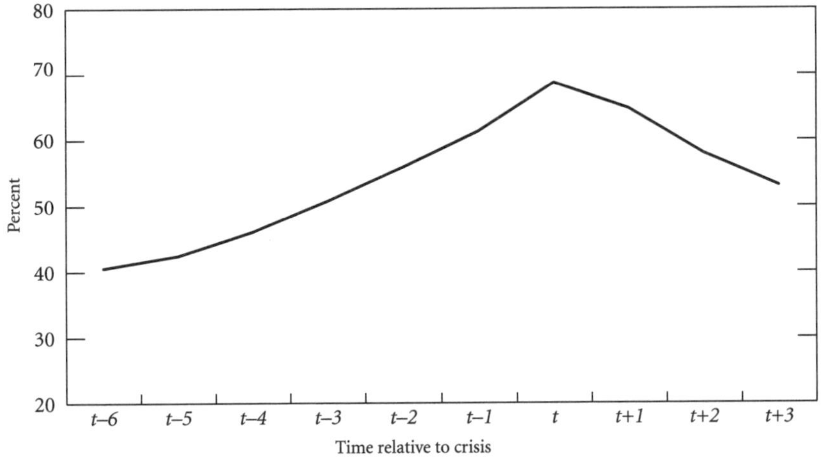

Time relative to crisis

Source: Duenwald, Gueorguiev, and Schaechter (2005).
[1]Finland, Indonesia, Korea, Mexico, Norway, Philippines, Sweden, and Thailand.

Although credit growth has resulted in a reduction of banks' holdings of government securities, this has so far led to only a modest increase in treasury bill rates. Moreover, while imports and the trade and current account deficits are rising, RBI reserves of $160 billion as of end-April 2006 are large. The key risk in the Indian case, therefore, appears to be credit risk.

In cases when rapid credit growth did lead to a banking crisis, it was usually due to a failure by banks and supervisors to maintain asset quality, properly account for risks, and ensure that adequate buffers were built in anticipation of a possible downturn. In times of rapid credit growth, the mere quantity of loan applications makes risk assessment difficult, and often results in a decreased quality of new loans. An additional source of concern in the Indian case comes from the fact that the current rapid credit growth is in part due to cyclical factors (and risk tends to be underestimated during booms and overestimated in recessions), and is accompanied by considerable exuberance in asset markets, suggesting the possibility of asset overvaluation.[8]

---

[8]Real estate prices in major metropolitan areas (such as Bangalore, Kolkata, and Mumbai) have increased at an annual rate of about 20 percent since 2003, with prices accelerating in the second half of 2004. Until the end of 2005, the Indian stock market had been growing at an annual rate of about 37 percent since early 2004.

Table 6.5. Nonperforming Assets (NPAs), March 2005

	Public Banks	Private Banks	Foreign Banks	All Banks
NPAs to gross loans	5.5	4.4	2.8	5.2
Provisioning ratio	61.3	50.0	62.8	59.7
Net NPAs to capital	13.6	9.5	4.5	11.7
NPA ratios in				
Priority sectors	7.5	3.2	1.8	6.7
Agriculture	6.4	2.2	8.1	5.6
Small-scale industry	11.6	11.1	2.7	11.3
Others	6.4	1.9	1.3	5.3
Consumer loans	2.5	1.7	2.4	2.2
Mortgage loans	2.4	1.0	1.1	1.9
Credit card debt	25.0	11.4	5.4	7.9

Source: Reserve Bank of India.

The aggregate nonperforming asset (NPA) ratio of the Indian banking system is currently low, although it may increase in the future. The aggregate nonperforming loan (NPL) ratio was 5 percent at end-March 2005, after having steadily decreased for the last five years. However, the most recent decreases in the NPL ratio are in part due to credit growth itself, as a growing share of the stock of loans is relatively new. Deterioration in asset quality typically occurs with a lag of one to two years, since a loan is classified as nonperforming only after it has not been serviced for a certain time. Furthermore, the NPA ratio is highest in public banks, which dominate the sector, and in lending to priority sectors, which is the biggest contributor to the overall credit growth (Table 6.5). While these numbers are not high enough for serious concern at the moment, they suggest that the policy of encouraging banks to increase their lending to priority sectors should at the least be conditional on appropriate credit assessment by banks.

Rapid credit growth also puts pressure on banks' capital. New loans to the private sector increase risk-weighted assets, making it more difficult for banks to satisfy the capital adequacy requirement. So far, however, capital adequacy of the system appears sound. The aggregate capital adequacy ratio (CAR) was at 12.8 percent as of end-March 2005, and only two banks out of 87 were violating the RBI requirement of 9 percent. Nevertheless, there are indications that some banks may have started to feel pressure on their capital. At end-March 2005, seven banks had a CAR between 9 percent and 10 percent (against only one bank a year before), and there were reports of some banks issuing significant amounts of subordinated debt to shore up their Tier II capital.

Stress Tests

Stress tests can be used to assess the vulnerability of the Indian banking system to credit risk. Three scenarios were considered by the IMF staff: (1) an increase in provisioning to the levels consistent with international best practices;[9] (2) an increase in NPLs by 25 percent; and (3) an increase in NPLs due to a portion of the "new" loans becoming nonperforming. In the third scenario, we assume that all loans made in the last two years are currently performing. Then, we assess the effect of these "new" loans becoming nonperforming at the same NPL rate that the "old" loans currently have. Assuming that the NPL ratio of the "old" loans reflects the average quality of risk assessment mechanisms currently in place and the average riskiness of lending in India, this is a fairly realistic scenario.

The results of the stress tests indicate that the Indian banking system as a whole is resilient to the tightening of provisioning requirements and to the deterioration in credit quality that typically accompanies periods of rapid credit growth (Table 6.6). No group of banks would experience serious capitalization problems as a result of increased provisioning or a 25 percent increase in NPLs. In the third scenario, which has the biggest effect on banks' capitalization, most groups of banks still remain above or very close to the capital adequacy requirement of 9 percent. The only exception are old private banks, whose aggregate CAR falls to 6 percent, but these banks together account for less than 6 percent of the market. Capital adequacy of all of the six largest banks in the country remains above 8 percent in this scenario. However, the next four banks (accounting for 12 percent of the system's assets) would see their capital adequacy fall to the levels of 4–7 percent. While this is a significant reduction compared with their current levels of capitalization, it need not present a systemic risk for the banking sector, and the affected banks should be able to restore their capital adequacy relatively quickly through new capital injections, consolidation, or other means.

The analysis above suggests that, while the recent rapid credit growth does present some risks, at the moment those risks do not appear to be significant. There are currently no signs of serious asset quality problems in the banking system, the aggregate ratio of credit to deposits is still moderate, capital adequacy ratios are sufficiently high, and the NPA ratios are low.

---

[9]Current regulations require provisioning of 20 percent on all substandard loans (defined as 3–12 months overdue), gradually increasing to 100 percent for loans that are more than three years overdue. In the stress tests, we test the effect of introducing a more stringent requirement of 25 percent provisioning on all substandard loans, and 100 percent provisioning on all loans that are overdue for more than 12 months.

Table 6.6. Stress Tests: Capital Adequacy Ratio Under Various Scenarios

	All Banks	Public Banks	Old Private Banks	New Private Banks	Foreign Banks	Ten Largest Banks
Actual at end-March 2005	12.8	12.8	12.5	12.1	14.1	12.7
Stress tests scenarios						
Increased provisioning	12.0	11.9	10.7	11.7	13.8	11.8
NPLs increase by 25 percent	10.4	10.0	7.5	11.1	13.2	10.1
New loans become NPLs at						
the same rate as old loans	9.4	8.8	6.0	10.7	12.8	9.0
Memorandum item:						
Market share (assets)	100.0	74.8	5.8	12.5	6.8	55.4

Sources: Reserve Bank of India; and IMF staff estimates.

Nevertheless, credit developments need to be closely monitored, to ensure that potential risks do not materialize.

Sound financial policies (including prudential rules and regulations) play a crucial role in allowing the level of stress in the financial system to be contained (Das and others, 2005). The RBI has already taken several steps to respond to potential risks. In 2004 and 2005, it increased the risk weights on consumer and housing loans, and on commercial real estate and capital market exposures.[10] It also tightened loan classification rules in line with the international best practices, by requiring that a loan be classified as nonperforming after it has not been serviced for 90 days, instead of the previous 180 days. More recently, general provisioning for nonpriority sector loans was increased from 0.25 percent to 0.4 percent.

The RBI is also working on reducing potential risks from the expansion of consumer credit. Consumer credit is still at low levels in India, and the NPL ratios are low (2.2 percent for all retail loans, 1.9 percent for housing loans, and 7.9 percent for credit card debt). However, the rapid rise in credit card debt (36 percent in 2004/05), as well as the already sizable share of nonperforming loans and reports of unfair market practices, point to the possibility of future problems. Experience of other countries (notably Korea) shows that developments in this area need to be closely monitored, especially in an environment where the concept of consumer credit is new for most borrowers. The RBI has recently issued a set of guidelines for credit card operations, aimed at raising consumer awareness and punishing unfair market practices.

---

[10]Risk weights on housing loans went up from 50 percent to 75 percent, and weights on consumer credit and capital market and commercial real estate exposures were raised from 100 percent to 125 percent, above those recommended in the Basel Capital Accord.

Figure 6.6. Banks' Credit to the Private Sector, 2004
(In percent of GDP)

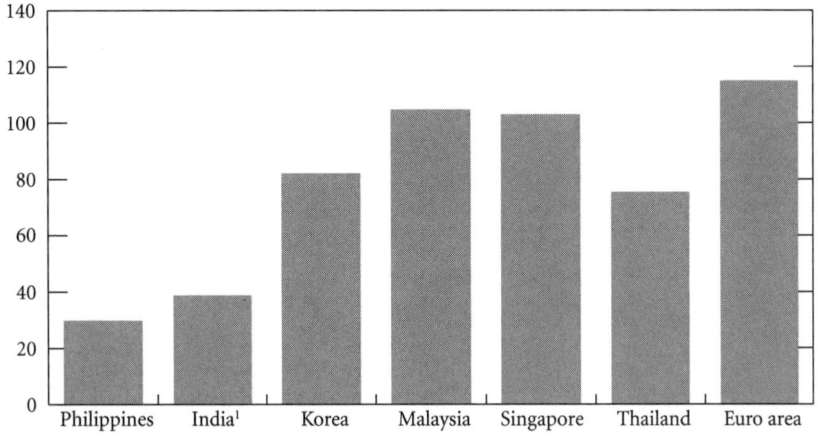

Source: IMF, *International Financial Statistics.*
[1]Data for India are for end-March 2005.

Nevertheless, additional prudential steps could be considered, especially if rapid credit growth continues. Experience of other countries that had periods of high credit growth can be useful. Hilbers and others (2005) explored the policy options that are available to counter and reduce the risks resulting from fast credit growth. The Indian authorities have indicated that they are considering the scope for additional steps, including the further tightening of loan classification norms and the introduction of "special mention" loans that would require provisions (International Monetary Fund, 2006).

Remaining Obstacles to Financial Development

The improving financial soundness of the banking sector and the absence of major risks provide an opportunity to devote more attention to developmental issues, and to accelerate banking reforms.

Despite all the remarkable progress of the last decades, India still lags behind the major industrial countries in financial sector development. The ratio of private sector credit to GDP grew from 33 percent in 2002 to around 40 percent in 2005—a level that may be impressive by developing countries standards but that is significantly lower than the levels in many other Asian countries, Western Europe, or North America (Figure 6.6). Many types of credit—in particular retail credit—still remain at very low levels, as banks in India have

Figure 6.7. Access of Indian Households to Formal Finance[1]
(In percent)

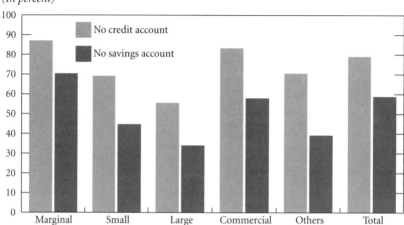

Source: Srivastava (2004).
[1]Marginal farming households are those with landholding of less than one acre; small with one to four acres; large with four or more acres. Commercial households are with or without land, but with income from nonfarm sources exceeding half of total household income.

tended to invest a large share of their deposits in government securities. Government securities still account for 31 percent of banking system assets, while net loans account for about 50 percent. Although growing rapidly, retail loans (which include housing loans, consumer durables, credit card receivables, and other personal loans) are still small at about 7 percent of GDP.

Furthermore, although Indian banking has become more inclusive over the years, the majority of rural population (including large farmers) still does not have access to finance from a formal source (Srivastava, 2004; and Basu, 2005) (Figure 6.7). This happens in spite of the fact that Indian banks typically exceed the government's target for the loan growth in priority sectors. The demographic branch penetration in India (6.3 branches per 100,000 people) is also lower than the developing Asia average of 7.5 (Beck, Demirgüç-Kunt, and Martinez Peria, 2005). This leads rural households to rely heavily on informal finance, where the interests charged averaged 48 percent a year in 2003.

To compensate for the lack of finance from the formal banks, some new innovative microfinance approaches have been developed, including the self-help group (SHG) bank linkage, which received strong support from the government. However, the reach of microfinance institutions has been modest, and in any case microfinance cannot substitute for the efficient formal financial sector (Basu, 2005; and Basu and Srivastava, 2005).

Another potential source of finance for rural households are rural coop-erative banks. However, many of them are in financial distress, with NPAs reaching 35 percent in some banks. More than a third of rural cooperatives are undercapitalized, and about a fourth are unprofitable. These banks also present a significant regulatory burden, given their large number and a number of differences in the regulatory frameworks for cooperatives and scheduled commercial banks.

Priority Sector Lending

One of the reasons for the continued failure of the Indian financial sys-tem to provide finance to the underprivileged population is the continued reliance on priority sector lending as a means to provide finance to rural areas. A recent World Bank report (Srivastava, 2004) noted that the directed lending norms that require banks to allocate 40 percent of their lending to the "priority sectors" have not generated the intended results, as access to finance of the rural households, as well as of the small and medium-sized enterprises (SMEs), remains at a very low level.

Lending in rural areas and to the SMEs remains a high-risk and high-cost proposition for banks. Uncertainty about the borrowers' ability to repay, in the absence of credit information (and of proper accounting in the case of SMEs), drives up default risk. In addition, transaction costs are high, due to the small loan size, high frequency of transactions, large geographical spread, and widespread illiteracy (Srivastava, 2004). As a result, most banks prefer to get around the priority lending requirement by subscribing to other eligible instruments. Similar programs of directed lending in other countries were also typically shown to be unsuccessful in improving access to credit for the targeted groups.

A substantial impact on financial sector development could be achieved by a shift from the heavy reliance on priority sector lending to removing roadblocks to lending, such as remaining difficulties in recovering assets, lack of well-developed credit registries, and weak accounting practices in SMEs. The passage of the new Securitization and Debt Recovery legislation in 2002 and 2004,[11] and the creation of the new credit registry in 2005, were

---

[11]The Securitization and Reconstruction of Financial Assets and Enforcement of Security Interest Act was passed in 2002. The Act confers powers on secured creditors to take pos-session and sell assets kept as security if a default is committed by the borrower in repay-ing secured debt. The Act also aims to regulate securitization, reconstruct financial assets, and enforce security interests. Some minor amendments to the Act were later made in the Enforcement of Security Interest and Recovery of Debts Laws (Amendment) Act in 2004.

both significant positive developments, but collateral requirements and limits on microfinance continue to constrain potential.

Dominance of Public Sector Banks

Another major obstacle to faster financial sector development in India is the continued dominance of public sector banks. Public banks account for 75 percent of banking system assets, 78 percent of deposits, and 67 percent of capital. Public banks have also played the major role in recent rapid growth in domestic credit. In contrast, foreign banks currently account for about 7 percent of total assets of the banking system, 5 percent of deposits, and 11 percent of capital.

The public sector also accounts for a significant share of banking sector credit, reflecting the important role public enterprises play in the Indian economy. Bank credit to the public sector in India accounts for nearly 40 percent of total banking sector credit, or slightly over 20 percent of GDP, which is higher than in many other Asian emerging market countries.[12]

A recent study argues that large public sector borrowing from the banking system may slow financial deepening, by affecting structural characteristics of the banking system (Hauner, 2006). In particular, it finds that high levels of public sector borrowing have a negative effect on standard indicators of financial sector depth, and that banks lending mainly to the public sector tend to be more profitable but less efficient.

Other recent studies (La Porta, Lopez-de-Silanes, and Shleifer, 2002) found that government ownership in banks tends to be significant in countries with low levels of per capita income, underdeveloped financial systems, interventionist and inefficient governments, and poor protection of property rights. They also found that government ownership of banks is associated with slower subsequent financial development and lower subsequent growth in per capita income, in particular with slower growth of productivity. These findings seem to support the view that government control of financial institutions tends to politicize resource allocation, soften budget constraints, and lower economic efficiency (Kornai, 1979; and Shleifer and Vishny, 1994), and stands in sharp contrast with the "development" view of government ownership (Gerschenkron, 1962; and Myrdal, 1968). Public banks can have a different objective function than

---

[12]Bank credit to the public sector accounts for about 50 percent of total banking sector credit in Indonesia, 6 percent in Malaysia, 33 percent in Pakistan and the Philippines, 23 percent in Sri Lanka, and 8 percent in Thailand.

Table 6.7. Key Financial Soundness Indicators by Bank Ownership, End-March 2005
(In percent)

	All Banks	State Banks	Domestic Private Banks	Foreign Banks
Market share (in assets)	100.0	74.4	18.8	6.8
Capital to risk-weighted assets	12.8	12.9	12.2	14.0
Tier I capital to risk-weighted assets	8.4	8.0	8.5	11.2
Gross NPLs to gross loans	5.2	5.5	4.4	2.8
Net NPLs to capital	11.7	13.6	9.5	4.5
Personnel expenses to total income	15.3	17.2	9.0	10.3
Return on assets	0.9	0.9	0.8	1.3
Return on equity	13.6	14.7	11.7	10.8

Source: Reserve Bank of India.

private banks. As a result, they tend to provide credit based on considerations such as economic development needs, without efficiency considerations or sufficient assessment of risks.

The relatively slow pace of financial development in India and the lack of success in providing access to finance to poor and rural communities seem to support the pessimistic view of effects of government ownership in the banking sector. Furthermore, key financial soundness indicators of public banks in India tend to be worse than those of foreign and domestic private banks (Table 6.7). Efficiency indicators (such as the ratio of personnel expenses to total income) are also much stronger in domestic private and foreign banks than in public banks.

The authorities are well aware of the need to further deregulate the banking sector, and are taking steps in that direction. In early 2005, the RBI announced a series of banking reforms, designed to give public banks greater autonomy and to provide guidelines for foreign bank expansion. The RBI sees it as a new step in the continuing process of financial market liberalization. The intention of the reforms is to increase public banks' efficiency, while providing them breathing space by keeping some restrictions on foreign competition until 2009. From 2005, foreign banks are allowed to establish wholly owned subsidiaries (previously only branches were allowed). In addition, the RBI plans to amend legislation to eliminate the 10 percent cap on the voting rights of foreign banks. However, any acquisition of 5 percent or more by a foreign bank will still require RBI approval, and foreign direct investment (FDI) is limited to private banks identified for restructuring, with a limit of 74 percent. Full national treatment for wholly owned subsidiaries of foreign banks and the expansion of FDI to nondistressed banks is not envisaged until 2009.

These measures are a welcome step. While presence of foreign banks will not by itself solve all the problems of financial development,[13] larger foreign bank presence should enhance the competitiveness of the banking sector, and widen access of qualified borrowers to financing (Mathieson, Schinasi, and Claessens, 2000; and Moreno and Villar, 2005). Currently, although foreign banks can engage in all financial sector activities, foreign presence in the Indian banking system (as captured by balance sheet data) is lower than in some other Asian emerging market countries, and significantly lower than in Latin America and Eastern Europe.[14] Bringing forward the target dates for lifting remaining restrictions on foreign ownership from 2009 could therefore help to improve efficiency of the banking system.

More generally, however, efficiency gains could be achieved by increasing private involvement in the banking sector, domestic as well as foreign. An important step here would be allowing some public banks to reduce their government share below 51 percent. In addition to efficiency considerations, this step should make it easier for public banks to deal with the rapid credit growth and the need to meet Basel II capital norms, which Indian banks will be required to implement from end-March 2007. Fast credit growth is already putting pressure on capital adequacy of some banks, and it is expected that a number of public banks with government ownership close to the 51 percent floor would need additional capital to satisfy the Basel II requirements. Without access to new private capital, banks would have to resort to the new instruments approved by the RBI in 2006 (such as perpetual preferential nonvoting shares), which may not necessarily be the most efficient way to raise capital.

To conclude, India is currently in a fortunate position where a relatively sound financial system provides the opportunity to take a significant step toward increasing the efficiency of the financial sector. Prudential issues remain important, as recent rapid credit growth poses a number of potential risks, that need to be closely monitored. But the soundness of the banking sector combined with its resilience to potential shocks present a unique opportunity to accelerate the banking sector reforms. The key steps here would be to reduce reliance on priority sector lending targets as a way to

---

[13]Many recent studies on the role of foreign banks in developing countries find that foreign banks help improve risk management and increase technical know-how and efficiency. Others, however, suggest that foreign banks contribute little to financial deepening, preferring to "cherry pick" borrowers and generally shying away from providing credit to small and medium-sized enterprises (Detragiache, Gupta, and Tressel, 2005; and Gormley, 2005).

[14]In contrast, foreign shareholders account for 21 percent of total trading in the Indian stock market—a level similar to other Asian countries.

provide finance to rural areas and SMEs, and to allow more private owner-ship in the banking system, domestic as well as foreign.

References

Al Jalal, A., J. Boyd, and G. De Nicoló, "Bank Risk Taking and Competition Revisited: New Theory and New Evidence," forthcoming IMF Working Paper.

Basu, P., ed., 2005, *India's Financial Sector: Recent Reforms, Future Challenges* (New Delhi: Macmillan; and Washington: World Bank).

————, and P. Srivastava, 2005, "Exploring Possibilities: Microfinance and Rural Credit Access for the Poor in India," *Economic and Political Weekly*, Vol. 40, No. 17, pp. 1747–56.

Beck, T., A. Demirgüç-Kunt, and R. Levine, 2000, "A New Database on the Structure and Development of the Financial Sector," *World Bank Economic Review*, Vol. 14, pp. 597–605.

————, 2003, "Bank Concentration and Crises," NBER Working Paper No. 9921 (Cambridge, Massachusetts: National Bureau of Economic Research).

Beck, T., A. Demirgüç-Kunt, and M.S. Martinez Peria, 2005, "Reaching Out: Access to and Use of Banking Services Across Countries," World Bank Policy Research Working Paper No. 3754 (Washington: World Bank).

Boyd, J., and G. De Nicoló, 2005, "The Theory of Bank Risk Taking and Competition Revisited," *Journal of Finance*, Vol. 60, No. 3, pp. 1329–43.

Das, U.S., P. Iossifov, R. Podpiera, and D. Rozhkov, 2005, "Quality of Financial Policies and Financial System Stress," IMF Working Paper No. 05/173 (Washington: International Monetary Fund).

Dell'Ariccia, G., 2006, "Credit Booms: The Good, the Bad, and the Ugly?" in *Thailand: Selected Issues*, IMF Country Report No. 06/19 (Washington: International Monetary Fund).

Detragiache, E., P. Gupta, and T. Tressel, 2005, "Finance in Lower Income Countries: An Empirical Exploration," IMF Working Paper No. 05/167 (Washington: International Monetary Fund).

Duenwald, C., N. Gueorguiev, and A. Schaechter, 2005, "Too Much of a Good Thing? Credit Booms in Transition Economies: The Cases of Bulgaria, Romania, and Ukraine," IMF Working Paper No. 05/128 (Washington: International Monetary Fund).

Favara, G., 2003, "An Empirical Reassessment of the Relationship Between Finance and Growth," IMF Working Paper No. 03/123 (Washington: International Monetary Fund).

Gerschenkron, A., 1962, *Economic Backwardness in Historical Perspective* (Cambridge, Massachusetts: Harvard University Press).

Gormley, T., 2005, "Banking Competition in Developing Countries: Does Foreign Bank Entry Improve Credit Access?" (unpublished).

Gurley, J.G., and E.S. Shaw, 1955, "Financial Aspects of Economic Development," *American Economic Review,* Vol. 45 (September), pp. 515–38.

Hauner, D., 2006, "Fiscal Policy and Financial Development," IMF Working Paper No. 06/26 (Washington: International Monetary Fund).

Hilbers, P., I. Otker-Robe, C. Pazarbasioglu, and G. Johnsen, 2005, "Assessing and Managing Rapid Credit Growth and the Role of Supervisory and Prudential Policies," IMF Working Paper No. 05/151 (Washington: International Monetary Fund).

International Monetary Fund, 2006, *India: Staff Report for the 2005 Article IV Consultation,* IMF Country Report No. 06/55 (Washington: International Monetary Fund).

Kaminsky, G., and C. Reinhart, 1999, "The Twin Crises: The Causes of Banking and Balance of Payments Problems," *American Economic Review,* Vol. 89, No. 3, pp. 473–500.

King, R.G., and R. Levine, 1993, "Finance and Growth: Schumpeter Might Be Right," *Quarterly Journal of Economics,* Vol. 108, No. 3, pp. 717–37.

Koeva, P., 2003, "The Performance of Indian Banks During Financial Liberalization," IMF Working Paper No. 03/150 (Washington: International Monetary Fund).

Kornai, J., 1979, "Resource-Constrained Versus Demand-Constrained Systems," *Econometrica,* Vol. 47, No. 4, pp. 801–19.

La Porta, R., F. Lopez-de-Silanes, and A. Shleifer, 2002, "Government Ownership of Banks," *Journal of Finance,* Vol. 57, No. 1, pp. 265–301.

Levine, R., 1997, "Financial Development and Economic Growth: Views and Agenda," *Journal of Economic Literature,* Vol. 35, No. 2, pp. 688–726.

Mathieson, D., G. Schinasi, and S. Claessens, eds., 2000, *International Capital Markets: Developments, Prospects, and Key Policy Issues,* World Economic and Financial Surveys (Washington: International Monetary Fund).

Moreno, R., and A. Villar, 2005, "The Increased Role of Foreign Bank Entry in Emerging Markets," in *Globalization and Monetary Policy in Emerging Markets,* BIS Paper No. 23 (Basel: Bank for International Settlements).

Myrdal, G., 1968, *Asian Drama* (Pantheon Books: New York).

Rajan, R., and L. Zingales, 1998, "Financial Dependence and Growth," *American Economic Review,* Vol. 88, No. 3, pp. 559–86.

Schumpeter, J.A., 1911, *The Theory of Economic Development* (Cambridge, Massachusetts: Harvard University Press).

Sharma, V.K., and C. Sinha, 2006, "The Corporate Debt Market in India," in *Developing Corporate Bond Markets in India,* BIS Paper No. 26 (Basel: Bank for International Settlements).

Shleifer, A., and R. Vishny, 1994, "Politicians and Firms," *Quarterly Journal of Economics* Vol. 109, No. 4, pp. 995–1025.

Srivastava, P., 2004, *Scaling-Up Access to Finance for India's Rural Poor* (Washington: World Bank).

7

Reining in State Deficits

CATRIONA PURFIELD AND MARK FLANAGAN

A major factor underlying India's large general government deficit and debt burden has been the deterioration of state government finances. State governments play an important role in implementing fiscal policies in India, undertaking more than half of general government spending. However, until recently they only received a little under 40 percent of government revenues. The imbalance in their finances has been aggravated by various special factors in recent years including large civil service pay increases granted by the Fifth Pay Commission in 1997, increased tax competition among the states, a rising interest burden, and low tax buoyancy during the growth slowdown of 2001–04 (Table 7.1). As a result, by end-March 2005 state government debt accounted for over one-third of the general government's total burden of almost 80 percent of GDP. In the fiscal year 2004 states also accounted for about half of the general government deficit of 9.1 percent of GDP (up from only a quarter a decade earlier).

While more recent indicators suggest that the states' fiscal position has begun to improve, problems remain. The aggregate state debt-to-GDP ratio of 33 percent accounts for 320 percent of state own revenues while the interest bill continues to consume more than a quarter of state own revenues. The situation is even more serious for some individual states, with debt approaching 100 percent of GDP in some special category states, and debt-to-revenue ratios as high as 400 percent (in the middle-income state of West Bengal). A lack of free resources is also constraining states' ability to maintain existing infrastructure and invest in new projects, and limiting options to expand social spending.

Table 7.1. Trends in State Finances
(In percent of GDP)

	1993–96	2002–03	2002/03	2003/04	2004/05 Estimate
	Average	Average			
Revenue	12.0	11.4	11.3	11.1	11.7
Expenditure	14.6	15.4	15.4	15.5	15.3
Revenue balance	–0.6	–1.9	–2.2	–2.2	–1.3
Overall balance	–2.6	–4.0	–4.1	–4.4	–3.6
Debt	19.3	32.6	31.9	33.0	32.8

Source: Reserve Bank of India.

This chapter examines how India's federal system may have created incentives for fiscal indiscipline at the state level and reviews the steps being taken to improve the system. First, it highlights those features of India's system of federal relations that have given rise to macroeconomic and fiscal problems in other countries. Next, it tests empirically whether the institutional characteristics of India's federal system have in fact contributed to states' fiscal problems. The chapter then reviews recent policy changes aimed at addressing state deficits, assesses whether these recommendations are likely to improve aggregate state finances, and examines their implications at the individual state level. Finally, drawing on international practice, the chapter considers some additional measures that could be taken to strengthen India's fiscal federalism framework.

India's Federal System in an International Context

International evidence suggests that decentralization can contribute to large and persistent general government deficits. Studies by Dabla-Norris and Wade (2002), Rodden (2002), and Tanzi (2000) find incentives for responsible fiscal behavior and hard-budget constraints are undermined when the federal framework is characterized by a high degree of dependence on transfers, lack of constraints on subnational indebtedness, lack of clarity in the respective roles of each tier of government, and weak budget institutions.

In an international context, the level of states' transfer dependence in India is relatively high. Central government grants account for a larger share of the states' revenue and a slightly higher share of expenditure than is typical in most decentralized systems (Table 7.2). Moreover, states have little control over the use of these grants. The split in responsibility for

Table 7.2. Subnational Autonomy in an International Context
(Average for 1990–97)

	Measures of Subnational Autonomy					
	Tax autonomy[1]	Tax sharing[2]	Grants share of revenue	Grant dependence[3]	Vertical gap[4]	Vertical gap after grants
India's states	46.9	32.4	42.4	34.7	−38.5	−22.1
Europe[5]						
Austria	51.5	88.1	22.8	23.5	. . .	. . .
Belgium	36.1	45.9	55.1	55.9	2.8	1.3
Denmark	47.8	4.8	43.1	43.1	−0.1	−0.1
Finland	46.5	11.4	33.0	33.4	1.6	1.1
France	45.1	0.0	35.2	34.7	−4.3	−2.8
Germany	61.0	86.5	11.4	10.3	−9.2	−6.9
Sweden	72.7	0.0	18.4	17.7	−5.4	−4.4
Average	51.5	33.8	31.3	31.2	−2.4	−1.9
Central and Eastern Europe and former Soviet Union[6]						
Belarus	71.9	93.8	22.6	22.7	−0.9	−1.0
Bulgaria	56.2	90.0	40.8	40.9	0.2	0.2
Czech Republic	47.4	91.7	29.4	29.0	−2.0	−1.4
Estonia	64.7	89.2	25.5	24.4	−6.6	−5.0
Hungary	19.3	67.4	58.6	59.3	2.1	1.3
Lithuania	67.0	100.0	27.6	27.6	−0.2	−0.2
Mongolia	49.5	. . .	41.3	41.4	0.3	0.0
Romania	51.8	75.0	38.1	38.8	3.1	1.8
Slovenia	59.7	90–100	21.9	22.6	3.4	2.7
Average	54.2	87.8	34.0	34.1	−0.1	−0.2
Latin America[3]						
Argentina	79.1	64.0	12.4	11.5	−9.2	−8.1
Bolivia	41.9	93.0	24.4	19.4	−4.0	−3.3
Mexico	65.2	100.0	18.9	18.7	−4.3	−4.0
Peru	8.4	. . .	70.4	71.0	2.2	0.0
Average	48.7	85.7	31.5	30.1	−3.8	−3.8
Other						
Australia	35.9	. . .	37.4	38.1	2.4	1.6
Canada	65.6	. . .	13.6	12.6	−9.5	−7.0
China[7]	53.0	. . .	53.4	36.9	−0.7	−0.3
Israel	33.9	. . .	40.6	38.1	−10.9	−6.5
South Africa	15.2	0.0	64.7	62.9	−10.6	−2.5
United States	55.0	. . .	15.2	5.4	5.4	3.9
Average	43.1	. . .	37.5	32.3	−4.0	−1.8

Sources: IMF, *Government Finance Statistics (GFS)* and *International Financial Statistics*; and IMF staff calculations.

[1]Ratio of tax revenue (including shared taxes) to total subnational revenues, including grants.
[2]Ratio of shared taxes from central government to total subnational tax revenue.
[3]Ratio of central grants to total consolidated expenditure of subnational governments.
[4]Deficit as a share of subnational nongrant revenue; a positive number implies a surplus.
[5]Tax share ratios from Ebel and Yilmaz (2002).
[6]Tax share ratios from Dabla-Norris and Wade (2002).
[7]Tax autonomy measured from *GFS* data for 1995–99. Other measures use data reported in Ahmad and others (2002). Subnational governments receive 25 percent of domestic value-added tax, the business tax, enterprises income taxes on state enterprises, the personal income tax, and a number of smaller taxes. Rates on these taxes are generally decided by the center.

grant allocations between the Finance and the Planning Commissions[1] is also unusual, and it leads to coordination problems, creates incentives for states to overstate revenue needs, and allows larger and politically stronger states to bargain for larger transfers.[2] Moreover, shared taxes account for about one-third of state tax revenues, and since these are pooled and divided across states by the Finance Commission, revenue collection incentives may suffer.

Even after the operation of the transfer system, the level of imbalance in state finances that remains is unrivaled. The state-level deficit in India still amounts to 22 percent of total states' nongrant revenue, including shared taxes and grants from the central government. Elsewhere, state-level finances are typically closer to balance after the operation of tax sharing and grant arrangements.

Indian states close this imbalance mainly through borrowing, and India's borrowing regime has been comparatively liberal by international standards.[3] Many developing countries prohibit or ban local borrowing (e.g., China and Indonesia). Most that permit borrowing impose numerical ceilings on subnational indebtedness, usually in the form of ceilings on the debt stock or debt service. Where ceilings are absent, hard-budget constraints are often enforced by legally prohibiting central government guarantees of subnational debt and state guarantees of public enterprise debt (e.g., South Africa and the Czech Republic). India's borrowing regime has been closer to that of advanced economies. Indian states are able to borrow domestically, although they need to seek central government approval if they are indebted to the center (which all states are). External borrowing by states is explicitly prohibited by the constitution. Until recently, the central government did not subject states to an explicit aggregate borrowing ceiling, choosing instead only to subject a state's market borrowings to caps. With states obliged to take 100 percent of the debt issued by small savings schemes, they were able to easily finance their growing deficits.

The combination of (de facto or de jure) soft-budget constraints and high transfer dependence has generated serious fiscal problems in other countries. Brazil and Argentina are well-known examples where the central

---

[1]The Finance Commission is a constitutional body established every five years to determine how federal revenues should be shared between the central and state governments, and among the states. The Planning Commission administers funds to states in support of their five-year development plans.

[2]See Rao and Singh (2001).

[3]The index developed by Rodden (2002) assesses the extent to which higher levels of government place constraints on subnational borrowing and whether subnational governments can tap financing via their ownership of public enterprises and banks.

government's inability to credibly commit to a policy of no subnational bail-outs led to moral hazard problems. The ability to tap state-owned banks and enterprises has also softened budget constraints in Germany and the Czech Republic. A weak regulatory borrowing framework contributed to subnational debt problems in Colombia, the Czech Republic, and South Africa.

Explaining State Fiscal Performance

We turn now to testing empirically the importance of transfer dependence and soft-budget constraints in explaining states' fiscal performance, using annual data from India's 15 largest states between 1985 and 2000. Fiscal performance is proxied using two measures: (1) The ratio of the budget deficit in state i to total expenditure in state i (which measures the share of state expenditure not covered by revenue and helps control for the large differences in the size of state governments); and (2) the ratio of the deficit in state i to gross state domestic product (GSDP) in state i. Fiscal performance is modeled as a function of the following:

Transfer dependence. States that rely more heavily on transfers from the central government have fewer incentives to be fiscally responsible. Once the link between taxes and benefits is broken, states may try to offload the cost of extra spending on the central government and bailout expectations are likely to be higher. The degree of transfer dependence in a state is measured as the sum of grants and shared revenue received by state i in period t as a share of state i's revenue in period t.

Soft-budget constraints. Soft sources of central government finance for states can generate moral hazard: having condoned the borrowing, it is difficult in future for the central government to deny assistance to states in financial stress. States' expectations for a bailout are likely to increase the higher the level of their central government debts. Such borrowing dependency is measured by the stock of central government loans to GSDP in state i in period t.

The extent of decentralization. It could also be more difficult for a state to control deficits if it is responsible for implementing a greater share of general government expenditure. However, if a state collects a greater share of general government revenue, the link between expenditure and revenue is stronger, creating better incentives for fiscal discipline. A state's expenditure (revenue) share in period t is measured relative to general government expenditure (revenue).

Contagion. Shortfalls in shared taxes can quickly lead to a widening deficit at both tiers of government. The inability of the central government to control its own deficits may also signal deficit tolerance or future offloading of unfunded expenditure mandates on states. We measure these spillover effects using the ratio of the central government deficit to central government expenditure in each period.

State-specific structural and economic characteristics. The hypothesis here is that a state would have greater difficulty controlling deficits the greater its reliance on agriculture, the larger its population, the greater the share of its population living in poverty, or the lower its real per capita income.

Table 7.3 presents the results with the upper section using the ratio of state deficit to expenditure as the dependent variable and the lower section using the deficit to GSDP.[4] A Hausman test favors the random effects (Model 3) over the fixed effects specification.

The results confirm that the combination of high transfer dependence and soft-budget constraints significantly weaken state fiscal discipline: Transfer and borrowing dependency are individually significant. States that implement a larger share of general government spending have significantly higher deficits, while those that account for greater share of general government revenues have much lower deficits. Larger deficits at the central government level are also found to have resulted in significantly larger state-level deficits. With the exception of *poverty,* most state-specific characteristics are found to be insignificant in explaining cross-state divergence in fiscal performance. Although per capita incomes are found to be statistically significant, the impact on state deficits is very small. Model 4, which includes a time-specific dummy variable to capture the effects of the Fifth Pay Commission, finds that the pay awards—which also fed into higher pension spending—caused the ratio of states' deficit to expenditure to ratchet upward by close to 4½ percentage points.

Transfer dependence and growing expectations of central government bailouts may have created upward pressure on state deficits over time. To test this hypothesis, Table 7.4 presents the results of using the one-step robust Arellano and Bond generalized method of moments (GMM) estimator where the key explanatory variable is the change in borrowing dependency measured by the change in loans outstanding from the central government.[5] The results suggest that since the mid-1980s, the ratio of the

---

[4]See Purfield (2004) for further details.

[5]The GMM estimator uses first differences to remove fixed effects in the error terms, and instrumental variable estimation, where the instruments are the lagged explanatory variables (in differences) and the dependent variable lagged twice to control for endogeneity. An Arellano-Bond test rejects the null of no first-order autocorrelation in the differenced residuals, and it is not possible to reject the null of no second-order autocorrelation.

Table 7.3. Estimates of State Deficits and Transfer Dependence[1]

	Instrumental Variable Estimates							
	Model 1 Two-Stage Least-Squares Pooled		Model 2 Fixed Effects		Model 3 Random Effects		Model 4 Random Effects	
	Coefficient	Standard errors	Coefficient	Standard errors	Coefficient	Standard errors	Coefficient	Standard errors
Dependent variable: state deficit/expenditure								
Transfer dependence measure	0.1461	0.0557***	0.0463	0.1288	0.1555	0.0836**	0.1034	0.0834
Borrowing dependency	0.7709	0.1104***	0.3851	0.2728	0.5637	0.1948***	0.4931	0.1970**
Ratio of states expenditure to general government expenditure	1.6454	0.4923***	1.1750	0.5429**	1.7433	0.4714***	1.3673	0.4791***
Ratio of states revenue to general government revenue	-2.8492	0.5205***	-2.8267	0.5285***	-3.1372	0.4857***	-2.4549	0.5194***
Central government deficit to expenditure ratio	0.9870	0.2290***	1.0778	0.2264***	1.1678	0.2127***	0.9112	0.2230***
Share of agriculture in GSDP	-0.1704	0.0752**	-0.0659	0.1561	-0.1099	0.1153	-0.0292	0.1178
Share of population living below the poverty line	-0.1497	0.0595**	-0.3415	0.1191***	-0.2424	0.0876***	-0.2363	0.0864***
State population	0.0113	0.0140	0.2515	0.0990**	0.0431	0.0333	0.0378	0.0333
Per capita income	0.0003	0.0002	0.0002	0.0002	0.0002	0.0002	0.0000	0.0002
1997–2000 dummy variable							4.4897	1.3975***
Constant	35.2550	16.7045**	51.9221	19.2975***	40.4937	16.4826**	36.1998	16.1772**
R^2	0.4783		0.1256		0.4510		0.4642	
Groups	14.0000		14.0000		14.0000		14.0000	
Dependent variable: state deficit/GSDP								
Transfer dependence measure	0.0233	0.0126*	-0.0314	0.0282	0.0117	0.0189	-0.0006	0.0188
Borrowing dependency	0.1837	0.0250***	0.2059	0.0598***	0.2009	0.0441***	0.1853	0.0445***
Ratio of states expenditure to general government expenditure	0.4829	0.1113***	0.3583	0.1191***	0.4519	0.1048***	0.3655	0.1062
Ratio of states expenditure to general government expenditure ($t-1$)	-0.6856	0.1177***	-0.5848	0.1159***	-0.6630	0.1079***	-0.5049	0.1150***
Ratio of states revenue to general government revenue	0.2462	0.0518***	0.2269	0.0497***	0.2524	0.0472***	0.1929	0.0493***
Central government deficit to expenditure ratio	-0.0409	0.0170**	-0.0840	0.0342**	-0.0585	0.0260**	-0.0399	0.0265
Share of agriculture in GSDP	-0.0108	0.0134	0.0205	0.0217	-0.0166	0.0197	-0.0151	0.0194
Share of population living below the poverty line	-0.0067	0.0032**	0.0205	0.0217	-0.0010	0.0077	-0.0025	0.0077
State population	0.0000	0.0000	0.0000	0.0000	0.0000	0.0000	-0.0001	0.0000***
Per capita income								
1997–2000 dummy variable							1.0397	0.3098***
Constant	4.0018	3.7760	8.0820	4.2318*	4.6718	3.6744	3.6515	3.5973
R^2	0.4653		0.1410		0.4452		0.4833	
Groups	14.0000		14.0000		14.0000		14.0000	

Source: IMF staff calculations.
[1] *** $p(z) <0.01$; ** $p(z) <0.05$; * $p(z) <0.1$.

Table 7.4. Dynamic Panel Estimates of the Evolution of State Deficits[1]

	Model 5		Model 6	
	Coefficient	Robust standard errors	Coefficient	Robust standard errors
Dependent variable: Δ in state deficit/expenditure				
State deficit/expenditure $(t-1)$	0.2840	0.0779***	0.3416	0.1163***
State deficit/expenditure $(t-2)$	−0.0798	0.0938	−0.0890	0.1017
ΔTransfer dependence measure	0.0438	0.1751		
Δ Borrowing dependency	0.9416	0.3331***		
Δ Borrowing dependency*transfer dependence measure			0.0166	0.0067**
Δ Ratio of states expenditure to general government expenditure	1.2078	1.0818	1.1832	1.0767
Δ Ratio of states revenue to general government revenue	−2.4760	0.8999***	−2.6257	0.8406***
Δ Central government deficit to expenditure ratio	0.9362	0.3506***	0.9838	0.3274***
Δ Share of agriculture in GSDP	−0.0706	0.2281	0.0707	0.1980
Δ Share of population living below the poverty line	−0.3701	0.2088*	−0.2859	0.2250
Δ State population	0.1780	0.1021*	0.1599	0.0898
Δ Per capita income	0.0001	0.0002	0.0001	0.0003
Constant	0.2063	0.5679	0.2400	0.5819
Wald chi²(11)	702.5		344.9	
Groups	14		14	
Number of observations	168		168	
Dependent variable: Δstate deficit/GSDP				
State deficit/GSDP $(t-1)$	0.1619	0.0691**	0.2589	0.0890***
State deficit/GSDP $(t-2)$	−0.1954	0.0717***	−0.2048	0.0905**
Δ Transfer dependence measure	−0.0181	0.0278		
Δ Borrowing dependency	0.3657	0.0818***		
Δ Borrowing dependency*transfer dependence measure			0.0055	0.0012***
Δ Ratio of states expenditure to general government expenditure	0.2057	0.2303	0.1938	0.2416
Δ Ratio of states revenue to general government revenue	−0.4284	0.1938**	−0.5022	0.1866***
Δ Central government deficit to expenditure ratio	0.1720	0.0766**	0.1934	0.0774**
Δ Share of agriculture in GSDP	−0.0646	0.0529	−0.0380	0.0543
Δ Share of population living below the poverty line	−0.0293	0.0416	0.0066	0.0489
Δ State population	−0.0047	0.0324	−0.0028	0.0300
Δ Per capita income	−0.0001	0.0001	−0.0001	0.0001
Constant	0.1952	0.1394	0.1869	0.1604
Wald chi²(11)	228.3		544.1	
Groups	14		14	
Number of observations	168		168	

Source: IMF staff calculations.
[1] *** p(z) <0.01; ** p(z) <0.05; * p(z) <0.1.

deficit to state expenditure rose by almost 1 percent for each 1 percent of GSDP increase in states' indebtedness to the central government (Model 5). It is also feasible that transfer dependency and bailout expectations could interact to cause the states' deficit to rise over time. States have an incentive to increase expenditure knowing that the central government will be under pressure to provide assistance. This could be especially relevant in India where the revenue-sharing ratios are fixed for five-year intervals and states can use evidence of their past deficits to argue for larger transfers at the time of review. Model 6 includes a multiplicative term to capture such interactions and it confirms that bailout expectations, as measured by the stock of loans outstanding to the central government, coupled with transfer dependency, contributed to states' rising deficit.

Fixing the Problem

Mindful of the growing problem in state finances and the shortcomings in the existing federal system, the 2004 Twelfth Finance Commission (TFC) reassessed the system of fiscal federal relations. It made three key recommendations, which are now being implemented:

- States now receive a higher revenue share and higher grants. These additional transfers are expected to help to close the gap between states' expenditure commitments and their revenues. While the TFC made some effort to adjust for inadequate fiscal effort in its calculations of grants, this may yet present a risk in terms of incentives for fiscal responsibility.
- States can benefit from conditional debt restructuring and relief provided they pass and then implement fiscal responsibility legislation (FRL) targeting revenue balance by 2008/09 and a 3 percent of GDP overall deficit by 2009/10. This would provide an incentive toward fiscal discipline in the states.
- States also now confront a stricter borrowing regime, with the center setting global ceilings on borrowings and henceforth only lending to fiscally weak states. This will help address the issue of soft-budget constraints and moral hazard.

The TFC's framework is expected to have a considerable direct impact on general government finances. The direct impact—due to a higher revenue share, higher grants, and interest relief—can be assessed relative to a baseline reflecting a continuation of revenue and spending ratios at levels realized during 2004/05 (Table 7.5). The comparison shows that:

- States' revenue and overall deficits could drop by as much as 0.6 percent of GDP due to higher direct and untied transfers. In any event,

**Table 7.5. Projected Impact of Twelfth Finance Commission
Recommendations on Fiscal Baseline**
(In percent of GDP)

	2005/06	2006/07	2007/08	2008/09	2009/10
States					
Total deficit impact	−0.59	−0.44	−0.40	−0.34	−0.31
Tax revenues	0.22	0.22	0.22	0.22	0.22
Nontax revenues (tied and plan grants)	0.38	0.40	0.33	0.25	0.19
Interest	−0.12	−0.11	−0.10	−0.09	−0.08
Spending of tied and plan grants	0.13	0.28	0.25	0.21	0.18
Center					
Total deficit impact (1 + 2)	0.16	0.14	0.04	−0.07	−0.15
1. Total revenue deficit impact	0.72	0.73	0.64	0.56	0.49
Tax revenues	−0.22	−0.22	−0.22	−0.22	−0.22
Nontax revenues (interest)	−0.12	−0.11	−0.10	−0.09	−0.08
Transfers (tied grants)	0.28	0.30	0.22	0.15	0.09
Transfers (plan grants)[1]	0.10	0.10	0.10	0.10	0.10
2. Impact on net lending	−0.56	−0.58	−0.61	−0.62	−0.64
New loans[2]	−0.82	−0.82	−0.82	−0.82	−0.82
Repayments (maximum debt relief)	−0.26	−0.23	−0.21	−0.19	−0.17
General government: total deficit impact	0.13	0.28	0.25	0.21	0.18

Sources: Government of India, *Report of the Twelfth Finance Commission;* and IMF staff estimates.
[1]Discretionary.
[2]As in 2005–06 budget.

provisial estimates of the 2005/06 outturn (compiled from states' revised budget estimates) suggest the state-level fiscal deficit declined to 3.3 percent of GDP in 2005/06, a reduction of only 0.3 percent relative to the 2004/05 outturn.

- States will need to undertake considerable fiscal adjustment in future years just to maintain their deficit at 2005/06 levels. The challenge is driven by the fact that grants from the center are (1) fixed in nominal terms, and thus declining in terms of GDP; and (2) shifting in their composition away from untied gap-filling grants toward tied grants (which must be spent).
- The central government will have to undertake more fiscal adjustment upfront to achieve the targets specified in its own fiscal responsibility legislation. In 2005/06, the center's revenue deficit would have deteriorated by about 0.7 percent of GDP other things equal, though the overall central government deficit would have remained broadly unchanged if the center stopped lending to states as planned. In the event, however, the central government was able to overperform on

Table 7.6. State Fiscal Adjustment Scenarios

(In percent of GDP)

| | 2004/05 | | 2009/10 | | | |
	Actual	Twelfth Finance Commission (TFC)	TFC	IMF-base	IMF-low	IMF-high
Total revenues	11.7	11.6	13.2	13.3	12.8	13.9
Tax	8.4	8.4	9.7	9.9	9.4	10.6
Of which: own tax	5.9	5.9	6.8	6.7	6.3	7.1
Nontax	3.3	3.2	3.5	3.4	3.4	3.3
Of which: own nontax	1.5	1.2	1.4	1.3	1.3	1.3
Total expenditures	15.3	16.2	16.3	16.3	16.4	16.5
Revenue expenditure	13.1	13.6	13.2	13.4	13.8	13.4
Of which: interest	2.8	2.9	2.0	2.8	3.2	2.7
Capital expenditure	2.5	2.6	3.1	2.9	2.6	3.0
Revenue balance	−1.3	−2.0	0.0	−0.3	−1.2	0.3
Overall balance	−3.6	−4.5	−3.0	−3.1	−3.6	−2.5
Debt (end-year)	32.8	30.3	30.8	31.8	34.1	29.6
Memorandum items:						
Growth rate	...	...	7.0	6.5	6.0	8.0
Real interest rate	...	...	1.9	4.2	5.2	5.7

Sources: Government of India, *Report of the Twelfth Finance Commission;* and IMF staff estimates.

the budget slightly, despite lower interest receipts from states, thanks to expenditure savings.

- The general government fiscal deficit could deteriorate by an amount equal to the additional tied spending by the states. However, the TFC recommended that the center withdraw from spending in areas which are states' responsibility to offset the impact of the higher state spending.

Scenarios for Aggregate State Fiscal Adjustment

Three scenarios are developed here, covering baseline, high growth, and low growth cases to assess whether the adjustment anticipated by the TFC is on track (Table 7.6).[6] The baseline assumes growth will continue

---

[6]States are in a better initial position than the TFC envisioned: the expected 4½ percent of GDP overall deficit and 2 percent of GDP revenue deficit for 2004/05 are well above the provisional outturn estimates. However, the TFC used optimistic growth and real interest rate assumptions—about 1 percent above and ¾ percent below the respective historical averages—suggesting that forecast debt improvements could have been optimistic.

at its recent average, while the high and low cases are about one standard deviation above and below the TFC's baseline growth assumption. In the baseline scenario, revenue buoyancy is assumed to be in line with recent trends, but rises and falls moderately under the different growth assumptions. In each scenario, states try to raise both primary revenue spending (reflecting the need for operations and maintenance and social spending), and capital spending (with a view to achieve the TFC's target of a total investment increase of ½ percent of GDP). However, if the scenario shows a burgeoning deficit, states are assumed to restrain their spending. Finally, since the aggregate state deficit path differs across the scenarios, the total debt and interest relief received by states is allowed to vary across scenarios: over three-fourths of states (on a value-weighted basis) receive the debt relief in the high growth scenario, but less than half do in the low growth scenario.

With these assumptions several important results emerge (Figure 7.1 and Table 7.6):

- States, in aggregate, are broadly on track to achieve the TFC fiscal targets. Under the baseline, the revenue deficit is cut by about 1¼ percent, to ⅓ percent of GDP, and the overall deficit falls by slightly under 1 percent to just over 3 percent of GDP by 2009/10. Capital spending also rises to 3 percent of GDP.
- However, broad achievement of TFC targets would not be sufficient to achieve a sustainable reduction in state debt ratios. Under the baseline, state debt falls initially by about 1 percent of GDP, but rises to almost 32 percent of GDP by the end of the period. Even in the TFC's scenario, debt reductions were extremely gradual and a small drop in growth is all it takes to reverse debt dynamics.
- Results are sensitive to growth and interest rate assumptions. In the low growth scenario, targets would be missed by a wide margin and debt would rise throughout the period. States are forced to substantially curtail investment by the end of the period to cope with a rising interest burden. In the high growth scenario, all targets are achieved with room to spare.

Fiscal Adjustment in Individual States

Even if states in aggregate achieve a sustainable debt level, some states may yet face significant fiscal stress. Since states face widely varying initial fiscal conditions and diverse growth prospects, some are likely to

Figure 7.1. India: Fiscal Outcomes Under Adjustment Scenarios

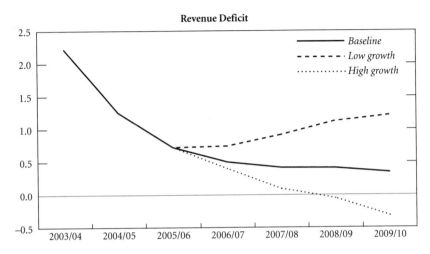

Revenue Deficit

Source: IMF staff calculations.

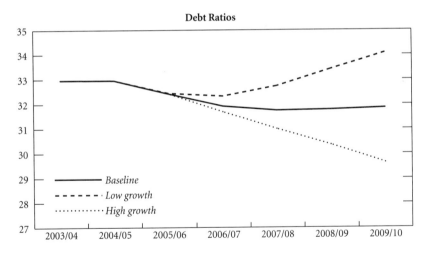

Debt Ratios

Source: IMF staff calculations.

require more fiscal adjustment and/or debt relief than others to achieve a sustainable debt position. To evaluate the impact on individual states, we consider whether a state would achieve a debt stabilizing primary balance if it were to implement the full TFC fiscal adjustment (i.e., revenue balance and an overall deficit of 3 percent of GDP) up front and were also to be given all of the proposed debt rescheduling and relief in the first year.[7]

In calculating debt scenarios for individual states, relatively favorable assumptions are used. For each state, the historic state growth rate is used, adjusted for the difference between projected growth for the economy as a whole under the baseline macroeconomic scenario (Table 7.5) and past growth for the economy as a whole. States are assumed to face the same interest rate on new borrowing, approximately the rate on small savings (the largest source for state borrowing at the moment). This rate is assumed to evolve in line with, but remain above, market rates. In reality, however, weaker states would almost surely face a harsher borrowing environment. At the same time, if the adjustment were to be phased instead of undertaken upfront, the initial debt ratio would be higher for many states. On both counts, debt dynamics would be worse.

Even with these favorable assumptions, analysis of the general category states suggests that many of them would indeed continue to face significant fiscal stress (Table 7.7):[8]

- The primary adjustment required by the TFC varies greatly across them. Some states are already in sustainable positions (e.g., Haryana), but others face gaps exceeding 4 percent of GDP (e.g., Rajasthan). For states facing large adjustments this would not likely be feasible over a five-year period without deep cuts to key programs.
- Not all states would achieve a debt stabilizing primary balance. Four states would face a need for a further small primary adjustment of about ½ percent of GDP to become sustainable.[9] If states instead can only implement a maximum adjustment equal to 10 percent of their initial spending level, then a further two states (Rajasthan and Gujarat) would also fall short of sustainability.
- Finally, for those states that do succeed in reducing debt, their burden—as measured by debt-to-revenue and interest-to-revenue ratios—can nonetheless remain very high (e.g., 360 percent and 37

---

[7]The debt stabilizing primary balance can be calculated as the nominal interest rate minus the nominal growth rate multiplied by the initial debt ratio and deflated by the nominal growth rate.

[8]Data were not available to assess special category states. However, their average debt ratio in 2004/05 was 13 percent of GDP higher than the average for general category states, suggesting that the problem might be more acute for many of them. It is also noteworthy that the high growth scenario does not improve the outcome, since interest and growth rates are projected to move up in tandem.

[9]The residual adjustment for two of the states declines to under ¼ percent of GDP if they simply maintain their current deficit, rather than loosening to achieve TFC targets.

Table 7.7. Sustainability of State Debts Post-TFC: Baseline Scenario[1]

	Debt 2004/05	Debt Post-relief	Debt Relief	Required Primary Adjust-ment	Incen-tive[2]	Primary Balance[3] Debt stabi-lizing	Pro-jected	Gap[4]	Debt/ Reve-nue	Interest/ Reve-nue
Andhra Pradesh	33.4	30.9	2.5	−0.1	−0.1	−0.3	0.2	0.4	1.9	0.2
Bihar	56.0	49.1	6.9	0.5	0.1	0.3	1.3	1.0	1.8	0.2
Gujarat	37.3	35.3	2.0	2.0	1.0	−0.3	−0.3	0.1	2.6	0.2
Haryana	27.2	26.4	0.8	−1.9	−2.5	−0.5	−0.2	0.3	2.3	0.2
Karnataka	32.6	30.3	2.3	−0.3	−0.1	−0.1	−0.6	−0.5	1.5	0.1
Kerala	40.8	37.7	3.1	1.8	0.6	−0.6	0.0	0.7	2.3	0.2
Madhya Pradesh	43.5	40.7	2.8	4.2	1.5	0.2	−0.3	−0.4	2.0	0.1
Maharashtra	31.0	29.7	1.3	2.2	1.7	−0.1	−0.6	−0.5	2.2	0.2
Orissa	69.0	64.3	4.7	2.4	0.5	0.5	2.1	1.7	2.7	0.2
Punjab	53.9	51.8	2.1	2.5	1.2	0.5	1.1	0.7	2.4	0.2
Rajasthan	58.9	57.0	1.9	4.3	2.2	0.2	1.4	1.2	2.8	0.2
Tamil Nadu	27.9	26.2	1.7	−0.3	−0.2	0.0	−0.6	−0.5	1.9	0.2
Uttar Pradesh	51.3	48.2	3.1	2.1	0.7	0.3	1.1	0.8	2.7	0.2
West Bengal	44.5	42.7	1.8	2.5	1.3	−0.9	1.4	2.3	3.6	0.4

Sources: World Bank; and IMF staff estimates.
[1]Assumes that all debt relief and fiscal adjustment are to be realized up-front.
[2]Amount of adjustment required to realize 1 percent of GDP in debt relief.
[3]Assumes an overall deficit of 3 percent of GDP.
[4]When a positive gap exists, the overall debt level would be declining.

percent in West Bengal). This signals that significant crowding out of other budget items is likely.

The analysis also highlights that the debt relief incentive scheme, while a positive step, may prove insufficient to motivate a full adjustment effort in some states. While the central government is providing considerable resources to the states in aggregate, for many states the debt relief is minor relative to their total outstanding liabilities, and relative to the amount of primary adjustment they need to undertake (Table 7.7; see also Kurian, 2005). From another perspective, for debt relief equivalent to only 8½ percent of total transfers they are already set to receive, states would have to undertake very politically difficult policy reforms. For states where there is no present consensus, and which face a very large adjustment requirement, the incentive on offer may prove inadequate.[10]

---

[10]Another category of state—those that have already achieved the FRL deficit targets—may choose not to participate altogether. This would allow them to raise their overall deficit (and thus capital spending), which would otherwise be capped at present levels by TFC requirements.

Some Further Improvements to the Federal System

Given the long-standing nature of the problem in the states, and the risks to achieving TFC targets, there is good reason to consider ways in which the borrowing and incentive regime could be strengthened. On the borrowing side much can be done in the short term; however, on the incentive side, due to the constitutional prerogative of Finance Commissions over the design of fiscal federal relations, some of the more attractive options may need to await the next Finance Commission, in 2009.

India could, in the near term, take a number of measures to strengthen the borrowing regime:

- The central government could set its *borrowing ceilings* more in line with FRL adjustment targets and sustainability considerations. It could also harden the rules for approval of new borrowing: as in some countries with FRLs (e.g., Brazil, Colombia, and Ecuador), and it could condition approval of borrowing on demonstrating compliance with the FRL. Ultimately credibility will be cemented only when the system is tested (e.g., when growth and revenues unexpectedly fall short) and the government does not raise borrowing limits.

- In terms of *market discipline*, the various soft sources of finance need to be progressively restricted and eliminated, and information provision improved. In this context, consideration could be given to removing states' obligation to borrow fully the resources from small savings schemes (allowing the schemes to pursue other investment options), and to bringing the administered interest rates on these schemes in line with market rates. Some countries penalize lenders for assisting subnational governments in borrowing beyond their legal limits—for instance, Brazil requires immediate repayment with no interest—and such sanctions could alter lenders' incentives in India.

- Finally, it would help to improve both market discipline and the credibility of administrative control if India were to legally rule out future bailouts as in the Czech Republic and South Africa.

The government could also, at the same time, pursue greater cooperation with states, with peer pressure as a sanction. Under a cooperative approach, negotiations with subnational governments determine a global borrowing ceiling, which is then apportioned to the various government entities (see Ahmad, Albino-War, and Singh, 2005). Enforcement can be through an independent intergovernmental entity (e.g., Austria) or through a subnational government association (e.g., Denmark), and should involve some form of financial sanction. In Spain, for instance, subnational governments that violate agreed borrowing ceilings are required to contribute to any fines assessed by the European Union (under the Stability and Growth Pact). In India, the central government regularly engages the states on their individual borrowing plans, and has plans to set up a borrowing council (involving the Ministry of Finance, the RBI, the Planning Ministry, and states). This council could become a forum for the determination of a global all-state borrowing ceiling, and for agreement on sanctions for exceeding state-specific targets.

In terms of the incentive regime, stronger requirements on information provision and stronger sanctions would help make it more effective:

- A major problem to overcome in making the incentive regime more effective is information provision. Key issues would include establishing standardized definitions, accounting systems, and classifications; upgrading and standardizing information technology systems; and ensuring that states maintain databases on all financing sources. The central government could also increase the incentive for states to improve information provision by suspending grants when it is inadequate. Brazil and Ecuador have applied information-related conditionalities in their FRLs, with Ecuador requiring information provision within 15 days of the date set out in the FRL, upon penalty of suspension of grants (see Webb, 2004).

- The center can encourage states to amend their FRLs to incorporate sanctions for nonperformance. The FRLs (or related legislation) would hold accountable those individuals who were responsible for any breaches of the law. Examples of sanctions include financial reimbursement and loss of employment. The Brazilian framework again provides an example, and while it has not been formally tested, observers see it as having changed civil servant behavior (see Webb, 2004).

Looking forward to the next Finance Commission, the center may also consider grants that are more tightly linked to fiscal performance, to provide a stronger institutional sanction. This could prove especially useful for states that ultimately do not abide by TFC recommendations. Brazil, Ecuador, and Peru have all embedded provisions to suspend grants in their FRLs due to poor fiscal performance. In Peru, the suspension is temporary (for 90 days), and this can avoid worsening the subnational authorities' fiscal situation. Brazil is seen as having enjoyed good success with its framework, and indeed subnational balances have improved markedly since its introduction (see Webb, 2004). Constitutional issues arise in India, however, insofar as the revenue share cannot be subject to conditions. An option might then be to reduce the revenue share, and to use the freed funds to create an equivalent (and ex ante fixed) grant for each state. This grant could be suspended at least temporarily if a subnational government fails to meet its fiscal adjustment targets.

Conclusions

This chapter finds evidence that institutional factors have played an important role in explaining both the differences in fiscal performance across Indian states as well as the deterioration in their combined deficit over time. The results of the econometric analysis suggest that states with greater access to central government transfers have tended to have larger deficits, and this negative relationship has been amplified the higher a state's reliance on central government loans. This finding reflects the fact that states may have little incentive to rein in deficits when they expect—on the basis of their past experience—central government bailouts.

The recommendations of the TFC represent a step forward in addressing these adverse incentives and the long-standing problems with state finances in India. However, other steps are needed to supplement the framework. The extra resources available to states will give adjustment a significant push, but a stronger adjustment strategy, both in the aggregate and for individual states, would improve overall and individual state prospects. Strengthening borrowing controls will be critical to outcomes, and in this context there is a need to tighten administrative controls, to remove impediments to more market discipline, and to reform the small savings schemes. At the same time, the conditionality on fiscal performance could be strengthened, with a focus in particular on sanctions at the state level for not meeting targets, information provision, and sanctions by the center (in the form of withheld grants) for fiscal performance shortfalls.

References

Ahmad, Ehtisham, Li Keping, Thomas Richardson, and Raju Singh, 2002, "Recentralization in China?" IMF Working Paper No. 02/168 (Washington: International Monetary Fund).

Ahmad, Ehtisham, Maria Albino-War, and Raju Singh, 2005, "Subnational Public Financial Management: Institutions and Macroeconomic Considerations," IMF Working Paper No. 05/108 (Washington: International Monetary Fund).

Dabla-Norris, Era, and Paul Wade, 2002, "The Challenge of Fiscal Decentralization in Transition Countries," IMF Working Paper No. 02/103 (Washington: International Monetary Fund).

Ebel, Robert D., and Serdar Yilmaz, 2002, "On the Measurement and Impact of Fiscal Decentralization," Policy Research Working Paper No. 2809 (Washington: World Bank).

Government of India, 2004, *Report of the Twelfth Finance Commission 2005–10* (New Delhi).

Kurian, N. J., 2005, "Debt Relief for States," *Economic and Political Weekly*, Vol. 40, No. 31, pp. 3429–34.

Purfield, Catriona, 2004, "The Decentralization Dilemma in India," IMF Working Paper No. 04/32 (Washington: International Monetary Fund).

Rao, M. Govinda, and Nirvikar Singh, 2001, "Federalism in India: Political Economy and Reform," Department of Economics Working Paper No. 484 (Santa Cruz, California: University of California).

Rodden, Jonathan, 2002, "The Dilemma of Fiscal Federalism: Grants and Fiscal Performance around the World," *American Journal of Political Science,* Vol. 46, No. 3, pp. 670–87.

Tanzi, Vito, 2000, "On Fiscal Federalism: Issues to Worry About," paper presented at a conference on "Fiscal Decentralization" at the International Monetary Fund, Washington, November 20.

Webb, Steven, 2004, "Fiscal Responsibility Laws for Subnational Discipline: The Latin American Experience," Policy Research Working Paper No. 3309 (Washington: World Bank).

8

Creating Fiscal Space: Medium-Term Directions for Tax Reform

MARK FLANAGAN

Tax reform figures prominently in India's plans for fiscal consolidation and to generate fiscal space for infrastructure investment. Successive Indian governments have devoted considerable effort to developing a tax reform strategy: the 2003 Kelkar Task Force laid out a strategy for direct and indirect taxation and the Fiscal Responsibility and Budget Management Act (FRBMA) road map (Ministry of Finance, 2004) and Twelfth Finance Commission report (Government of India, 2004) both highlighted how tax reform could contribute to fiscal adjustment. Increases in revenue are expected to contribute almost 3 percent of GDP in fiscal adjustment at the center, and about 1 percent of GDP in the states, permitting 1½ percent of GDP in extra annual investment at the general government level.

International experience has shown that revenue-based consolidation strategies can be successful, but are a more difficult route to take. The earlier literature on fiscal consolidation had emphasized expenditure-based adjustment (Alesina and Perotti, 1996). More recent work has cast a more positive light on revenue-based experiences (Gupta and others, 2004; and Tsibouris and others, 2006), especially when a country begins its adjustment at a low initial revenue-to-GDP ratio and has developed well-defined tax reform plans that are phased in gradually (as in India at present). However, successful revenue-based consolidations are less common than expenditure-based consolidations even at low revenue levels, mainly reflecting constraints on the capacity of tax administrations. Countries have also had

Figure 8.1. General Government Revenue and Deficit
(In percent of GDP)

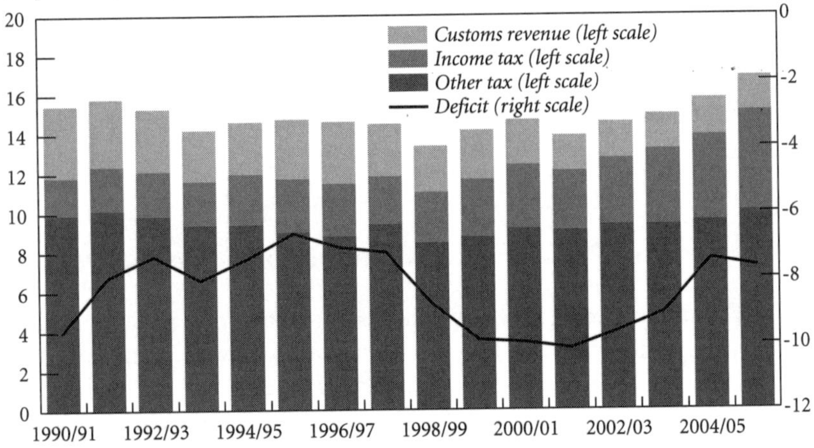

Customs revenue (left scale)
Income tax (left scale)
Other tax (left scale)
Deficit (right scale)

Source: Country authorities; and IMF staff estimates.

more difficulties protecting revenue-based gains against new revenue erosions and expenditure incursions.[1]

To date, India's revenue strategy has shown some success. Measures have been passed to broaden the corporate income tax (CIT) base, efforts have been made to improve tax administration, and, after many years of negotiations and planning, a state-level value-added tax (VAT) has been introduced. Early returns from the VAT have been encouraging, with half-year 2005/06 indirect tax receipts up by close to 15 percent in those states implementing it. Growth in CIT and personal income tax (PIT) collections have been enough of late to offset the drag to revenues from continuing trade tax reforms; since 1993, the average effective tariff rate has dropped from 34 percent to 17 percent, and trade-related revenues have fallen by 1 percent of GDP (Figure 8.1).

The time is ripe in India for further tax reform. To meet FRBMA deficit reduction targets, the center must raise its gross tax collection ratio by another 2½ percent of GDP, to a little over 13 percent of GDP, by 2008/09. With progress on some planned measures behind schedule, and sizable spending commitments on the horizon, new measures may need to be identified. Past international studies have emphasized that tax reforms undertaken at a measured pace within a stable macroeconomic environment—the present situation in India—stand a greater chance of success.

---

[1]One possibility is that expenditure cutbacks are less reversible, for example if canceling programs permanently weakens the lobby groups promoting them.

This chapter looks at India's tax reform options in more detail. It first examines India's revenue performance in international perspective to identify areas of potential collection gains. Then it considers India's existing tax reform strategy, noting where gaps remain. The next section discusses an important gap: the level of the PIT threshold. The chapter concludes by discussing strategies for reinvigorating and sustaining base-broadening tax reforms.

India's Revenue Performance in International Perspective

International comparisons provide insight into India's revenue collection effort and directions for future reforms. In selecting relevant comparators, account must be taken of several factors that are key for establishing taxable capacity: (1) per capita income adjusted for purchasing power parity (PPP) (it is infeasible to tax a subsistence level of income); (2) the structure of output (certain sectors, such as agriculture, are difficult to tax); and (3) openness to trade and capital flows (a more open economy faces more mobile tax bases). From an administrative angle, it is also important to consider population—the challenge of efficiently administering a tax system grows at least in proportion with the number of taxpayers.

It is useful to consider two groups of comparators for India. In the first group are countries in India's PPP-adjusted per capita income range that are also broadly similar to India in terms of economic structure (China, Egypt, Indonesia, Pakistan, the Philippines, Sri Lanka, and Vietnam). In the second group are countries whose structural characteristics place them at a more advanced state of development (Brazil, Colombia, Mexico, Russia, South Africa, Turkey, and Ukraine). Table 8.1 highlights the differences between these two samples.

India's revenue collections compare very favorably to the first group of comparators (Table 8.2). Total general government revenues exceed the level realized in direct comparators by almost 2 percent of GDP. The higher performance is mainly due to indirect taxation (sales taxes and excises). India is very much in line with income tax, customs and nontax revenue collection efforts in these other countries. This good performance is not driven by comparisons against the weakest members of the group—India outperforms both China and the Philippines, the two highest income comparators in the group.

However, against more mature emerging market countries, there are some revealing differences (Table 8.2). These more advanced economies collect some 13 percent of GDP more in general government revenues than

Table 8.1. India and Other Economies: Socioeconomic Characteristics

	Population 2004–05 (In millions)	Income PPP GNI 2003 (Per capita)	Income Rank[1]	Income Distribution (Gini)	Output Structure 2003 (In percent of GDP) Agriculture	Output Structure 2003 (In percent of GDP) Services	Global Integration 2003 (In percent of GDP) Goods	Global Integration 2003 (In percent of GDP) Capital	Global Integration FDI	Infrastructure Power 2002 (Consumption per capita)	Infrastructure Mobiles 2003 (per 1,000)
India	1,091	2,880	146	32.5	22.8	50.7	21.1	3.1	0.8	380	25
Comparators											
China	1,288	4,980	119	44.7	15.0	33.0	60.1	14.3	4.5	987	215
Egypt	68	3,940	132	34.4	16.0	50.0	20.7	8.6	0.3	1,073	84
Indonesia	215	3,210	142	34.3	17.0	40.0	44.9	4.0	1.7	411	87
Pakistan	148	2,040	159	33.0	23.0	53.0	30.3	2.8	0.7	363	18
Philippines	82	4,640	128	46.1	14.0	53.0	94.3	39.9	0.6	459	270
Sri Lanka	19	3,740	136	33.2	19.0	55.0	64.7	2.4	1.4	297	73
Vietnam	81	2,490	151	37.0	19.0	...	115.0	5.8	4.0	374	34
Average[2]	82	3,577		37.5	17.3	47.3	61.4	11.1	1.9	566	112
Mature emerging market countries											
Brazil	177	7,510	86	59.3	6.0	75.0	25.1	6.7	2.1	1,776	264
Colombia	45	6,410	97	57.6	12.0	58.0	33.8	12.6	3.4	817	141
Mexico	102	8,980	80	54.6	4.0	70.0	54.9	5.4	2.0	1,660	291
Russia	143	8,950	82	31.0	5.0	61.0	48.2	19.6	5.0	4,291	249
South Africa	46	10,130	76	57.8	4.0	65.0	48.5	6.1	1.0	3,860	364
Turkey	71	6,710	94	40.0	13.0	65.0	48.2	6.8	0.9	1,458	394
Ukraine	48	5,430	112	29.0	14.0	46.0	93.1	14.2	2.9	2,229	136
Average[2]	71	7,731		47.0	8.3	62.9	50.3	10.2	2.5	2,299	263

Sources: World Bank; and IMF, *International Financial Statistics*.
[1]Of 208 total jurisdictions.
[2]Median for population.

Table 8.2. India and Other Economies: General Government Revenues
(In percent of GDP)

	Total	Tax	Income			Property	Goods and Services			International Trade	Social Contributions	Other	Grants	Nontax
			Total	Personal income tax	Corporate income tax		Total	VAT	Excises					
India	20.30	16.86	5.02	1.75	3.28	0.74	8.65		...	1.76	0.00	0.68	0.09	3.90
Comparators														
China	19.41	17.64	4.33	1.27	2.89	0.57	10.85	6.74	...	0.76	0.00	1.13	0.00	1.78
Egypt	20.54	14.17	6.14	2.27	3.87	0.03	5.44	2.48	1.12	1.50	1.06	0.00	0.53	5.34
Indonesia	17.99	12.47	6.32	1.38	4.94	0.61	4.91	3.15	1.77	0.54	0.00	0.08	0.02	5.50
Pakistan	14.45	10.02	2.80	0.40	2.40	0.15	5.32	3.66	1.25	1.76	0.00	0.00	0.30	4.13
Philippines	17.66	14.85	5.76	3.05	2.71	0.44	6.10	2.88	1.59	0.97	1.58	0.00	0.00	2.81
Sri Lanka	16.44	14.61	2.04	1.22	0.82	0.19	9.57	6.23	3.24	2.02	0.17	0.62	0.43	1.40
Vietnam	22.70	16.50	5.70	0.50	5.20	0.04	8.20	5.90	1.80	2.60	0.00	0.00	0.20	6.00
Average	18.46	14.32	4.73	1.44	3.26	0.29	7.20	4.43	1.79	1.45	0.40	0.26	0.21	3.85
Mature emerging market countries														
Brazil	33.62	29.75	5.66	...	...	...	10.52	8.71	...	0.48	12.30	0.80	...	3.86
Colombia	30.13	20.28	6.13	...	...	...	9.82	5.82	2.87	0.87	2.74	0.72	...	9.86
Mexico	26.05	19.50	5.67	3.32	2.35	0.31	9.91	3.84	1.84	0.41	3.38	0.09	0.00	6.55
Russia	38.61	36.08	8.62	3.43	5.19	...	11.03	6.39	1.47	5.13	7.83	3.46	0.00	2.53
South Africa	24.95	24.35	13.63	7.71	5.49	0.40	9.53	7.12	2.41	0.99	0.00	0.79	0.00	0.60
Turkey	39.67	32.90	7.75	5.15	2.61	1.13	15.91	8.15	6.63	0.28	6.79	1.07	0.00	6.77
Ukraine	39.74	33.91	10.06	4.15	5.91	0.66	11.16	6.67	2.35	1.77	8.71	1.56	0.00	5.83
Average	33.25	28.11	8.22	4.75	4.31	0.63	11.13	6.67	2.93	1.42	5.96	1.21	0.00	5.14

Sources: Country authorities; and IMF staff estimates.

does India. The largest difference is in payroll (social contribution) levies: all but one of the comparators has a formal social security system funded in this way while India does not. However, differences are broad based including an almost 3 percentage point gap in the PIT collection, and a gap of about 2½ percent of GDP for goods and services taxes (GST). India also collects a little less in nontax revenues, perhaps reflecting more efficient use of state assets elsewhere.

Part of the difference against mature emerging market countries will disappear over time as the structure of India's economy shifts. If the share of agriculture in Indian output were to fall by 13 percentage points in favor of manufacturing and services (which would move its economic structure into line with more mature emerging market countries), this could yield close to 1 percent of GDP in additional revenue. However, it would take a long time for this shift in economic structure to occur—20 years, given the present differential between agricultural and nonagricultural growth rates. And there would still be a large gap in total revenues relative to the mature emerging market countries if nothing else in the tax system changed.

Medium-Term Directions and Strategies for Tax Reform

International comparisons suggest that India's greatest revenue-raising opportunities lie in the goods and services and income taxation areas, and prospects for strengthening each of these areas are good. In fact, plans are already well laid out in India for reform of the GST, and many aspects of the PIT and CIT reform agenda have also been identified. The thrust of the proposals, consistent with international experience of successful tax reform episodes, is to broaden tax bases.

Goods and Services Taxation

There is already a general strategy to address indirect tax shortfalls. The Kelkar Commission report and FRBMA road map both highlighted the need to move toward a broad-based and integrated GST. Key steps include (1) extending the state-level VAT to all states, and incorporating services into the base; (2) eliminating the tax on interstate trade (central sales tax (CST)); (3) expanding the service tax base at the center (for instance, to incorporate further financial and legal services); (4) integrating the central VAT and services tax into a new central-level GST applied at the retail stage; (5) broadening the GST base by eliminating exemptions (including for small-scale industries and specific regions); and (6) introducing a comprehensive

GST (having a common base at the central and state level, but allowing rates to be fixed separately, subject to some limitations).[2] The government is already moving forward on several of these steps.[3]

There is ample opportunity, in moving to a broad-based GST, to close the revenue gap with more mature emerging market countries. In general, international experience has shown that the introduction of a VAT often leads to higher revenues due to base broadening and compliance improvements (Tsibouris and others, 2006; and Thirsk, 1997). Looking more specifically at India, estimates suggest that eliminating exemptions for small-scale industries and for specific regions could generate an additional ¼ percent of GDP in annual revenue (Bagchi and others, 2005). Expanding the service tax base could alone generate 1 percent of GDP (FRBMA report; see Ministry of Finance, 2004). In terms of compliance, the sharp distinction in India between a good and a service along with the availability of scale- and location-based exemptions have given companies an incentive to reorganize production and distribution processes to minimize taxes. This has led to many drawn-out disputes with the tax authorities, and to complicated and costly-to-administer rules for imputing taxable values. There is thus much scope for compliance-based revenue gains, although the precise amount and timing would be difficult to predict.[4]

An integrated GST is best viewed, however, as a medium-term reform. Some steps would involve difficult center-state negotiations; for instance, elimination of the CST would produce winners and losers among the states (depending on whether they are net exporters to other states), and is raising issues of compensation. Others, like service taxation at the state level, involve constitutional issues. Even once these impediments are overcome, international experience has shown that implementing a full GST can take substantial lead time, in order to put in place appropriate administrative arrangements and to train taxpayers. The challenge is magnified for India, given the need to introduce a system of joint or unified audit and establish channels for adequate information exchange between different tax administrations. Taking adequate time to get this right is crucial. Unprepared

---

[2]This approach can be characterized as a dual VAT. An alternative approach in a fiscal federal system is the CVAT, which imposes a creditable tax on interstate trade to minimize opportunities for cross-border fraud. See Bird and Gendron (2005) for a discussion of the merits and demerits of each of these approaches.

[3]There is also a need to review remaining excises on energy products, alcohol, and tobacco.

[4]*The Report of the Task Force on Implementation of the FRBMA* (Ministry of Finance, 2004) foresaw compliance-driven revenue improvements of about ½ percent of GDP through the service tax alone.

administrations could face significant revenue leakages, to the detriment of public support for the VAT. At the same time, if taxpayers have difficulty complying with changes, pressures for reversal of reform could become intense (Gillis, 1989; and Thirsk, 1997).

Personal Income Taxation

India has already reformed key elements of its PIT regime. In the 2005/06 budget, thresholds were increased dramatically, rates were lowered modestly, and a variety of savings-related exemptions were consolidated into one deduction. The government is now considering modalities for taxing withdrawals from small savings funds.[5] Small savings incentives cost the government in the range of ¼ percent of GDP annually in forgone income tax revenue (Ministry of Finance, 2002a). However, the FRBMA road map suggested grandfathering many existing savings schemes, which would limit near-term revenue gains.

There remain important base-broadening measures, however, that the Indian authorities could take. These would not be easy—well-organized vested interests would need to be confronted—but could yield some ¾ percent of GDP a year:

- *Tightening the tax treatment of charities.* Charities are generally exempt from taxes when they perform activities of social value that are not for profit. At present in India, however, trusts carry on many activities that are for profit, and surveys have suggested that business income may represent 50–60 percent of their total income. This leads to revenue losses of almost 0.2 percent of GDP a year and distorts competition and horizontal equity (Bagchi and others, 2005).
- *Subjecting agricultural income to taxation.*[6] Besides creating horizontal equity problems, the exemption has led to significant evasion. High administrative and compliance costs could provide a rationale for some special treatment, but the present high income tax threshold in India (see below), which would eliminate all small and many medium-sized farmers from the tax net, already accommodates this

---

[5]Deposits, withdrawals, and interest earned are exempt from taxation; international practice has moved toward exemptions for deposits and interest only (Ministry of Finance, 2004).

[6]See Bagchi and others (2005) for a discussion of the arguments in favor of an agricultural exemption, and why they fail in the Indian context.

Table 8.3. India and Other Economies: Structure of the Personal Income Tax System

	Revenue (In percent of GDP)	Rates				Thresholds[1]		
		No.	Minimum	Maximum	Surcharge	Minimum rate	Maximum rate	Social[2]
India	1.75	3.00	10.0	30.0	10	315	788	631
Mature emerging market countries								
Brazil	...	2.00	15.0	27.5		132	264	237
Colombia	...	many	...	35.0		0	1474	0
Mexico	3.32	5.00	3.0	32.0		7	124	121
Russia	3.43	1.00	13.0	13.0		4	4	43
South Africa	7.71	6.00	18.0	40.0		120	1,030	135
Turkey	5.15	4.00	15.0	35.0		0	678	44
Ukraine	4.15	1.00	13.0	13.0		33	33	60
Average	4.75	3.17	12.8	27.9		42	515	91
Other								
China	1.27	9.00	5.0	45.0		184	678	...
Philippines	3.05	7.00	5.0	32.0		17	861	...

Sources: PricewaterhouseCoopers (2003b); country authorities; and IMF staff estimates.
[1]In percent of per capita GDP.
[2]For a married taxpayer with two children earning the per capita income and taking advantage of all savings, dependent, and education deductions.

concern.[7] The exemption is estimated to cost ¼ percent of GDP a year (Bagchi and others, 2005).

Eliminating the tax deductibility of mortgage interest. This deduction raises issues of vertical equity—high-income taxpayers who face higher marginal tax rates receive a larger benefit—and distorts investment incentives.[8] Its elimination could bring an additional 0.2 percent of GDP a year in revenue (Ministry of Finance, 2002a).

India's high income tax threshold would also restrain the growth of revenues over the medium term, but addressing this is not part of the current reform strategy. Compared to PIT systems in more mature emerging market countries, India's threshold for income taxation is very high relative to per capita income, even adjusting for different deductions available (Table 8.3).[9]

[7]The vast majority of developing countries do not exempt agricultural income from taxation (Khan, 2001). However, difficulties in measuring income in the agricultural sector have led to widespread use of presumptive methods of taxation.
[8]See Ministry of Finance (2002a) for a discussion of the pros and cons of the deduction. Among countries surveyed in the Kelkar report, one-half of high-income countries and one-quarter of emerging market and low-income countries had such a provision.
[9]This is also before accounting for the fact that social considerations are partly built into the threshold in India: it is 25 percent higher for women, and 50 percent higher for retirees. Such a design is uncommon, although South Africa also applies a higher threshold for the aged.

Figure 8.2. Evolution of the Personal Income Threshold
(Ratio to per capita income)

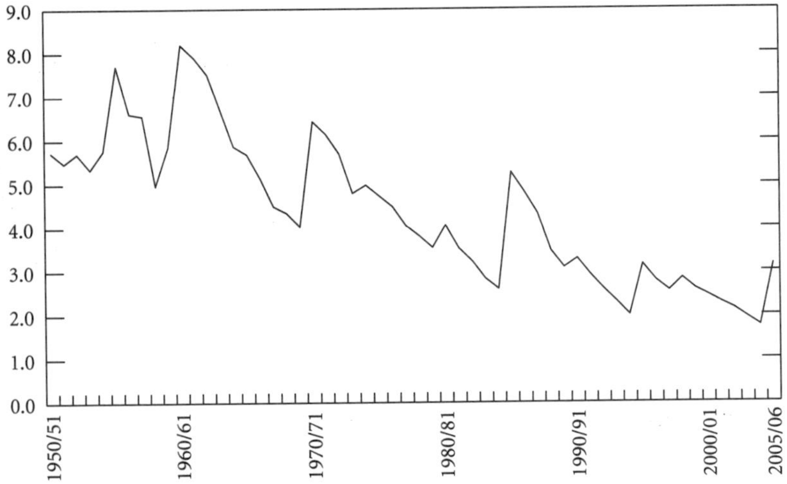

Sources: Ministry of Finance (2002a); and IMF staff estimates.

The amount of tax revenue forgone may be significant: perhaps 1⅓ percent of GDP.[10] The PIT threshold has just been raised in India, breaking a long decline over the past 40 years relative to average income (Figure 8.2). This issue is considered in more detail in the section "The Income Tax Threshold" below.

Corporate Income Taxation

Many aspects of India's corporate tax regime are now in line with international practice, but low revenue productivity signals too narrow a base. India's corporate tax rate remains high, but it has done a good deal of late to bring its other CIT provisions in line with international practice (Table 8.4). However, even with these changes, the productivity of the corporate tax lags more mature emerging market countries. This indicates significant leakage through exemptions, and India does maintain extensive tax holidays, including for export-related activities, specific sectors, and regions.

---

[10]Calculated using 2003 data and assuming a threshold of 40 percent of per capita income, 35 million current taxpayers, and 70 million new nonagricultural taxpayers with an average income of Rs 20,000 and savings deductions of Rs 4,000. Calculations also include agriculture, beyond the value of ending the exemption, and are made using data from Bagchi and others (2005). The gains should be understood as relevant for the medium term.

Table 8.4. India and Other Economies: Structure of the Corporate Income Tax System

	Revenue (In percent of GDP)	Revenue Productivity (Revenue/rate)	Rate[1]	Minimum Tax	Loss Carry Forward[2]	Depreciation Rate[3]	Investment Incentives		
							Lower CIT rate	Accelerated depreciation	Income tax holidays
India	3.28	0.10	33.7	7.5	8	15	No	Yes	Yes
Mature emerging market countries									
Brazil	...	...	25.5	No	Nlim (cap)	10 to 20	No	Yes	Yes
Colombia	...	...	36.7	Yes	8 (cap)	10	No	Yes	Yes
Mexico	2.35	0.07	32.0	1.8	10	...	Yes	Yes	No
Russia	5.19	0.22	24.0	No	10 (cap)	5 to 100	Yes	Yes	No
South Africa	5.49	0.18	30.0	No	Nlim	20	No	Yes	No
Turkey	2.61	0.09	30.0	No	5	6.6 to 50	No	Yes	Yes
Ukraine	5.91	0.24	25.0	No	Nlim	24 to 40	No	No	No
Average	4.31	0.16	29.0						
Other									
China	2.89	0.09	33.0	No	8	10	No	No	Yes
Philippines	2.71	0.08	32.0	2.0	3	...	No	No	Yes

Sources: PricewaterhouseCoopers (2003b); country authorities; and IMF staff estimates.
[1]Including surcharges.
[2]Number of years; "Nlim" denotes no limit; "cap" indicates that the amount in any one year is capped.
[3]Machinery and equipment, under straight line method.

The direct cost of holidays for regions, exports, and the construction sector alone has been estimated at some ½ percent of GDP (Bagchi and others, 2005), and there is little evidence that these holidays have generated significant investment or employment.[11] One result of excessive leakage in India has been a proliferation of other corporate taxes (e.g., the minimum tax and wealth tax), which complicate the tax system and raise administrative and compliance costs. Recent practice in more mature emerging market countries has been to reduce or eliminate tax holidays.[12]

The need to broaden the corporate tax base has long been recognized in India. The Kelkar Report (Ministry of Finance, 2002a) and FRBMA road map (Ministry of Finance, 2004) advocated the removal of tax holidays and discussed options including upfront elimination, a rapid two- to three-year phaseout, and sunset clauses with no new entrants. Time consistency would argue in favor of the first option: a phase-out would allow vested interests to lobby for continuation. The government has been pursuing the third route, but some setbacks are evident: in the 2005/06 budget, exemptions covering research and development facilities in specific sectors and investments in Jammu and Kashmir were extended by two years, and new tax benefits have been offered to corporates operating within special economic zones. A key issue, considered in the section "Creating an Environment for Reform," is how to create an environment in which base-broadening measures would stand more of a chance of success.

The Income Tax Threshold

Elaborating a strategy to increase the PIT threshold over the medium term should be a focus for the Indian authorities. International experience suggests that having well-specified tax reform plans is important: sudden political or economic events often provide an unexpected impetus to reform.[13] Doing nothing would allow inflation to erode the threshold (so-called "bracket creep"), but this would require 25 years to bring the threshold into line with the average in more mature emerging market countries. Moreover, without an explicit strategy, there is a significant risk that the

---

[11]See Bagchi and others (2005). Aggarwal (2004) considers export zones and finds that exports per employment unit declined sharply after a period, as the incentives could not compensate for poor governance and infrastructure in the zones.

[12]See Zee, Stotsky, and Ley (2002) for a discussion of the merits and demerits of various types of investment incentives. Income tax holidays are considered to be among the worst. South Africa's practice—budget subsidies—is an example of a more transparent approach.

[13]See Thirsk (1997).

threshold will eventually be raised again, leaving the problem in place even as India develops into a more mature emerging market.

Several arguments have been put forward in India in favor of a high threshold:[14]

- *Tax administration constraints.* Due to resource constraints and organizational shortcomings the tax administration is unable to challenge effectively taxpayers' declarations, allowing them to underdeclare income. They tend to do so at levels just above the threshold, and thus a higher threshold may even enhance revenues.
- *High compliance costs for taxpayers.* These raise the social cost of extracting resources from the private sector. Chattopadhyay and Das Gupta (2002) have estimated compliance costs in India to be well above those in developed countries.
- *Social considerations.* There is no formal social security system in India, so that a higher level of exemption may be needed to allow Indians to self-insure.
- *The high level of indirect taxation relative to comparable developing countries.* A higher threshold may ensure that the effective rate of tax on labor (i.e., including consumption taxes) is reasonable in India for low income earners.

The arguments in favor of a high threshold have merit, but are less compelling from a medium-term perspective. Tax administration reforms, for instance the expansion of the taxpayer identification number (TDS system), computerization, introduction of a large taxpayer unit, and expanded collection of third party information, should strengthen tax administration. The information technology revolution should at the same time rapidly reduce compliance costs for taxpayers. In addition, the government has prioritized the enhancement of social spending over the medium term, and is introducing elements of a safety net. Finally, in the medium term, India will join the ranks of more mature emerging markets, and compared to them, its level of goods and services taxation lags.

Improvements in tax administration and better targeted social spending could open the door to a change in the threshold. As administrative and compliance costs fall and the government becomes more effective at redistributing income, political opposition could lessen. A formal social security system funded by a payroll tax is not necessarily needed but, if India does follow the lead of more mature emerging markets and introduces one, the

---

[14]See, for instance, Ministry of Finance (2004).

payroll tax could promote better compliance, given the benefit motivation for payroll tax payment and the administrative synergies in payroll tax and PIT collection.

Creating an Environment for Reform

International experience suggests that successful tax reform, in particular, base broadening, requires focused efforts to build and maintain public support. In this regard, improvements in simplicity and horizontal equity (fairness) proved to be strong selling points in generating public support for tax reform; vertical equity and economic efficiency—while important from a theoretical perspective—did not (Thirsk, 1997). Moreover, tax base broadening also seems to be associated with successful revenue-based fiscal consolidation episodes, perhaps due to improved efficiency and macroeconomic outcomes (Tsibouris and others, 2006).[15]

To promote a broader tax base, many emerging market countries have become more transparent about the revenue forgone from various exemptions, that is, tax expenditures. Brazil, Mexico, Turkey, and Ukraine report tax expenditures and Russia and the Philippines have partial reporting.[16] Indeed, in some cases this seems to have had a direct impact on subsequent policy (e.g., Ukraine).[17] The Kelkar commission and FRBMA road map recognized the importance of transparency about tax expenditures, and the Ministry of Finance has been working on estimates for major items. Box 8.1 discusses the key issues to consider in this process.

Maintaining a broad tax base also requires careful administration. Budget process controls are important and are reasonable in India: the Ministry of Finance is required to vet and cost all new tax expenditure proposals and can propose alternative modalities for delivering support (e.g., on-budget subsidies). Moreover, the FRBMA in India effectively requires that new measures with a cost be compensated elsewhere. However, the system has

---

[15]See Chapter 9 for a discussion of the growth-enhancing impact that a tax base broadening and rate reduction reform could have.

[16]China, Colombia, and South Africa do not report tax expenditures. Beyond emerging markets, all G-7 countries except Japan report tax expenditures (although Italy's reporting is partial). Among higher income Asian economies, Korea also reports tax expenditures. Source: IMF Report on Observance of Standards and Codes, various reports.

[17]The Ukrainian authorities began publishing tax expenditure estimates in 2002, and efforts were made to broaden the tax base. Steady successes were followed by sweeping reform in 2005, when a new government sought resources to fund social initiatives.

Box 8.1. Enhancing Transparency About Tax Expenditures

Improving transparency about tax expenditures requires consideration of several issues (Craig and Allan, 2001):

- *Definitions.* The two most commonly used approaches are the conceptual and reference law approaches. In the former, tax expenditures are defined relative to a pure theoretical baseline (e.g., a single rate VAT). In the latter, only exemptions relative to the existing tax law are considered (e.g., lower rate of VAT would not be considered a tax expenditure). The conceptual approach produces the widest accounting, but should be tempered to reflect administrative feasibility.
- *Measurement.* The standard approach is to focus only on the direct reduction of tax liability and to avoid assumptions about a behavioral response. Estimation can be done using survey or other data, but over time tax forms and filing requirements can be adapted to permit more exact measurement. A de minimis rule—the exclusion of small items—can be used to reduce the administrative burden of measurement.
- *Publication.* The budget documents should ideally include information covering the past two years, plus the projection, and should distinguish any new initiatives. The documents should spell out the estimation methodology and discuss the risks to revenues, and budget implementation, from misestimation.
- *Ex post assessment and audit.* Standard compliance audit is appropriate, but value-for-money audit is crucial. The Auditor General should ask whether the instrument achieved the policy goal. If this is not feasible, specialized studies can be undertaken, as has been done in India for tax holidays in the northeastern region. Any assessment should be published.

---

failed in practice to stem the flow of exemptions, and recent legislation on special economic zones evolved to include extensive tax holiday provisions. An option to exert greater control would be to make all steps of the process more transparent, including what would now be internal Ministry of Finance deliberations on alternative subsidy mechanisms.

To protect CIT revenues, India may also need to address risks from harmful international tax competition. As India enters into bilateral and regional free trade arrangements, and companies are able to supply the Indian domestic market from other locations, the various jurisdictions may compete for mobile tax bases.[18] Tax coordination can help to reduce

---

[18]In India, before 2001, states competed for investment via incentives and lower tax rates. An agreement in 2001, which set floor rates of sales tax and eliminated some incentives, was widely seen as mitigating the problem. See Twelfth Finance Commission report (Government of India, 2004).

Table 8.5. Summary of Key Revenue Reforms

Measure	Potential Yield (In percent of GDP)
Goods and services taxation	1.25
Broaden service tax base	1.00
Eliminate exemptions	0.25
Compliance improvement	Large
Personal income taxation	2.25
Tax agriculture[1]	0.25
Tighten treatment of charities	0.20
Mortgage interest deduction	0.20
Interest exemptions	0.25
Raise threshold[2]	1.35
Corporate income taxation	0.50
Eliminate exemptions	0.50
Total	4.00

Source: Bagchi and others (2005); Ministry of Finance (2002a and 2002b); and IMF staff estimates.
[1]Yield at existing income tax threshold.
[2]Including agriculture.

the extent of competition. The least intrusive form would be a nonbinding code of conduct (as in the European Union). More developed forms would involve agreement on tax floors and on acceptable incentives (see Easson, 2004).

Conclusions

There is ample room for further revenue gains in India. The introduction of a GST, reduction of income tax thresholds, extension of income tax to the agricultural sector, and elimination of corporate tax exemptions would go a long way to raising India's revenue ratio over the medium term, to achieve revenue collection performance on par with more mature emerging market countries (Table 8.5).

Moving difficult reforms forward in India requires some thought about strategy. Fiscal federal agreements would be needed to secure a full GST and agricultural income taxation, while PIT reform would likely gain traction with improvements in the social safety net and tax administration reform. Corporate tax reforms may benefit from improvements in transparency, and from efforts to ensure appropriate tax coordination.

References

Aggarwal, Aradhna, 2004, "Export Processing Zones in India: Analysis of the Export Performance," ICRIER Working Paper No. 148 (New Delhi: Indian Council for Research on International Economic Relations).

Alesina, Alberto, and R. Perotti, 1996, "Fiscal Adjustments in OECD Countries: Composition and Macroeconomic Effects," NBER Working Paper No. 5730 (Cambridge, Massachusetts: National Bureau of Economic Research).

Bagchi, Amaresh, R.K. Rao, and B. Sen, 2005, "Raising the Tax-Ratio by Reining in the 'Tax Breaks'" (New Delhi: National Institute for Public Finance).

Bird, Richard, and P.P. Gendron, 2005, "VAT Revisited: A New Look at the Value Added Tax in Developing and Transition Countries," paper presented at the USAID Workshop for Practitioners on Tax on May 4 (Washington: U.S. Agency for International Development).

Chattopadhyay, Saumen, and A. Das Gupta, 2002, "The Compliance Cost of the Personal Income Tax and Its Determinants" (New Delhi: National Institute for Public Finance).

Craig, Jon, and William Allan, 2001, "Fiscal Transparency, Tax Expenditures, and Budget Processes: An International Perspective," *Proceedings of the Ninety-Fourth Annual Conference 2000*, pp. 258–64 (Washington: National Tax Association).

Easson, Alex, 2004, "Harmful Tax Competition: An Evaluation of the OECD Initiative," *Tax Notes International* (June 7), pp. 1037–77.

Gillis, Malcolm, ed., 1989, *Tax Reform in Developing Countries* (Durham, North Carolina: Duke University Press).

Government of India, 2004, *Report of the Twelfth Finance Commission* (New Delhi).

Gupta, Sanjeev, B. Clements, E. Baldacci, and C. Mulas-Granados, 2004, "The Persistence of Fiscal Adjustments in Developing Countries," *Applied Economics Letters*, Vol. 11, No. 4, pp. 209–12.

International Monetary Fund, Reports on Observance of Standards and Codes, various reports (Washington).

Khan, Mahmood, 2001, "Agricultural Taxation in Developing Countries: A Survey of Issues and Policy," *Agricultural Economics*, Vol. 24, No. 3, pp. 315–28.

Ministry of Finance, 2002a, *Report of the Task Force on Direct Taxes* (New Delhi: Government of India).

———, 2002b, *Report of the Task Force on Indirect Taxes* (New Delhi: Government of India).

———, 2004, *Report of the Task Force on Implementation of the Fiscal Responsibility and Budget Management Act, 2003* (New Delhi: Government of India).

———, 2005, *Budget 2005–06* (New Delhi: Government of India).

PricewaterhouseCoopers, 2003a, *Corporate Taxes 2004–05: Worldwide Summaries* (Toronto: John Wiley & Sons Canada Ltd.).

_____, 2003b, *Individual Taxes 2004–05: Worldwide Summaries* (Toronto: John Wiley & Sons Canada Ltd.).

Thirsk, Wayne, ed., 1997, *Tax Reform in Developing Countries* (Washington: World Bank).

Tsibouris, George C., Mark A. Horton, Mark J. Flanagan, and Wojciech S. Maliszewski, 2006, *Experience with Large Fiscal Adjustments*, IMF Occasional Paper No. 246 (Washington: International Monetary Fund).

Zee, Howell, J. Stotsky, and E. Ley, 2002, "Tax Incentives for Business Investment: A Primer for Policymakers in Developing Countries," *World Development*, Vol. 30, No. 9, pp. 1497–1516.

9

Making Tax Policy Pro-Growth

Hélène Poirson

Despite recent reforms to the personal and corporate income taxes and the introduction of a state value-added-tax (VAT) on goods in April 2005, India's competitiveness is hampered by the complexities and distortions of the domestic tax system. The tax system remains characterized by high marginal rates and a narrow tax base. The average tax intake and tax productivity are low by international standards, reflecting widespread tax evasion and—as discussed in Chapter 8—exemptions and tax holidays for various sectors and regions. Moreover, despite significant trade liberalization in recent years, India continues to rely heavily on trade taxes as a source of revenue. Trade taxes account for 12 percent of general government revenue, three times higher than the average for nonmember countries of the Organization for Economic Cooperation and Development (OECD).

A significant concern as India contemplates further liberalization—whether in the context of new regional and bilateral trade agreements or multilateral tariff reduction under the Doha round—is the potential impact on tax revenues. To ensure that any trade tax revenue losses are recouped, while maintaining the gains from the trade reform itself, the government's 2004 Fiscal Responsibility and Budget Management Act (FRBMA) road map envisages lower statutory personal and corporate income tax rates, the elimination of most exemptions and tax incentives, and the introduction of a national goods and services tax (GST) to both help improve tax revenue productivity and enhance economic efficiency.

The envisaged reforms, if implemented as a package, would not only help replace lost trade revenues but also make the tax system more investment friendly and less biased against exports. In particular, cuts in corporate and personal tax rates accompanied by base broadening to mitigate the revenue loss would help improve savings and investment rates, which are low by regional standards.[1] The introduction of a destination-based GST, by shifting the burden of indirect taxation from manufacturing to consumption, would enhance India's export prospects and increase India's attractiveness as an investment destination by contributing to the formation of a single internal Indian market.

While the empirical evidence is mixed and results are not robust, cross-country studies generally confirm the negative impact of a high tax burden on economic activity. Firm-level evidence and simulation results are the most conclusive, supporting the view that high tax rates have an adverse effect on growth and distort financing and investment decisions (Box 9.1). High tax rates may also contribute to the growth of the "shadow economy," carrying costs in terms of forgone tax receipts and lower productivity growth (Farrell, 2004; and Schneider and Klinglmair, 2004).

This chapter explores how tax policy can help generate a revenue-led adjustment while enhancing India's competitiveness and investment prospects. It first examines revenue performance in recent years and finds that it is characterized by (1) a continued high dependence on indirect taxes despite recent reforms, (2) low average effective tax rates and low tax productivity, and (3) high marginal tax rates and tax-induced distortions on investment and financing decisions. The next section finds that further reforms envisaged in the FRBMA road map would simultaneously improve tax productivity and lower the marginal tax burden and tax-induced distortions, but firms that rely on internal sources of funds or face problems borrowing would continue to face high marginal tax rates.

The Indian Tax System: Recent Revenue Performance and Issues

The Tax System

The authority to levy taxes in India is divided between the central government and the state governments. The central government levies direct taxes such as personal income tax (PIT) and corporate income tax (CIT); indirect taxes such as customs and excise duties and a service tax; and a

---

[1]National savings during 1999–2004 in India reached 24 percent of GDP on average annually, compared with 43 percent in China, 34 percent in Malaysia, and 32 percent in Korea.

Box 9.1. Empirical Evidence on Taxation and Growth

High labor taxation can have a negative impact on employment and growth by pushing up labor costs. In the presence of strong and decentralized labor unions, labor taxes are shifted into real wages, reducing labor demand; this, in turn, leads to substitution away from labor and downward pressure on the marginal product of capital, reducing investment and growth. Empirical evidence for European Union (EU) countries confirms this view.[1] High marginal effective tax rates (due to the combination of tax and benefit systems) can also affect labor supply decisions by affecting the choice between additional work and leisure.[2]

Consumption taxes should not in theory affect savings and investment decisions since future and current consumption are treated equally, and they remain neutral with respect to various sources of income. Empirical evidence is mixed, however. Some studies find that such taxes indeed have no impact on employment and growth,[3] but others find that—like income taxes, although to a lesser extent—they have a negative impact on growth by distorting the choice between labor and leisure, and also could depress savings.[4]

Corporate taxes raise the required rate of return on investment and thereby depress investment. In addition, corporate taxes tend to favor debt over equity financing or retained earnings, potentially leading to an inefficient allocation of resources, higher insolvency risks, and discrimination against smaller compa-

[1]See Daveri and Tabellini (2000).
[2]For example, see Organization for Economic Cooperation and Development (2001).
[3]See Daveri and Tabellini (2000) and Kneller, Bleaney, and Gemmell (1999).
[4]For example, see Milesi-Ferretti and Roubini (1995) and Tanzi and Zee (2000).

sales tax on interstate trade (central sales tax (CST)). States levy a VAT on goods, state sales taxes, and various local taxes. As in other developing countries, tax incentives feature prominently in India, with tax holidays being the preferred form of incentives (see Chapter 8). Such incentives may be important for some companies to offset other costs of doing business in India—such as still relatively high import duties, restrictive labor laws, and inadequate public infrastructure—but an unfortunate outcome has been to thin out the overall direct and indirect tax bases (Shome, 2004).

Since 1991, the tax structure has been substantially rationalized. Changes at the central government level include reducing customs and excise duties, lowering CIT rates, extending a form of VAT to some industries, and broadening the tax base to some services (Box 9.2). At the state level, the main reform has been the introduction in 2005 of the VAT—now in all but two states—after 10 years of delay.

nies that face more difficulties borrowing. Corporate taxes are also distortionary given the widespread use of rebates, exemptions, and special regimes for specific sectors or regions. This also benefits large companies that can lower their tax burden through tax planning and fiscal engineering.[5] Cross-country studies confirm a negative link between the tax burden (measured by tax revenue as a share of GDP) and growth for high-income countries, although the result does not hold for low- and middle-income countries, perhaps reflecting measurement problems.[6] Firm-level empirical results, as well as simulation results using computable general equilibrium models, also support the view that higher taxes negatively affect growth.[7]

Taxation of capital income—even when at a low level—appears to have a distortionary effect on savings. Cross-country studies find little evidence for the EU that taxes affect the aggregate level of savings, but they appear to influence its composition and location. Many EU countries tend to grant favorable treatment to specific savings instruments, such as retirement schemes and housing investment. Moreover, they generally apply a preferential treatment to nonresidents, thus distorting saving flows and potentially enhancing tax evasion possibilities associated with cross-border investment.[8]

---

[5]See Rao and Lukose (2002); Organization for Economic Cooperation and Development (2001); Joumard (2002); and Nicodème (2002).

[6]See Blankenau and Simpson (2004). The marginal or effective tax rate on corporates ideally should be used.

[7]See Fisman and Svensson (2000) and Feltenstein and Shah (1995).

[8]See Organization for Economic Cooperation and Development (2001).

How Has Revenue Performed in Recent Years?

After declining below 14 percent of GDP in 2001/02, India's general government tax revenue rebounded to 16¾ percent of GDP in 2005/06. This exceeds the average for Asian emerging market countries by 3¾ percentage points but is 3½ percentage points below the average for all emerging market countries. The decline in revenue in the 1990s occurred as major tax reforms were implemented, aimed at improving the buoyancy of revenues and increasing the share of direct taxes in total revenues. Direct tax revenues increased, but indirect tax collections declined, mainly due to tariff reductions.

Recent reforms have had some success in reversing the declining trend of revenues. The peak tariff reduction for nonagricultural imports advocated by the 2002 Kelkar committee reports on direct and indirect taxation

Box 9.2. Main Features of the Tax System (December 2005)

The principal direct taxes include PIT and CIT, state taxes on agricultural income, wealth tax, and various withholding taxes. The PIT is levied on non-agricultural income at rates of 10 percent to 31.5 percent. It applies to Indian residents and foreigners, on income earned in India. The exemption threshold of Rs 111,250 ($2,472) results in a relatively narrow tax base of about 40 million taxpayers. States levy some taxes on agricultural income (land revenue tax and agricultural income tax), but their combined incidence is considerably less than that of the PIT. A wealth tax is levied on net assets in excess of Rs 1.5 million (about $33,000). The CIT is levied at a rate of 33.66 percent for domestic companies (including surcharges), but with significant exemptions. Other corporate taxes include a 12.75 percent tax (including surcharges) on dividend distribution, a minimum alternative tax on profits, a tax on fringe benefits, and various withholding taxes on interest, royalties, and so on.

The main indirect taxes are the state VAT and sales taxes, central customs and excise duties, central service tax, and CST. The state VAT and sales taxes are levied on intrastate trade and the CST on interstate trade, at a rate that varies depending on the type of transaction and good. In VAT-implementing states, the VAT rates are 1, 4, and 12.5 percent. Sales taxes are also levied on specific items (e.g., petroleum products). The two states that have not implemented a VAT continue to levy state sales taxes. The center levies customs duties and a central excise duty (CENVAT) on goods manufactured or produced in India at a single rate of 16 percent, with some exceptions. The CENVAT base is truncated to manufacturing and eroded by a complex and extensive system of exemptions, including for small-scale industries and special economic zones. A service tax is levied by the center on some 71 services at a rate of 12 percent. Other minor taxes and duties imposed at both center and state level include stamp duty, taxes on land and buildings, and taxes on motor vehicles.

(Box 9.3) was fully implemented but the revenue loss was more than off-set by buoyant corporate tax collections. PIT revenues rose as a share of GDP, but only marginally, reflecting the extension of further exemptions, deductions, and rebates, while excise revenues as a share of GDP remained broadly unchanged. The states succeeded in raising sales tax collections, and, as mentioned earlier, a VAT was introduced in 2005.

Despite reforms, the tax structure remains dominated by indirect taxes. The share of revenue from indirect taxes exceeds two-thirds, slightly above the average for emerging Asian economies, and significantly above the average for all emerging market countries (54 percent). State taxes on commodities and services are the prominent source of general government

Box 9.3. Kelkar 2002 Reports' Proposals

As part of its overall reform agenda, the government in 2002 set up a tax reform task force (Kelkar task force) to propose a far-reaching reform agenda for direct and indirect taxes.[1] Proposals centered around the following elements.

- *A change in the exemption level and rate structure of the personal income tax and broadening of the base, as well as the elimination of most exemptions and replacement of allowances by credits.* A proposed constitutional amendment would allow the central government to tax agricultural income. The general exemption would be increased, the number of brackets reduced, and the highest marginal rate reduced to 30 percent. A range of special deductions would be eliminated with some converted into credits. The report also proposed changes to the taxation of capital income, specifically exempting dividends from Indian companies and long-term capital gains on equity.
- *A reduction in the rate and in the large number of deductions and exemptions of the corporate income tax.* The rate would be reduced from 35 percent (net of 2 percent surcharge) to 30 percent for domestic companies and from 40 percent to 35 percent for foreign companies. The minimum alternate tax would be eliminated.
- *A rationalization of the import tariff structure and export promotion schemes.* The existing 20 tariff rates, ranging up to 182 percent, would be reduced to a range of 0–20 percent for most goods, with higher rates—up to 150 percent—for certain agricultural products and "demerit" goods. Exemptions would be significantly narrowed.
- *Broadening the base of the CENVAT and moving it further toward a VAT.*

---

[1]See Ministry of Finance (2002a and 2002b).

revenue (representing nearly a third of the total tax intake), followed by central government excises (one-fifth of the total) (Table 9.1).

The overall tax burden on labor and capital income, as measured by the average effective tax rate (AETR), is low compared to advanced economies and higher-income emerging market countries in the region.[2]

---

[2]The AETR is measured as the ratio of tax collections to the notional tax base derived from national accounts. It is a standard indicator of the effective tax burden on categories of income or consumption. The measure summarizes the impact of various factors, including statutory tax rates, the effective tax base (accounting for tax evasion, exemptions, and the extent of informal activity), and the quality of tax administration. See Appendix 9.2 for details on the calculation of AETRs in India.

Table 9.1. Structure of General Government Tax Revenue, 2004/05

	In Billions of Rupees	In Percent of GDP	In Percent of Total
Central government	3,049.8	9.8	62.4
Corporate tax	835.7	2.7	17.1
Income tax	483.1	1.6	9.9
Excises	991.6	3.2	20.3
Customs	576.6	1.9	11.8
Other[1]	162.9	0.5	3.3
States and union territories[2]	1,834.7	5.9	37.6
Taxes on income	16.4	0.1	0.3
Taxes on property and capital transactions	215.3	0.7	4.4
Taxes on commodities and services	1,602.9	5.2	32.8
Total	4,884.5	15.7	100.0

Sources: Indian authorities; and IMF staff estimates.
[1]Mostly service tax.
[2]IMF staff estimates based on projected GDP growth and historical elasticities.

The AETR on labor, at 2 percent in 2001, is much lower than in the European Union, United States, or Japan, which range from 21 percent to 36 percent (Table 9.2).[3] This reflects India's narrow effective tax base and the lack of a social security system. The AETR on capital income is also low, owing to the wide coverage of tax incentives, low personal taxes on capital income, and a large informal sector. The operating surplus of unincorporated enterprises (a proxy for the share of the informal sector) accounted for three-quarters of the operating surplus of the economy in 2000/01. India's low AETRs on capital and labor match those of other low-income countries in the region (Sri Lanka and China), but are much below those of higher-income emerging market countries such as Korea and Thailand (Figure 9.1). These results suggest ample room for AETRs to increase further in India as income levels rise, without adversely affecting competitiveness. India's AETR on consumption is broadly average despite a tax base that largely excludes services. As in other countries in Asia, it has declined over time.

AETRs are relatively low in India mainly owing to low tax productivity.[4] For example, CIT tax productivity is much below the average for both OECD and non-OECD countries, reflecting a tax base thinned out by

---

[3]Estimates for non-OECD countries are not available.

[4]Tax productivity is calculated as the ratio of the effective to statutory tax rate (Kraemer and Zhang, 2004). It measures the extent to which revenues that should be received—given the rate and potential base of the tax—are actually being realized.

Table 9.2. Comparison of Average Effective Tax Rates, 1990–2000
(In percent)

| | Average Effective Tax Rate | | | Total Tax Wedge on Labor[1] |
	Labor	Capital	Consumption	
India[2]	1.6	5.2	15.0	15.9
Australia	20.9	30.7	12.1	30.5
Austria	39.6	24.3	16.2	51.2
Belgium	41.3	32.7	15.0	51.7
Canada	29.6	36.8	13.9	39.4
Czech Republic	41.5	21.6	13.0	47.2
Denmark	39.9	39.5	20.6	56.0
Finland	45.0	26.0	18.7	58.0
France	40.5	33.2	15.1	51.3
Germany	35.0	21.2	13.4	44.9
Greece	34.9	12.9	15.5	46.5
Hungary	...	14.7	22.2	...
Ireland	26.3	...	21.2	41.9
Italy	37.7	31.0	13.9	47.9
Japan	24.1	27.9	6.4	29.4
Korea	9.9	16.7	15.8	24.2
Netherlands	36.4	32.7	18.0	47.9
New Zealand	25.1	...	18.5	38.9
Norway	36.2	24.7	25.7	52.5
Poland	...	20.9	17.1	...
Portugal	23.9	17.6	19.9	39.0
Spain	30.7	20.0	14.5	40.8
Sweden	49.6	35.7	19.8	59.6
Switzerland	30.9	27.1	9.3	37.3
United Kingdom	22.6	34.0	15.7	34.8
United States	23.4	27.3	6.4	28.3
Unweighted average	32.4	26.5	15.9	43.4
EU15 average	38.0	28.7	17.8	48.9

Sources: Carey and Rabesona (2002); and IMF staff estimates for India.
[1]Combined effective tax rate on labor and consumption.
[2]Average 1993–2000, based on data availability.

exemptions and widespread tax evasion (Tables 9.3 and 9.4).[5] This suggests ample scope for increasing revenue without raising rates, via expansion of the taxpayer net, lifting of exemptions, and stepped-up tax administration. During the period 1993–2001, India increased AETRs on labor and capital despite reductions in statutory rates and continued widespread exemptions. This suggests that improved tax administration and compliance was the main factor underlying the improvement in tax productivity and resulting rise in AETRs.

---

[5]In Table 9.3, following the Kraemer-Zhang approach, we use the operating surplus of the economy (from national accounts) as the potential tax base. In Table 9.4, in the absence of such data for non-OECD countries, we use nominal GDP.

Figure 9.1. Selected Asian Countries: Average Effective Tax Rates (AETRs) on Labor, Capital, and Consumption
(In percent)

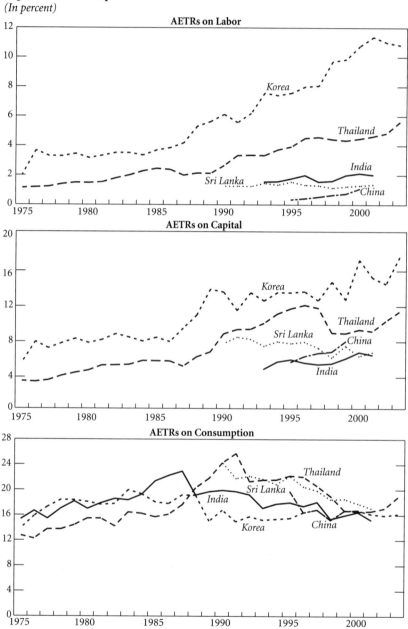

Source: Country authorities; and IMF staff estimates.

Table 9.3. Revenue Productivity of the Corporate Tax, 2001
(In percent)

	Statutory CIT Rate	Effective CIT Rate	Revenue Productivity[1]
India	35.9	3.5	9.7
France	33.3	8.9	26.8
Germany	38.9	2.1	5.3
Italy	37.0	6.7	18.2
Japan	40.9	8.7	21.2
Korea	29.7	9.6	32.4
United Kingdom	30.0	9.9	32.9
United States[2]	45.8	5.3	11.6
OECD average	32.3	9.6	29.7

Sources: Standard & Poor's; and IMF staff estimates for India and Korea.
[1]Ratio of effective CIT rate to statutory CIT rate.
[2]As of 2000.

Table 9.4. Revenue Productivity of the Corporate Tax, 2003
(In percent)

	Statutory CIT Rate[1]	Corporate Taxes/GDP[2]	Revenue Productivity[3]
India	35.9	2.3	6.4
Argentina	35.0	2.7	7.7
Bolivia	25.0	1.8	7.2
Chile (2001)	17.0	4.6	27.2
China	33.0	2.5	7.5
Colombia	35.0	4.7	13.4
Hungary	16.0	8.0	49.8
Indonesia	30.0	1.7	5.5
Mexico (2000)	33.0	5.0	15.3
Pakistan	35.0	3.6	10.2
Peru	30.0	3.4	11.4
Philippines	32.0	2.6	8.2
Poland	19.0	4.9	25.6
Russia	24.0	4.0	16.6
Singapore (2001)	22.0	8.0	36.5
South Africa	37.8	5.5	14.4
Thailand	30.0	3.0	10.0
Turkey	33.0	2.5	7.6
Ukraine	25.0	5.0	20.0
Uruguay	35.0	2.6	7.4
Venezuela	34.0	14.7	43.1
Average	29.0	4.5	17.2

Sources: KPMG; IMF, *Government Finance Statistics* and *International Financial Statistics*; and various country databases.
[1]As of January 1, 2004.
[2]Used as proxy for the effective CIT rate. For 2003, unless otherwise indicated.
[3]Ratio of corporate tax/GDP to statutory CIT rate.

The Burden of Taxation on Investors

Does the Indian income tax code affect incentives to invest? To investigate this, we calculate two standard indicators, the marginal effective tax wedge (METW) between the pretax and posttax return on capital, and the marginal effective tax rate (METR), defined as the ratio of the METW to the real required pretax rate of return.[6] By summarizing various tax effects, including the statutory CIT and personal tax rates on capital income, depreciation allowances, and inventory valuation method, the METW measures the potential cost of taxation to investors, which in turn affects their decision to invest. The AETR on capital income, although commonly used for this purpose, does not accurately reflect incentives, as it is backward looking and measures the average rather than marginal tax burden. Moreover, international comparisons using the AETR are difficult to interpret due to differences in accounting definitions and the timing of tax payments. Further, it does not incorporate personal tax provisions.

The marginal tax burden on capital in India is lower than the OECD average, but tax-induced distortions tend to be high. Firms that rely on internal financing are particularly penalized, as they face a marginal tax wedge almost one-third higher than the OECD average (Tables 9.5 and 9.6):

- *The marginal tax wedge (1.4 percent) is slightly below the OECD average.* This reflects low personal taxes, including the elimination of tax on long-term capital gains in 2004/05.
- *However, the standard deviation of the marginal tax wedge across investment assets is three times higher than the OECD average.* Inventory investment is treated more harshly than investments in machinery and buildings, so that firms that need to carry more inventories are penalized, more so than in OECD countries. The use of the FIFO (first in, first out) method for inventory valuation also entails a higher tax burden, as increases in the value of inventories due solely to inflation are taxed.
- *The standard deviation of the marginal tax wedge across financing sources is nearly twice as high as the OECD average.* The negative tax wedge enjoyed by debt financing means that the government is effectively subsidizing marginal debt-financed investments, more so

---

[6]See Appendix 9.2 for tax parameters used. See Organization for Economic Cooperation and Development (1991) for further details on the methodology and parameters. Indirect taxes impose additional costs on investment, but the METR approach focuses on direct taxation, thus understating the tax burden on investors. Comparable estimates have been published for OECD countries.

Table 9.5. Marginal Effective Tax Wedge by Investment Type[1]
(In percent)

	Standard Deviation[2]	Weighted Average	Machinery	Building	Inventories
			Investment Type		
India	1.3	1.4	1.2	0.2	2.7
Canada	1.0	3.6	2.7	4.1	5.1
Germany	0.4	1.2	0.9	1.4	1.9
Japan	1.0	2.0	1.0	3.1	2.8
United Kingdom	0.5	2.2	1.9	2.2	3.1
United States	0.4	1.9	1.5	2.5	2.0
OECD average	0.4	1.6	1.2	1.7	2.3

Sources: Dalsgaard (2001) based on OECD calculations; and IMF staff estimates for India.

[1]These indicators show the degree to which the personal and corporate tax systems scale up (or down) the pretax real rate of return that must be earned on an investment, given that the representative investor can earn a 4 percent real rate of return on a demand deposit. The estimates shown refer to 2004 for India, 1999 for other countries.

[2]The standard deviation across investment vehicles provides an indicator of the neutrality of the tax system toward corporate investment decisions. The lower the standard deviation, the more neutral the tax system.

than in OECD countries. Investments financed by new equity face a below-average tax wedge, thanks to relatively low dividend taxation. In contrast, investments financed by retained earnings face an above-average tax wedge, in excess of 2½ percent. Smaller firms that face problems in borrowing and tend to be more dependent on internal sources of funds are thus disadvantaged compared to larger firms (Rao and Lukose, 2002; and Joseph and others, 1998). The relatively large tax advantage of debt finance may also have contributed to relatively high financial leverage in India, exacerbating firms' vulnerability. The average debt-to-equity ratio for Indian companies is high relative to their counterparts in Asian countries and elsewhere, and—even before the recent credit boom (Chapter 6)—had risen to 1.4 in 2002 from a low of 1.2 in 1996 (Topalova, 2004).

A related result is that corporates that have only limited access to debt financing, particularly smaller firms, face a high effective marginal tax rate. The METR for investments financed by retained earnings or equity is nearly 33 percent, compared with the OECD average of 22 percent, reflecting a relatively high CIT rate.[7]

---

[7]The METR calculated here follows the methodology of Devereux, Griffith, and Klemm (2002) and ignores any personal taxes, focusing on the marginal tax burden at the firm level.

Table 9.6. Marginal Effective Tax Wedge by Financing Source[1]
(In percent)

	Standard Deviation[2]	Sources of Financing		
		Retained earnings	New equity	Debt
India	1.6	2.6	2.5	−0.2
France	2.9	3.6	7.7	0.7
Germany	0.7	0.9	2.5	1.3
Italy	0.4	1.3	1.3	0.4
Japan	2.3	3.3	5.5	−0.1
Korea	0.5	0.6	1.6	1.6
United Kingdom	0.5	2.9	2.4	1.6
United States	1.5	1.7	4.8	1.4
OECD average[3]	0.9	2.0	3.2	1.0

Sources: Joumard (2002) based on OECD calculations; and IMF staff estimates for India.

[1]These indicators show the degree to which the personal and corporate tax systems scale up (or down) the pretax real rate of return that must be earned on an investment, given that the representative investor can earn a 4 percent real rate of return on a demand deposit. The representative investor is supposed to be a resident person, taxed at the top marginal income tax rate (see OECD, 1991). The estimates shown refer to 2004 for India, to 1999 for other countries.

[2]The standard deviation across financing instruments provides an indicator of the neutrality of the tax system toward corporate financing decisions. The lower the standard deviation, the more neutral the tax system.

[3]Weighted average across available countries (weights based on 1995 GDPs and PPPs).

The prevalence of tax incentives for special sectors and regions in India means that the marginal tax burden also varies greatly across sectors and regions. The marginal tax wedge for a firm that benefits from a corporate tax exemption is only 0.4 percent, 1 percentage point lower than that of a firm that does not enjoy the tax holiday. Other incentives, such as accelerated depreciation provisions, also result in a lower marginal tax burden for benefiting firms. Such large variations in METWs in turn can result in large distortions to investment decisions and allocative efficiency.

Priorities for Reforms

The facts highlighted above suggest that a tax reform combining lower statutory rates with base broadening could help achieve a pro-growth fiscal adjustment in India. AETR and tax productivity estimates suggest ample scope for raising direct tax revenue through the removal of exemptions and improved tax administration and compliance. In addition to reducing tax-induced distortions, the removal of exemptions would create room for further lowering statutory rates, which in turn would enhance the return on investment and further improve the neutrality of the tax system. With investors pursuing high-return investments rather than tax benefits, growth would tend to rise. Meanwhile, the planned introduction of a national VAT on goods and services (GST) would help improve the revenue productivity of domestic indirect taxes, helping recoup expected trade revenue losses, and also enhance economic efficiency. These broad directions for tax reform were highlighted in the government's 2004 FRBMA road map.

An Assessment of the FRBMA Road Map Tax Proposals

The road map proposes a number of changes to income taxation and the introduction of a national GST.

- *Direct tax measures include further reductions in statutory rates.* The road map proposes a reduction of the CIT rate to 30 percent and elimination of the surcharge; reduction of the general depreciation rate to 15 percent; elimination of the withholding tax on distribution of dividends; and elimination of the long-term capital gains tax. Several measures, including the reduction in the CIT and depreciation rates and the elimination of the long-term capital gains tax, have been implemented over the last two years. This has contributed to lowering the marginal tax wedge and reducing its variation across investment assets, thus increasing the return on investment and contributing to economic efficiency. The implementation of remaining measures would help consolidate those gains.
- *Introduction of the GST and further reduction in customs duties are the hallmarks of proposed indirect tax reforms.* The GST would replace the existing state VAT, CST, central excise duties, and central service tax. Tariffs have already dropped in the last two budgets and the government envisages further cuts in coming years to bring them down to levels in member countries of the Association of South East Asian Nations.
- *The reforms also envisage a significant increase in tax productivity via the removal of most exemptions and incentives, expansion of the taxpayer net, and increased reliance on information technology to improve tax administration and compliance.* The computerization of tax administration— including increased tax withholding at the source, the introduction of a tax information network and a tax information system to track interstate transactions, and the computerization of customs—is well under way. The planned introduction of large taxpayer units in major cities in 2006 should help reduce compliance and transaction costs for large taxpayers. However, most exemptions remain in place. The

Table 9.7. Tax Wedges Under Current Versus Reformed Tax System
(In percent)

Type of Investment	Mode of Financing				Standard Deviation[1]
	Retained earnings	New equity	Debt	Weighted average	
Tax system, 2005–06[2]					
Machinery	2.4	2.3	−0.4	1.2	1.6
	44.0	*42.8*	*−13.5*	*27.6*	
Buildings	1.3	1.2	−1.3	0.2	1.5
	30.3	*28.6*	*−74.5*	*4.8*	
Inventories	4.1	3.9	0.9	2.7	1.8
	57.1	*56.3*	*23.7*	*46.7*	
Weighted average	2.6	2.5	−0.2	1.4	1.6
	46.4	*45.3*	*−6.6*	*31.1*	
Standard deviation[1]	1.4	1.4	1.1	1.3	
Tax system, FRBMA road map[2]					
Machinery	2.1	2.1	−0.3	1.0	1.3
	39.9	*39.9*	*−9.9*	*24.9*	
Buildings	1.1	1.1	−1.1	0.1	1.3
	26.7	*26.7*	*−56.1*	*4.4*	
Inventories	3.5	3.5	0.9	2.4	1.5
	53.1	*53.1*	*22.6*	*43.2*	
Weighted average	2.3	2.3	−0.1	1.2	1.4
	42.3	*42.3*	*−4.0*	*28.2*	
Standard deviation[1]	1.2	1.2	1.0	1.1	

Source: IMF staff estimates.

[1]The standard deviation measures the neutrality of the tax system with respect to corporate financing and investment decisions. The lower the standard deviation, the more neutral the tax system.

[2]Corresponding marginal effective tax rates are reported in italics.

government announced that it would let existing corporate tax exemptions lapse, but extended sunset clauses in some cases, and introduced new incentives in the context of the 2005 Special Economic Zones Act. New services have been added to the tax net over the last two years, but the move toward a GST will require further expansion of the service tax base and the removal of most excise exemptions, including for small-scale industries and selected areas.

Implementation of remaining tax reforms would further decrease the marginal tax burden on investment and reduce tax-induced distortions. The METW would decrease to 1.2 percent, thanks to lower personal taxes (Table 9.7). Neutrality with respect to sources of financing would improve, but firms that rely on internal financing (mainly smaller firms) would remain relatively penalized. The marginal tax wedge faced by such firms would remain ¼ percentage point above the OECD average. Neutrality with respect to investment patterns would also improve, but the standard deviation of the METW across investment assets would remain more than double the OECD average, suggesting scope for further improvements.

To mitigate potentially excessive reliance on debt finance and help further improve the neutrality of the tax system, additional measures can be considered. These include limiting the deductibility of interest to a percentage of net taxable income; limiting debt for the purposes of income tax (e.g., debt-to-equity ratios in Canada are limited to 2, in Germany to 1.5, and in Japan to 3); limiting interest to a referential rate (e.g., in Portugal, the 12-month Euribor plus 1.5 percent); or introducing an allowance for corporate equity.[8]

The recent introduction of a state VAT is a major step toward the GST. By allowing full integration of goods and services taxation at the national level, a GST should help secure further gains in economic efficiency, with favorable effects on investment and exports. However, successful introduction will require bringing remaining states into the VAT, phasing out the CST, and reaching agreement with states on the sharing of GST revenues.[9]

Base-broadening measures envisaged by the road map would imply a significant increase in tax productivity and economic efficiency gains as tax-induced distortions are reduced. For example, corporate tax revenue is projected in the FRBMA road map to nearly double from 2.3 percent of GDP in 2003/04 to 4.2 percent of GDP by 2008/09, despite a lower CIT rate, as most exemptions are eliminated. CIT tax productivity would more than double to 14 percent by 2008/09 (nearing the non-OECD average). The removal of most tax incentives would also result in lower variation of the marginal tax burden across sectors and regions, contributing to higher economic efficiency. Meanwhile, the proposed introduction of a GST with few exemptions should help enhance indirect tax productivity and improve economic efficiency by harmonizing tax rates across states. Moreover, a truly destination-based GST would allow the emergence of a single Indian market, greatly enhancing India's attractiveness as an investment destination.

---

[8]The notional rate of return on invested equity is deductible under the CIT in Croatia (1994–2001), and imputed equity return is taxed at a reduced rate in Austria and Italy (until 2001).

[9]The Indian constitution currently gives the center the exclusive right to tax services, while precluding it from taxing retail sales. To introduce the GST, a "grand bargain" therefore needs to be struck between the center and the states. Specifically, the latter would agree to let the center tax sales, in exchange for a share of GST revenues.

Appendix 9.1. Average Effective Tax Rates Based on Macroeconomic Data

The AETR on labor is derived in two steps. First, the effective tax rate on total household income is calculated as the ratio of individual income tax and household income, including operating surplus of unincorporated enterprises, property income, and wage income. Second, the AETR on labor is calculated by dividing the sum of taxes paid on labor income (tax on wages and salaries—calculated by applying the household income AETR to wage income[10]—social security contributions, and other payroll taxes) by the sum of wages and salaries and employer-paid social security contributions.

The AETR on capital is obtained by dividing the sum of taxes paid by capital (corporate income tax, household taxes on capital income, and various property taxes) by the net operating surplus of the economy.

The AETR on consumption is calculated as the sum of domestic taxes on goods and services, taxes on exports, and import duties, divided by the sum of private and government nonwage consumption, net of indirect taxes. Indirect taxes are excluded in the denominator to reflect the common practice of expressing indirect tax rates as a percentage of the price before tax.

More recent studies, however, have argued that it is preferable to express the consumption tax base in gross terms (i.e., including indirect tax rates in the denominator), to improve comparability with the tax ratios on labor and capital and facilitate calculating a combined AETR on labor and consumption (Carey and Rabesona, 2002). We therefore also present this alternative (revised) estimate together with the original Mendoza and others (1994) estimate.

---

[10]Labor and capital income of households are assumed to be taxed at the same rate.

Appendix 9.2. Tax Parameter Data, December 2005

	In percent
Corporate tax system	
Corporate tax rate on retained earnings	33.66
Inventory valuation	First in, first out
Long-term capital gains tax rate	0.00
Dividend distribution tax rate	12.75
Tax depreciation rates	
For machinery	15.00
For buildings	10.00
Depreciation method	Declining balance
Personal tax system	
Interest income tax rate	10.71
Dividend income tax rate	0.00
Short-term capital gains tax rate	10.20
Long-term capital gains tax rate	0.00
Proportion of assets realized each period	10.00

Source: Indian authorities.

References

Blankenau, W., and N.B. Simpson, 2004, "Public Education Expenditures and Growth," *Journal of Development Economics,* Vol. 73, No. 2, pp. 583–605.

Carey, David, and Josette Rabesona, 2002, "Tax Ratios on Labour and Capital Income and on Consumption," OECD *Economic Studies,* No. 35, Vol. 2, pp. 129–74.

Dalsgaard, Thomas, 2001, "The Tax System in New Zealand: An Appraisal and Options for Change," Economics Department Working Paper No. 281 (Paris: Organization for Economic Cooperation and Development).

Daveri, F., and G. Tabellini, 2000, "Unemployment, Growth and Taxation in Industrial Countries," *Economic Policy,* Vol. 15, No. 30 (April), pp. 47–104.

Devereux, Michael, Rachel Griffith, and Alexander Klemm, 2002, "Corporate Income Tax Reforms and International Tax Competition," *Economic Policy,* Vol. 17, No. 35 (October), pp. 450–95.

Farrell, Diana, 2004, "Boost Growth by Reducing the Informal Economy," *Asian Wall Street Journal,* October 18.

Feltenstein, A., and A. Shah, 1995, "General Equilibrium Effects of Investment Incentives in Mexico," *Journal of Development Economics,* Vol. 46, No. 2, pp. 253–69.

Fisman, R., and J. Svensson, 2000, "Are Corruption and Taxation Really Harmful to Growth? Firm Level Evidence" (unpublished; New York: Columbia University).

Joseph, Mathew, Rupa Nitsure, L. Bhagirathi, and Madan Sabnavis, 1998, "India's Economic Reforms: Private Corporate Sector Response," paper presented to 1998 ABAS International Conference on Emerging Economies (Budapest).

Joumard, Isabelle, 2002, "Tax Systems in European Union Countries," *OECD Economic Studies*, No. 34, pp. 91–151.

Kneller, R., M.F. Bleaney, and N. Gemmell, 1999, "Fiscal Policy and Growth: Evidence from OECD Countries," *Journal of Public Economics*, Vol. 74, No. 2, pp. 171–90.

KPMG, 2004, *Corporate Tax Rate Survey*; available via the Internet at www.kpmg.com.

Kraemer, Moritz, and Eileen Zhang, 2004, "Flexibility in Taxing Times—A New Index of Governments' Revenue-Raising Potential" (London: Standard & Poor's).

Mendoza, Enrique, Assaf Razin, and Linda Tesar, 1994, "Effective Tax Rates in Macro-economics: Cross-Country Estimates of Tax Rates on Factor Incomes and Consumption," *Journal of Monetary Economics*, Vol. 34, No. 3, pp. 297–323.

Milesi-Ferretti, Gian-Maria, and Nouriel Roubini, 1995, "Growth Effects of Income and Consumption Taxes: Positive and Normative Analysis," NBER Working Paper No. 5317 (Cambridge, Massachusetts: National Bureau of Economic Research).

Ministry of Finance, 2002a, *Report of the Task Force on Indirect Taxes* (New Delhi: Government of India).

———, 2002b, *Report of the Task Force on Direct Taxes* (New Delhi: Government of India).

Nicodème, G., 2002, "Sector and Size Effects on Effective Corporate Taxation," Economic Paper No. 175 (Brussels: European Commission).

Organization for Economic Cooperation and Development, 1991, *Taxing Profits in a Global Economy* (Paris).

———, 2001, *Tax and the Economy: A Comparative Assessment of OECD Countries*, OECD Tax Policy Studies, No. 6 (Paris).

Rao, S. Narayan, and Jijo Lukose, 2002, "An Empirical Study on the Determinants of the Capital Structure of Listed Indian Firms" (unpublished; Mumbai: Indian Institute of Technology).

Schneider, Friedrich, and Robert Klinglmair, 2004, "Shadow Economies Around the World: What Do We Know?" CESifo Working Paper No. 1167 (Munich: Center for Economic Studies and Ifo Institute for Economic Research).

Shome, Parthasarathi, 2004, "India: Resource Mobilization Through Taxation" (unpublished; Washington: International Monetary Fund).

Tanzi, Vito, and Howell Zee, 2000, "Taxation and the Household Saving Rate: Evidence from OECD Countries," *Banca Nazionale del Lavoro Quarterly Review*, Vol. 53 (March), pp. 31–43.

Topalova, Petia, 2004, "Overview of the Indian Corporate Sector: 1989–2002," IMF Working Paper No. 04/64 (Washington: International Monetary Fund).

10

Understanding the Growth Momentum in India's Services

ENRIC FERNANDEZ AND POONAM GUPTA

A striking feature of India's growth performance over the past 15 years has been the strength of the services sector.[1] The sector has benefited tremendously from the globalization of services and the increasing openness of the Indian economy to trade and foreign direct investment (FDI). Indeed, the services sector has benefited far more than has industry. Thus, India has become a leading exporter of services in the global economy with a share in global exports of services that is more than double its share of global exports of merchandise (Table 10.1). The most visible and well-known dimension of this phenomenon has been the takeoff in exports of software and services based on information technology (IT). But the growth in services has been broader than this and has also involved domestically consumed services. The pickup in growth since the 1990s has been most remarkable in business services, which includes the IT sector, and telecommunications, a sector that has witnessed a phenomenal expansion in domestic demand. This chapter shows that important roles have been played by economic reforms, and growing external demand for services exports in explaining the growth momentum of the services sector. The chapter also discusses the growth potential, in particular, of the IT sector and the challenges India faces in realizing this potential.

---

[1]The chapter is largely based on papers by Gupta (2005) and Gordon and Gupta (2004).

Table 10.1. Leading Exporters of Goods and Services, 2004

Rank	Merchandise	Share in World Trade	Rank	Services	Share in World Trade	Rank	Services Other Than Travel and Transportation	Share in World Trade
1	Germany	10.0	1	United States	15.0	1	United States	16.7
2	United States	8.9	2	United Kingdom	8.1	2	United Kingdom	11.8
3	China	6.5	3	Germany	6.3	3	Germany	7.3
4	Japan	6.2	4	France	5.1	4	Japan	5.2
5	France	4.9	5	Japan	4.5	5	France	4.3
6	Netherlands	3.9	6	Spain	4.0	6	Ireland	4.0
7	Italy	3.8	7	Italy	3.9	7	Netherlands	3.9
8	United Kingdom	3.8	8	Netherlands	3.4	8	Italy	3.3
9	Canada	3.5	9	China	2.9	9	India	3.1
10	Belgium	3.3	10	Hong Kong SAR	2.5	10	Belgium	2.8
...			...					
30	India	0.8	16	India	1.9			

Source: World Trade Organization, *International Trade Statistics 2005*.

Table 10.2. Sectoral Growth Rates[1]

| | Average Growth and Coefficient of Variation (CV) (In percent a year; CV in parentheses) | | | |
	1951–80	1981–90	1991–2000	2001–05
Agriculture	2.1	4.4	3.0	2.0
	(3.1)	(1.4)	(1.3)	(3.2)
Industry	5.3	6.8	5.8	6.2
	(0.7)	(0.3)	(0.6)	(0.2)
Services	4.5	6.6	7.6	7.6
	(0.3)	(0.2)	(0.3)	(0.2)
GDP	3.5	5.9	5.8	5.9
	(1.0)	(0.4)	(0.3)	(0.3)

Sources: Central Statistical Organisation; and IMF staff estimates.
[1]Underlying data are for fiscal years ending in March.

Sectoral Growth Rates

The growth of services picked up sharply in the 1980s and has since accelerated further. Since the takeoff in reforms in 1991, the services sector has grown faster than industry with an average growth rate of more than 7½ percent a year (Table 10.2). In the last three years, growth in services has increased by a full percentage point above this recent historical trend and in the first half of 2005/06 it reached 10 percent. This increase has coincided with an explosion in the growth rate of exports of services (see discussion below). Growth in the services sector has also been less cyclical than the growth of industry and especially agriculture. The coefficient of variation (CV) for the annual growth in services is less than one-tenth the CV for growth in agriculture.

The remarkable growth of the services sector in India is not unique but has come early in the development process. As an economy matures, its sectoral growth pattern typically evolves in two stages. In the first stage, both industry and services grow faster than agriculture, and their share in total output increases. In the second stage, services tend to grow faster than the rest of the economy, and its share in GDP continues to increase, accompanied by a stagnant or declining share of the industrial sector. Though the Indian experience fits in this pattern, services have overtaken the industrial sector faster and at a lower level of income than in other countries. Consequently, India's services share of GDP is now higher than the average for other low-income countries (Figure 10.1). This outcome results, at least in part, from constraints that have affected industry disproportionately, such as poor infrastructure, labor restrictions, and reservations for small-scale industries.

Interestingly, the substantial rise in the share of services in GDP has not been accompanied by a commensurate increase in the shares of employment

Figure 10.1. International Comparisons of Shares of Services and Industry in GDP, 2003
(In percent)

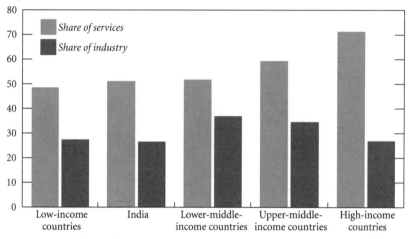

Source: World Bank, *World Development Indicators*.

and capital used by the sector (Table 10.3). This suggests that technological improvements or efficiency gains arising from liberalization have played an important role in the sector's growth performance. Productivity improvements in services may also indicate that the growth in services has been concentrated in subsectors that are more dependent on skilled labor rather than on unskilled labor or capital.

Which Services Have Grown Rapidly?

The acceleration in services growth has not been uniform across activities. The acceleration was most pronounced in business services, starting in the 1980s albeit from a low base and picking up further in the 1990s–2000s; communication, in the 1990s and picking up further in 2000s; and banking, in the 1980s and 1990s (Table 10.4). While the increase in growth in the trade subsector has been less spectacular, its contribution to growth in the 1990s–2000s has been significant given its higher share in GDP. Growth in the insurance sector has also risen in the current decade after a sluggish performance in the previous decade.

The communication and business services subsectors alone have contributed 0.75 percentage point to overall GDP growth in the 2000s. Their

Table 10.3. Share of Services Sector in GDP, Employment, and Capital Stock
(In percent of total)

	GDP	Employment	Capital Stock
1970	32.1	20.0	43.7
1980	37.7	18.9	44.0
1990	40.7	24.4	47.0
1994	42.8	20.4	46.6
2000	48.3	22.5	43.3
2004	51.4	23.5	44.2

Sources: Hansda (2002); Central Statistical Organisation, National Accounts; National Sample Survey Organisation; and IMF staff estimates.

contribution to GDP growth has increased from 0.2 percentage point in the 1990s and 0.1 percentage point recorded in the 1980s. By 2004, the last year for which a detailed breakdown of growth by sector is available, both sectors had a combined value added similar to the banking system but were contributing 2.5 times as much to growth.

Explaining Services Sector Growth

The growth of the services sector in recent years reflects a number of factors. These include a switch to a more service-input-intensive method of organizing production, that is, splintering (see Bhagwati, 1984); rapid growth in the final demand for services from domestic and foreign consumers; and technological advances, whereby new activities or products have emerged. Important policy reforms were also made starting in the early 1990s, including deregulation, privatization, and opening up to FDI, which were also conducive to the growth of the services sector.

Using input-output coefficients and sectoral shares in output, it is possible to illustrate that splintering has had some impact on services growth. The matrices for different years show that the use of service sector inputs accounted for 31 percent of all intermediate inputs used in 1998/99 (the latest available), up from 27 percent in both 1978/79 and 1989/90. The use of services inputs in industry increased to 17.8 percent of gross industrial output in 1998/99 from 14.1 percent of gross output in 1979/80, while the use of services inputs into agriculture, which is much lower, increased by less than 2 percentage points over the same period to about 5 percent of gross agricultural output. Thus, the input-output coefficients for services input into the nonservices sector increased by about 2.3 and 1.8 percentage points during the 1980s and 1990s, respectively. These coefficient changes

Table 10.4. Growth Rates and Sectoral Shares in GDP

Sector	Activities Included	Average Growth in 1950s–70s (Share in 1980)	Average Growth in 1980s (Share in 1990)	Average Growth in 1990s (Share in 2000)	Average Growth in 2000s (Share in 2004)
Communications	Postal services, money orders, telegrams, telephones, overseas communication services, and miscellaneous.	6.7 (1.0)	6.1 (1.0)	14.9 (2.2)	24.4 (4.3)
Business services	Software and business process outsourcing.	4.2 (0.2)	13.5 (0.3)	19.8 (1.1)	20.7 (1.8)
Insurance	Life, postal life, and nonlife.	7.1 (0.5)	10.9 (0.8)	6.7 (0.7)	14.4 (0.9)
Hotels and restaurants	Services rendered by hotels and other lodging establishments, restaurants, cafes, and other eating and drinking places.	4.8 (0.7)	6.5 (0.7)	9.3 (1.0)	8.5 (1.1)
Trade (distribution services)	Wholesale and retail trade in commodities, both produced at home (including exports) and imported, purchase and selling agents, brokers and auctioneers.	4.8 (11.7)	5.9 (11.9)	7.3 (13.6)	7.4 (14.5)
Transport by other means	Road, water, air transport, and services incidental to transport.	6.3 (3.6)	6.3 (3.8)	6.9 (4.2)	7.0 (4.4)
Personal services	Domestic, laundry, barber, beauty shops, tailoring, and others.	1.7 (1.6)	2.4 (1.1)	5.0 (1.0)	6.9 (1.1)
Community services	Education, research, scientific, medical, health, religious, and other community.	4.8 (4.0)	6.5 (4.3)	8.4 (5.5)	6.7 (5.7)
Railways		4.2 (1.5)	4.5 (1.4)	3.6 (1.1)	5.8 (1.1)
Other social and personal services	Recreation, entertainment, radio and television broadcast, and sanitary services.	3.4 (1.1)	4.3 (1.0)	2.8 (0.7)	5.4 (0.7)
Banking	Banks, banking department of the Reserve Bank of India, post office saving bank, nonbank financial institution, cooperative credit societies, and employees provident fund.	7.2 (1.9)	11.9 (3.4)	12.7 (6.3)	4.3 (6.0)
Public administration, defence		6.1 (5.3)	7.0 (6.0)	6.1 (6.1)	3.1 (5.6)

Source: IMF staff calculations from data provided by the Central Statistical Organisation.

($\Delta\theta$) would have increased output demand for services (Y_S) (as a first-round effect) by

$$\Delta Y_S = \Delta\theta \, Y_{NS}, \tag{1}$$

where Y_{NS} is nonservice output.

Adding additional variables on both sides of this formula (VA denotes value added in the services or nonservices sector and TVA denotes total value added) allows the use of the input-output tables to estimate the impact of splintering:

$$(Y_S/VA_S) \, (VA_S/TVA) \, (\Delta Y_S/Y_S) = \Delta\theta \, (Y_{NS}/VA_{NS}) \, (VA_{NS}/TVA). \tag{2}$$

Evaluating this formula at the average output-value-added ratio and value-added shares in each decade indicates that splintering may have added about 0.6 percentage point to annual services growth during the 1980s and 0.5 percentage point during the 1990s.[2]

A rise in domestic demand for services reflecting higher incomes appears to also have some merit in explaining the pickup in services growth in some subsectors. Available data indicate that private final consumption expenditure on certain categories of services has increased sharply since the 1990s. This has been the case, in particular, for transport services and medical care and health services, which have experienced an increase in their shares of expenditure in GDP of 2½ and 2 percentage points of GDP, respectively, over 1990–2004. The fact that the relative price of both types of these services also increased over the period (relative to the GDP deflator) further suggests that income effects may have played a role in raising demand. In contrast, while expenditure on communication has also risen sharply over the period, its relative price has plummetted (falling by more than 60 percent since 1990).[3] In this case, although income effects may help explain the rise in private expenditure, falling prices as a result of technological advances and deregulation are likely to have played a much bigger role. The still relatively low levels of telephone penetration suggest that growth in telecommunications can remain high for many years (Figure 10.2).

Technological advances (and, ironically, a technological glitch—the millennium bug) appear to have played an important role in raising foreign demand in the most dynamic sectors. Due to the revolution in IT and telecommunication sectors it has become possible to deliver services over

---

[2]The output-to-value-added ratios are averaged over the years for which input-output tables are available.

[3]Private final consumption expenditure on communication rose by ½ percent of GDP at current prices over 1990–2004 but, at constant prices, it increased by 2 percentage points.

Figure 10.2. Telephone Penetration Rates

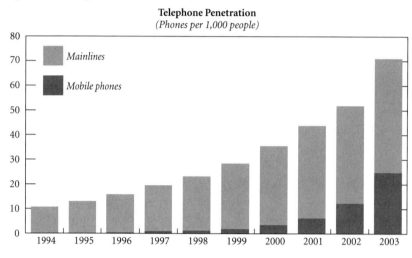

Source: World Bank, *World Development Indicators.*

long distances at a reasonable cost, increasing trade in services. India has been a particular beneficiary of this trend benefiting from the rapid growth in exports of software, business process outsourcing (BPO) activities and other business services, and telecommunications (Figure 10.3). Exports of services took off sharply in the second half of the 1990s, growing at an average rate of 18 percent a year from 1994/95 to 2003/04 (in U.S. dollars).

Figure 10.3. Service Exports

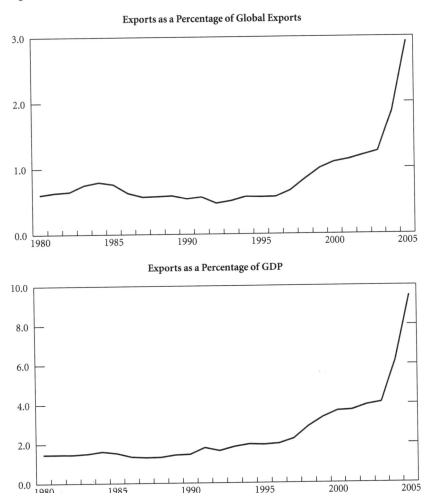

Source: IMF, *World Economic Outlook*.

Growth was especially rapid prior to 2000, as Indian companies took on the massive task of fixing the so-called millennium bug in computer codes.[4] More recently, in 2004/05 and the first half of 2005/06, services exports

<hr/>

[4]The millennium bug or Y2K problem arose because computer programs stored years with only two digits and the year 2000, represented by 00, would be interpreted by software as the year 1900. This could have caused computers to stop working or produce erroneous results.

have ballooned, with annual growth rates of more than 70 percent. Exports of software and BPO accounted for about one-third of services exports in 2004/05.[5] Future areas of growth for offshoring activities beyond IT services are likely to include industrial research and development, including in the pharmaceutical industry, medical research, and back-office functions.

Exports may have added an average of about 1 percentage point to services sector growth a year in the 1990s. In contrast, it is estimated that exports contributed a negligible amount to the increased growth rate of the services sector in the previous decade. To arrive at these estimates, the share of value added in services from exports is approximated by the share of services output that is exported, as given by the input-output tables of 1978/79, 1989/90, and 1998/99 (which is a good approximation if the share of value added in output of exported and domestically consumed services is similar). Then, that share is used to weigh the respective growth rates in the different time periods. While in 2000/01–2003/04, the contribution of services exports did not rise above the level of the 1990s, the growth rate experienced in 2004/05 (of around 60 percent in real terms) would imply an additional contribution to service sector growth of more than 5 percentage points in that year. This result does not seem plausible as the growth of value added in the services sector rose by much less (approximately 10 percent). This casts some doubt on the comparability of the data with previous years, as it would imply that the share of value added in exported services declined sharply in that year.

While the explanations above explore the proximate causes for the pickup in services growth, at a more fundamental level, policy changes appear to have been an important factor in allowing the services sector to respond dynamically to changes in demand and technology. The sector was an important beneficiary of liberalization reforms, including the opening up to the private sector and foreign investment (Box 10.1). To test for the significance of policy changes, a panel of 13 service activities is used. The time period used is 1970–2004, and the observations are averaged over 1970s, 1981–85, 1986–90, 1991–95, 1996–2000, and 2000–04, which results in six observations for each service subsector. The following regression equation with sectoral fixed effects is estimated by ordinary least squares:

$$GSER_{it} = C_i + \alpha GInd_t + \beta GAgr_t + \eta GTG_t + \gamma GTS_t + \delta RSer_{it} + \varepsilon_{it}. \quad (3)$$

[5]Unfortunately, there is no breakdown for exports of other types of business services and telecommunications, which are recorded together in a miscellaneous category. That category, excluding software and BPO, accounted for about one-third of services exports in 2004/05.

Box 10.1. Selected Policy Measures Affecting the Services Sector

Telecommunications
- Telecoms Policy of 1994 opened basic telecommunications services to private entrants, including foreign entrants.
- Telecom Regulatory Authority of India established (1997).
- New Telecoms Policy of 1999 further liberalized the sector, including for long-distance calls.
- Use of Internet telephony allowed for international services (2001).

Tourism
- FDI liberalized (1991/92).

Financial and insurance sectors
- Liberalization of private sector entry, including foreign participation (1992).
- Securities and Exchange Board of India is given statutory powers (1992).
- Access of companies to capital markets deregulated (1992).
- Insurance Regulatory and Development Authority established (1999).
- Private sector entry in insurance allowed, including foreign entities (2000).

Transport
- Private sector entry allowed in scheduled air transport services (1995).
- Foreign equity allowed (1997).
- Foreign investment in ports liberalized (1996–98).

The dependent variable, *GSER*, is average growth in activity i in period t. The right-hand side variables are average growth in industry (*GInd*), average growth in agriculture (*GAgr*), average growth in external volume of trade in goods (*GTG*), and average growth in the export of services (*GTS*) over period t. A dummy variable accounts for the fact whether reforms were carried out in each segment of services (*RSer*).[6]

---

[6]The dummy variable for reform measures is based on information provided in other studies and is assigned a value of 1 if the activity was opened up for FDI, external trade, or private ownership. The following observations were assigned a value of 1: hotels, from 1991 to 1995; transport other means, from 1996 to 2000; communication, from 1991 to 1995; banking, from 1986 to 1990; insurance, from 1996 to 2000; business services, from 1991 to 1995; and community services, from 1996 to 2000. The dummy was created using information in Mattoo and others (2003) and information provided by Arpita Mukherjee of the Indian Council for Research on International Economic Relations.

Table 10.5. Explaining Services Growth Using Panel Data, 1970–2004[1]

	I	II
Average growth rate of agriculture in period t	0.77	0.02
	0.80	0.05
Average growth rate of industrial sector in period t	1.36*	0.88*
	1.78	1.86
Average growth of external trade (exports + imports) of merchandise in period t	0.32	
	0.79	
Average growth of exports of services in period t	0.17*	0.13
	1.76	1.55
Reform dummy variable	5.34***	5.64***
	3.76	3.71
Dummy for the 1990s–2000s		−1.01
		−0.96
R^2, adj. R^2	0.63, 0.52	0.63, 0.52
F test for equality of intercept across units	3.20 (F-stat)	3.20 (F-stat)
	0.00 (p-value)	0.00 (p-value)

Source: Authors' calculations.

[1]Number of observations is 78 in each regression. ***, **, * indicate significance at 1 percent, 5 percent, and 10 percent levels, respectively. t-values are given below the coefficients in each cell.

The reform dummy has a positive, and the most significant, coefficient in the regressions (Table 10.5). Services growth is also significantly correlated with the growth in the industrial sector. As a robustness test, specification II introduces a time dummy for the 1990s–2000s but its coefficient is not significant after controlling for the reform-specific dummy. This suggests that it is liberalization per se that is contributing to growth.

Growth Experience and Key Challenges in the IT Sector

As mentioned above, the IT sector has grown very rapidly, at an annual rate of about 31 percent between 1998/99 and 2004/05, with turnover reaching $22 billion.[7] While IT software and services continue to account for close to 60 percent of the industry's turnover, growth has been increasingly driven by BPO activities. These accounted for 21 percent of total industry revenues in 2005 compared with just 7 percent in 2000 (Figure

---

[7]The IT sector encompasses software and services (ITS—systems integration, packaged software support and installation, application outsourcing, custom application development, etc.), IT-enabled services (ITES—human resources, customer care, payment services, finance, etc.), and hardware.

Figure 10.4. Composition of the Information Technology (IT) Sector
(Sales in millions of U.S. dollars and in percent of total)

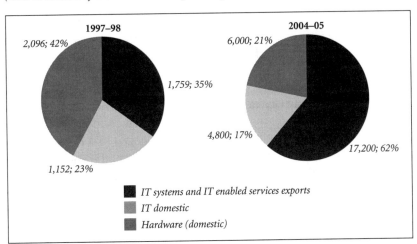

Source: National Association of Software and Service Companies.

10.4). The export market for IT services grew twice as fast as the domestic market, with average respective growth rates of 37 percent and 19 percent. In the last two years, however, domestic demand has been increasingly important, with annual growth picking up to around 25 percent.

The National Association of Software and Service Companies (NASS-COM) has set ambitious targets for the industry. Exports are targeted to grow by about 30 percent a year over the medium term, implying a very mild deceleration from the current pace of growth. Domestic sales are targeted to grow at the same pace as exports, as there appears to be significant untapped potential in sectors such as retail, telecommunications, banking, and small and medium-sized enterprises. It is estimated that the global IT/BPO offshoring market will amount to $110 billion by 2010, of which India could capture more than 50 percent (India's share in the global market is currently estimated at 44 percent).[8]

Despite rapid growth in recent years, employment in the IT sector remains a negligible fraction of the labor force. Employment has been growing by more than 25 percent a year in recent years. Nevertheless, total employment still amounts to only 1 million people. Industry estimates are that total direct employment could reach 2.3 million by 2010 and that 6.5

---

[8]NASSCOM-McKinsey (2005).

million jobs could be created indirectly. However, given India's need to generate employment for some 100 million new job entrants in the coming decade, its contribution to total employment will still be modest. This underscores the need to encourage the expansion of labor-intensive industries, including by tackling the two most important constraints faced by them: inadequate infrastructure—on power, roads, ports, and so on—and restrictive labor market regulations.

Looking forward, there are a number of external and domestic constraints that India may face in realizing the growth potential of the IT sector. The external factors include nontariff barriers such as visa restrictions, and the negative publicity in importing countries affected by offshoring. The greater bottleneck, however, is likely to be the shortage of skilled workers. Indeed, there is evidence that although wages in the IT sector have accelerated, the industry has also witnessed an increase in employee turnover rates.[9] India's universities have failed to expand in a manner commensurate with the growing demand for skilled labor. In this regard, there is a need to multiply institutions like the Indian Institutes of Technology and regional engineering colleges on which much of the current success of the software sector is based. To achieve this, private sector and foreign entry in the education sector should be encouraged. At the same time, to make urban centers attractive centers of employment for knowledge workers, urban infrastructure would need to be upgraded.

References

Bhagwati, Jagdish, 1984, "Splintering and Disembodiment of Services and Developing Nations," *World Economy*, Vol. 7 (June), pp. 133–43.

Farrell, Diana, Noshir Kaka, and Sascha Sturze, 2005, "Ensuring India's Offshoring Future," *The McKinsey Quarterly, 2005 Special Edition: Fulfilling India's Promise*; available via the Internet at www.mckinseyquarterly.com.

Gordon, James, and Poonam Gupta, 2004, "Understanding India's Services Revolution," IMF Working Paper No. 04/171 (Washington: International Monetary Fund).

Gupta, Poonam, 2005, "Understanding the Growth Momentum in India's Services," in *India: Selected Issues*, IMF Country Report No. 05/87 (Washington: International Monetary Fund).

---

[9]Wages for entry-level software developers rose by almost 50 percent between 2002 and 2004, while wages for project managers almost doubled (Farrell and others, 2005).

Hansda, Sanjay Kumar, 2002, "Services Sector in the Indian Economy: A Status Report," *RBI Staff Studies* (Mumbai: Reserve Bank of India, Department of Economic Analysis and Policy).

Mattoo, Aaditya, Deepak Mishra, and Anirudh Shinghal, 2004, *Sustaining India's Services Revolution: Access to Foreign Markets, Domestic Reform and International Negotiations* (Washington: World Bank).

NASSCOM-McKinsey, 2002, *Report on Strategies to Achieve the Indian IT Industry's Aspiration* (New Delhi: National Association of Software and Service Companies).

————, 2005, press release on the *Report on Extending India's Leadership in the Global IT and BPO Industries* (www.nasscom.org) (New Delhi: National Association of Software and Service Companies).

11

Realizing the Potential: The Case of India's Textile Sector

SONALI JAIN-CHANDRA AND ANANTHAKRISHNAN PRASAD

The removal in 2005 of quotas on textiles and clothing (T&C) presents important opportunities for India, but is also exposing key structural impediments to growth. India had been constrained by quotas, which suggests that it should benefit from their lifting in January 2005, under the Agreement on Textiles and Clothing (ATC). On the other hand, India now faces increased global competition, including from China. The Indian government is optimistic about export prospects—the National Textile Policy targets T&C exports to rise fourfold, to $50 billion by 2010—but the key question is: are policies in place to allow for such success?

Despite significant advantages, the Indian textile industry faces considerable constraints to reaching its potential. India has a competitive advantage stemming from its large and relatively low-cost labor force, a large domestic supply of fabrics, and the industry's ability to manufacture a wide range of products (United States International Trade Commission, 2004). India also has a strong and diverse raw material base for manufacturing natural and artificial fibers. Furthermore, India has large capacity in textiles and spinning, and India's textile industry spans the entire supply chain. However, whether India can benefit from the quota elimination will depend on the degree to which the existing constraints are removed. These include stringent labor market regulation, poor infrastructure, inadequate investment, and a legacy of unfavorable government policies.

This chapter examines the impact of the elimination of quotas on India. It first looks at how India has fared in the T&C industry over the last 10 years.

Table 11.1. Market Shares in Textiles and Clothing
(In percent)

	Textiles				Clothing			
	1995		2003		1995		2003	
	China	India	China	India	China	India	China	India
Exports to								
World	12.4	3.9	19.7	4.8	19.3	3.3	28.1	3.5
United States	11.6	6.3	19.8	8.4	14.9	3.3	16.9	3.2
European Union	7.8	10.2	13.9	9.5	13.8	6.4	20.5	5.0
Japan	31.0	3.0	48.0	3.0	57.0	1.0	80.0	1.0

Source: World Trade Organization.

Then it provides evidence, including from previous rounds of liberalization as well as economic modeling, of the likely impact of quota elimination on India. In the following section, we utilize a general equilibrium model to examine the impact of the elimination of the ATC quotas on India. Next, we focus on the specific constraints facing the Indian T&C sector, and conclude by discussing possible options for overcoming weakness.

Where Does India Stand in the Global Textile Industry?

The T&C sector is an important one for India. Textiles and clothing are significant items in India's export basket, accounting for nearly a quarter of Indian exports and around 3 percent of world T&C exports in 2003. In addition, this sector is the second largest generator of employment, providing jobs for 35 million people or around 10 percent of the work force. Thus, the T&C sector will need to play a key role as India looks to create jobs for its rapidly growing work force. Textiles and clothing exports are also a significant earner of foreign exchange, and contribute 4 percent and 14 percent to GDP and value added in manufacturing, respectively (Ministry of Textiles, *Annual Report, 2003–04*).

While India's market share of exports of both textiles and clothing has increased in recent years, it has lost ground to China in certain markets (Table 11.1). India has done reasonably well in the United States and Canada since 1995, but has lost ground in Europe, and plays a negligible role in the Japanese market. China, meanwhile, continues to surpass India as world leader in exports of T&C. A study by the United States International Trade Commission (2004) predicts that China will become the "supplier of choice" for most U.S. importers (the large apparel companies and retailers) because of its "ability to make almost any type of textile and apparel product at any quality level at a competitive price."

Table 11.2. Impact of Liberalization of Textiles and Clothing on Exports to the United States
(In percent)

	Impact of the Phase III Liberalization on Exports[1]	Impact of the 2005 Quota Elimination on Phase IV Products[2]	Impact of the 2005 Quota Elimination on Value of Exports of All T&C Products[3]	Impact of the 2005 Quota Elimination on Volume of Exports of All T&C Products[4]
Bangladesh	−52.4	27.5	22.1	19.4
China	298.5	241.8	65.7	46.6
Hong Kong SAR	−55.3	−26.0	−26.8	−24.2
India	21.3	34.2	29.1	24.2
Indonesia	−44.2	16.7	15.4	−1.4
Korea	−45.6	−38.0	−19.2	−13.4
Mexico	−14.9	−4.0	−4.0	−4.4
Pakistan	14.8	−0.4	10.5	5.9
Philippines	−53.4	−4.9	−2.4	−14.4
Thailand	−66.3	8.9	7.7	−4.6
Turkey	−16.9	−6.9	−2.5	−8.8

Sources: U.S. International Trade Commission; and U.S. Department of Commerce, Office of Textiles and Apparel.

[1]Change in exports to the United States of textile and clothing items liberalized during Phase III (2002–04).

[2]Change in the value of exports to the United States of Phase IV textile and clothing items since end-2004 (January–June 2005).

[3]Change in the value of exports to the United States of all textile and clothing items since end-2004 (January–June 2005).

[4]Change in the volume of exports to the United States of all textile and clothing items since end-2004 (January–June 2005).

Competing in the Post-Quota World: Initial Indications

The example of Japan can provide an early glimpse at how India might fare in a post-quota world—as Japan did not impose quotas in the pre-2005 period—and the picture that emerges provides some cause for concern. In particular, China accounted for nearly half and 80 percent, respectively, of Japan's T&C imports in 2003. Recently, imports from India have fallen, while those from Vietnam, Indonesia, and other member countries of the Association of South East Asian Nations (ASEAN) have risen notably.

Another indication of the possible impact after the abolition of quotas in 2005 comes from previous rounds of liberalization. Since 2002, when the so-called "Phase III" liberalization took place, Indian exports of products for which quotas were eliminated grew by a respectable 20 percent, but Chinese exports tripled (Table 11.2). A number of other countries, such as Bangladesh, Korea, Indonesia, the Philippines, and Thailand saw their T&C exports fall by 50 percent on average. So, while India has been able to maintain its place, previous liberalizations have hardly been a boon for its T&C industry.

**Table 11.3. Imports of Textile and Clothing in the
First Half of 2005 into the European Union**
(*In percent*)

	Change in Total Imports of Textile and Clothing[1]		Change in Liberalized Imports of Textile and Clothing[2]		
	Value	Volume	Value	Volume	Prices
Bangladesh	−7.2	5.0	−7.5	7.7	−15.2
China	35.3	40.4	80.3	119.0	−17.9
Hong Kong SAR	−51.9	−37.7	−55.3	−43.9	−20.0
India	11.0	6.0	10.5	5.2	4.8
Indonesia	−18.3	−13.9	−20.8	−17.0	−4.2
Korea	−23.2	−19.0	−51.8	−51.0	−1.7
Mexico	0.0	11.1	−12.1	15.0	−23.5
Pakistan	−16.8	−7.0	−11.9	−10.1	−8.9
Philippines	−34.7	−31.6	−37.3	−35.5	−2.9
Thailand	−14.0	12.7	−18.5	−12.1	−7.4
Turkey	1.8	1.7	2.8	3.1	−0.7

Source: European Commission.
[1]Change in total imports in January–May 2005, relative to 2004.
[2]Change in imports of products liberalized on January 1, 2005, during January–May 2005 relative to the corresponding period in 2004.

Early data on the impact of the recent elimination of quotas paint a broadly similar picture. U.S. data for the first half of 2005 confirm that exports of T&C from China have surged, India has held its ground, and some other exporters have faced sharp declines. As expected, China has tripled its T&C exports of liberalized product lines and saw a sharp increase in total textile exports (see Table 11.2). Export volumes from China rose by almost 50 percent in the first half of 2005. At the same time, prices of these liberalized goods fell sharply:[1] apparel prices fell by almost 8 percent; wool products by 30 percent; cotton coats, dresses, and knit shirts by more than 60 percent; and cotton trousers, skirts, and sweaters by almost 50 percent. India's textile exports to the United States grew robustly, faster than all major exporters with the exception of China. These trends are mirrored in member countries of the European Union (EU). Total EU imports from China grew three times as fast as those from India (in value terms) during January–May 2005 (Table 11.3). For products liberalized in January 2005, China's exports surged by 80 percent, while India posted a moderate growth of 10 percent. Surprisingly, while the prices of exports of most countries fell, Indian export prices rose.

Another way of understanding how India will fare in the new global environment for T&C is to use economic models. Here, results are mixed.

---

[1]Prices have fallen in the most competitive segments for which the quotas were binding. In other words, the quota premium was keeping the prices artificially high and these started falling once the quotas were removed.

While the literature mostly suggests that India stands to gain substantially from the liberalization, a few recent studies draw more negative conclusions. Differences in results reflect the methodologies used, including partial versus general equilibrium modeling, different base years for the data, differences in the sectoral and regional aggregations used, and the absence of preference schemes from the Global Trade Analysis Project (GTAP) database until recently (Table 11.4 contains a summary of the literature). We turn now to the GTAP model.

Modeling India's Potential in Textiles

The elimination of quotas on T&C is expected to have a significant impact on the production, exports, and employment in exporting countries and a positive impact on the welfare of consumers in importing countries. The quota-imposing countries—the United States, EU countries, and Canada—are expected to experience gains in welfare, despite a decline in production of T&C, through reduced consumer prices and increased efficiency following enhanced specialization. For developing countries the net effect will depend on two factors: while the terms of trade will deteriorate, quota-constrained exporters will experience an increase in efficiency as the distortionary trade regime is removed. Therefore, the elimination of quotas is widely expected to lead to winners and losers.

We use the computable general equilibrium model from the Global Trade Analysis Project (GTAP version 6) to simulate the impact of the elimination of quotas in the T&C sector. We simulate two scenarios to estimate the impact of the elimination of quotas on India. The first is a complete removal of the quotas, by eliminating the export tax equivalents (ETEs) of quotas under the Multifiber Arrangement (MFA) and the ATC.[2] The second scenario includes a 50 percent reduction of quotas on China, and a full removal of quotas (or equivalently ETEs) imposed on other countries.[3]

---

[2]The ETE measures the degree of restrictiveness of a quota. Exporters in countries where the quotas are binding need to buy the quota. Since the market clearing supply of quotas is not available, they sell at a premium imposing, in effect, a tax on exports. Therefore, increasing restrictiveness leads to rising ETEs. However, the removal of all ETEs may overestimate the impact of liberalization, since the GTAP model does not permit the elimination of simply those export taxes that are related to the MFA/ATC quota elimination.

[3]The simulated 50 percent reduction in China's export quotas is aimed at analyzing in a general sense the sensitivity of Scenario I to the presence of safeguards in general. The model is not sufficiently detailed to capture the precise impact of the current EU and U.S. limits on imports on specific Chinese T&C products.

Table 11.4. Summary of the Literature on the Effects of the Quota Elimination on India

Study	Methodology and Database	Results
Andriamananjara, Dean, and Spinanger (2004)	Computed from license prices and estimates an equation based on Krugman's intra-industry trade model.	Large increases in market shares expected for China, followed by India.
Cerra, Rivera, and Saxena (2005)	GTAP version 6, with 2001 as the base year. Static model.	Fall in India's economic welfare due to deterioration in the terms of trade in the clothing sector.
Chadha and others (2000)	Multicountry multisectoral computable general equilibrium with increasing returns to scale. GTAP version 4 with 1995 as base year.	India's welfare increases by $1.9 billion. India's textile and apparel exports rise by 19 percent and 54 percent, respectively, leading to increases of 4 percent and 29 percent in employment in these sectors.
Diao and Somwaru (2001)	UN database and regression analysis.	India's welfare increases by $7.3 billion in five years after the quota abolition, while market share rises marginally to 4.43 percent.
Elbehri, Hertel, and Martin (2003)	GTAP version 3, using 1992 as the base year and other data.	India's apparel output quadruples due to abolition of quotas. Boosting India's productivity to China's level would double the benefits from the ATC quota removal.
Kathuria, Martin, and Bhardwaj (2001)	GTAP and field work.	Total welfare will rise in India following the quota elimination.
Manole (2005)	GTAP version 6, with 2001 as the base year.	Quota removal results in a negative welfare effect of $267 million on India.
Nordas (2004)	Standard static GTAP version 5 model and parameters, with 1997 as base year.	Substantial increases in market shares for China and India; developing countries where quotas were not restrictive are likely to lose. India's market share in the United States is projected to remain at 5 percent for textiles, while its share of clothing is estimated to rise from 4 percent to 15 percent. India is projected to increase market share in the EU from 9 percent to 11 percent for textiles and from 6 percent to 9 percent for clothing.

This scenario aims to estimate the impact of the liberalization keeping in mind the somewhat more limited liberalization vis-à-vis China.

In 2005, quotas were imposed on Chinese exports of T&C using the textile-specific safeguard provision contained in China's protocol of accession to the World Trade Organization (WTO). Moreover, in June 2005, under the Shanghai Agreement between the EU and China, annual import

Table 11.5. Summary Table on the Impact of the Elimination of ATC Quotas on Exports
(In percent)

	Export Values	Export Volumes	Export Prices
	Scenario I—Full elimination of quotas		
Textiles			
India	5.6	10.3	−4.3
China	51.0	66.2	−9.2
Clothing			
India	−4.0	0.6	−4.7
China	85.1	113.5	−13.4
	Scenario II—Partial elimination of quotas on China[1]		
Textiles			
India	12.5	17.2	−4.0
China	19.6	24.7	−4.1
Clothing			
India	10.7	15.8	−4.4
China	36.7	46.4	−6.6

Source: Simulations using GTAP 6.0.

[1]This scenario assumes a complete elimination of quotas for all countries except China. For China, it assumes a 50 percent reduction in quotas.

restrictions were set for 10 categories of Chinese textile and clothing products, limits for many of which were reached early in the year. The United States has similarly placed restrictions on imports of about 30 T&C categories from China for the next three years. A key contribution of this chapter is to analyze incomplete liberalization in the presence of quotas on China and a focus on the impact on India.

Key results are as follows.[4]

• With full liberalization (Scenario I) textile exports from India are expected to grow by 6 percent (value terms), whereas clothing exports are expected to fall by 4 percent relative to the base year 2001 (Table 11.5). In the case of incomplete liberalization (Scenario II), both textiles and clothing exports from India are projected to grow, by 13 percent and 11 percent, respectively. Thus India, along with some other exporting countries, benefits from the temporary restrictions imposed on China.

---

[4]Results are in 2001 constant dollar terms. The regression results are relative to the base year 2001. The impact on welfare is measured by the change in equivalent variation. The equivalent variation is the income change, which at current prices would be equivalent to the proposed price change, that is, the income change needed to keep the utility of the consumer unchanged.

Table 11.6. Impact of the Elimination of ATC Quotas on GDP
(In percent)

	Consumption	Investment	Government	Exports	Imports	Total
	Scenario I—Full elimination of quotas					
India	0.0	0.1	0.0	0.0	0.2	0.0
China	2.2	2.5	2.1	3.5	4.7	2.1
	Scenario II—Partial elimination of quotas on China[1]					
India	0.4	0.5	0.4	0.8	0.9	0.4
China	1.0	1.0	1.0	1.5	1.8	1.0

Source: Simulations using GTAP 6.0.
[1]This scenario assumes a complete elimination of quotas for all countries except China. For China, it assumes a 50 percent reduction in quotas.

- The fall in export values in the first scenario is explained by the fall in prices rather than export volumes. In both scenarios, volumes of textile and clothing exports grow.
- As expected, prices of T&C exports fall with the lifting of the quotas. With the complete liberalization of the sector, Chinese exports are much more competitive as can be seen by a sharper fall in export prices.
- The impact on GDP is generally insignificant, except for China, where GDP rises by 2 percentage points due to tremendous gains in efficiency (Table 11.6). In the second scenario, India's GDP is projected to rise by ½ percentage point, while that of China's by 1 percentage point.
- World welfare would increase but India's welfare would drop, as a negative terms of trade effect would outweigh a rise in allocative efficiency effect (Table 11.7).[5] The negative effect on India is in contrast to a number of previous studies based on earlier versions of the GTAP database. The main welfare gains would accrue to consumers in the EU and the United States via reduced prices. Of the exporting countries, China would gain, despite a negative terms of trade effect, due to massive increases in efficiency. In the pre-2005 world, Chinese exports were severely restricted and faced binding quotas in many product categories. In Scenario II, we see a smaller increase in world welfare due to incomplete liberalization, and a smaller increase in the welfare of the United States, EU, and China. On the other hand, we see a smaller negative welfare effect on other exporting countries such as India, Mexico, and Bangladesh.

[5]The negative welfare effect for India is derived after taking into account the possible positive effect on domestic consumers because of the reduction in prices.

Table 11.7. Impact of the Elimination of ATC Quotas on Welfare
(In 2001 constant U.S. dollars)

		Decomposition		
	Total	Effect of allocative efficiency	Effect of terms of trade	Savings-investment effect
	Scenario I—Full elimination of quotas			
India	−449	66	−555[1]	40
China	2,855	9,260	−4,560	−1,845
United States	5,657	872	3,827	959
EU15	10,507	3,978	6,101	428
Total	13,846	13,779	50	17
	Scenario II—Partial elimination of quotas on China[2]			
India	−144	206	−364	14
China	2,768	5,271	−1,744	−760
United States	2,478	404	1,588	486
EU15	5,807	2,237	3,383	187
Total	8,565	8,551	11	3

Source: Simulations using GTAP 6.0.

[1]The breakdown of the terms of trade effect for India is food: 10; textiles: −325; clothing: −251; manufacturing: −10; and services: 20.

[2]This scenario assumes a complete elimination of quotas for all countries except China. For China, it assumes a 50 percent reduction in quotas.

These results should not, however, be interpreted to mean that India will be unable to benefit from the quota elimination. In particular, GTAP does not model the potential for India to strengthen its textile industry via domestic structural reforms. Furthermore, the simulations do not capture dynamic effects of, for instance, the impact of greater competition on productivity. Thus, the results should be seen as providing a warning that India may not do as well in the post-quota world as some expect if needed reforms are not pursued aggressively. In that regard, the results suggest also that the temporary quotas on Chinese exports provide a small window of opportunity to prepare for completely liberalized trade in 2008, when all quotas on China are to be lifted. We turn now to examine more closely the key constraints on India's textile industry and how they may be overcome.

What Is Constraining India's Potential in Textiles and Clothing?

Significant constraints facing the Indian T&C industry may be preventing it from realizing its export potential. The opportunities unleashed by the removal of the quotas are tempered in India by domestic policy constraints and a problematic business environment.

The absence of labor market flexibility and the legacy of reservation for small-scale industry are obstacles to achieving economies of scale.[6] Until recently, a number of T&C subsectors had been set aside for small-scale industry which has, perversely, precluded much-needed investment and modernization. Moreover, Indian manufacturers often set up several small plants instead of a single large one, to remain exempt from certain restrictive labor laws and onerous regulatory requirements. It should not be surprising, then, that India's T&C sector is dominated by small producers with little vertical integration in the apparel industry (United States International Trade Commission, 2004).

The failure to reap economies of scale—together with a generally difficult business environment—has limited investment and productivity gains. Investment in the textile industry has remained low and stagnant, varying between $1 billion and $1.5 billion annually during 2000–03. Moreover, foreign direct investment (FDI) in this sector has been insignificant, although the government has allowed foreign equity participation up to 100 percent in much of the sector. (See Chapter 5 for a discussion of constraints on FDI more generally.) Perhaps even more important than the funding that such investment could have generated is the fact that India has missed out on the associated technology transfer. Largely as a result of limited investment, productivity is low and, despite wages that are among the lowest in the world, labor costs per unit of production are relatively high. A study by the Reserve Bank of India (2004) finds a decline in total factor productivity growth in the textile sector in the 1990s. While capital intensity increased during the decade, growth in capital productivity in the textile sector slowed vis-à-vis the previous decade. Growth in labor productivity rose during the same period, but does not compare favorably with other countries. A lack of investment and innovation may also be constraining the quality of Indian T&C products. A recent study (World Bank, 2004) points to perceptions about the low quality and quality inconsistency for India's T&C products as a key problem for exporters.

Until recently, the excise tax regime for the textile sector was not conducive to new investment, although recent changes are a step in the right direction. The 2005/06 budget (Government of India, 2005) reduced excise duties for yarn and fiber, although blended and noncotton textiles contin-

---

[6]Small-scale industry is defined as one in which investment in fixed assets does not exceed Rs 10 million (about $0.2 million). Qualifying firms receive preferential treatment in a number of areas, including access to bank credit and lower tax rates.

ued to be subject to a higher tax regime. With the man-made fiber sector accounting for a large share of trade, rationalizing the taxation structure for this sector may strengthen competitiveness. In addition, the implementation of a value-added tax in most states in 2005/06 has made the tax system more export friendly (see Chapter 9).

Inadequate infrastructure and bureaucratic delays have contributed to long turnaround times in India. This is critical in today's world of global competition in which production can and does shift quickly to different locations. Poor roads, ports, and airports contribute to delivery times that are longer than for key competitors. Transportation times from India are long (see Chapter 4), and it is estimated that each additional day in transport is equivalent to an extra 0.8 percentage point increase in applied tariff rates (Hummels, 2001). The efficiency of customs processing is lower in India than in many other countries. Moreover, the price of industrial power in India is among the highest in the world, reflecting inadequate investment in the power sector as well as distortionary pricing, with large cross-subsidies from industry to consumers.

The Way Ahead

How can the Indian government ensure that its T&C industry is well prepared to deal with the new global environment? In general, the government should focus on creating an enabling environment—including via the provision of an adequate infrastructure—and on removing obstacles to investment, innovation, and job creation. By doing so, Indian enterprises will be empowered to enhance their productivity, increase product quality, and reduce delivery times. Goldman Sachs (2004) surveyed about 30 major wholesalers, manufacturers, and retailers globally to examine the impact of the elimination of textiles and apparel import quotas in 2005. Both U.S. and EU respondents cited product quality as the top consideration in sourcing decisions post quota elimination, followed by product cost, production speed, working conditions, access to inputs, and transportation speed. Most, if not all, of these issues can be addressed by improving the policy environment in which Indian textile firms operate.

- *Increased labor market flexibility is key to achieving economies of scale and much-needed flexibility in production.* A move to U.S.-style "hire and fire" policies is not in the cards in India and may not be desirable. However, raising the firm size threshold for exemption from various labor laws and regulatory requirements may lessen the incentive for Indian firms to remain inefficiently small. Special economic zones, if properly designed, could also help firms work around the restrictive labor laws and could enable the setting up of mega production plants similar in scale to those in China. Finally, a relaxation in contract labor law would be helpful in allowing businesses to respond to the rapid changes in demand that are typical in T&C, for example, by hiring temporary workers.

- *Steps to increase investment are needed to raise productivity.* In large part this will require broad changes in the business environment and economic infrastructure that are not specific to T&C. More specifically, India is considering allowing FDI in the retail segment, which could play an important role in improving distribution services for textiles and clothing.[7] In addition, technology will increasingly have a dominant influence in what was traditionally a labor-intensive industry. There may be a role for government to support the import of existing technology, investment in research and development, and technology transfer and diffusion both globally and domestically.

- *Continued efforts to enhance infrastructure and reduce customs red tape would have a large payoff.* Indian port capacities need to be increased. And the same applies for its airports. More firms internationally are expected to use air freight to tighten inventory and shorten delivery time, even if transport costs are higher, and the apparel industry is estimated to become one of the fastest growing air freight markets between 2004 and 2009. A policy of setting up textile clusters, linked to airports with emphasis on freight and business traffic, could be an option at least until ports and other capacities are enlarged. Increasing the efficiency in customs procedures, including by streamlining the administrative requirements to clear customs, expedite the customs procedures, and computerizing customs, would also be important in this regard. Moreover, power sector reforms—as contemplated in the 2003 Electricity Act—are needed to bring electricity costs down to internationally competitive levels. More specifically, in the T&C sector, use might be made of dedicated power delinked from State Electricity Boards, and better quality power in textile parks.

With the proper enabling environment, the private sector would be well placed to improve its capacity to compete in a market where prices are falling and more players are entering. In doing so, the following considerations will be critical:

---

[7]In China, foreign retailers will have the right to set up distribution networks through wholly foreign-owned enterprises, without any geographical or quantitative restrictions.

- To minimize lead times, firms should aim at integrating the supply chain and developing strong textile clusters, capable of handling all stages of production in a coordinated manner. In particular, the weaving and fabric processing sector—considered to be the weakest link in the supply chain because of inadequate investment and lack of technology—should be strengthened. There needs to be integration from weaving to garment making to reduce lead times, cut costs, and improve quality. There is also a need to forge business contacts between domestic clusters and retail groups.
- Greater emphasis should be placed on quality certification and branding to boost the quality of Indian fabric and garments.
- Developing expertise in designing, marketing, retailing, financing, and the gathering of market intelligence on foreign markets is important. To this end, FDI flows should be encouraged.
- Greater inroads need to be made into the area of upscale high-fashion and customized clothing segment. Extensive use of computer-aided design and manufacturing systems will aid innovation and reduce lead times. Greater emphasis is also needed on training to offer service-related skills and integrated solutions to prospective buyers. Some state governments are planning to set up training institutes to upgrade skills of personnel.
- Diversifying product bases—including moving into rapidly growing areas such as technical textile fabrics for packaging, sports textiles, medical and hygiene-related textiles, and military textiles—will also need to be part of the overall industry approach.

Conclusions

The dismantling of the MFA quota regime presents an opportunity for India to increase its market share in the world and to "go global". However, success is not guaranteed. The results of the simulations undertaken in this chapter do not present an especially optimistic scenario for India in terms of export growth of T&C in a quota-free world, as the decrease in prices will offset gains from higher export volumes. However, the presence of the safeguards on China provides India with a rare window of opportunity to undertake important reforms in labor markets, investment, and infrastructure, so it can realize its potential. If successful, such reforms will allow India to emerge much stronger and expand its share in world textiles and apparel markets at a much faster pace.

Appendix. Methodology and Data

The Global Trade Analysis Project (GTAP) database contains the bilateral trade, transport, and protection matrices that link all regions of the world. In turn, the regional matrices are derived from individual country input-output tables. The GTAP relates trade policy shocks to the medium-term changes in global production and trade flows. We use the standard general equilibrium closure for the simulations.

We present a regional aggregation model with 13 regions or countries and the major exporters and importers (as per the World Trade Organization data) of textiles and clothing. The countries or regions included are Bangladesh, China, EU15, Hong Kong SAR, India, Indonesia, Korea, Mexico, the Philippines, South Asia (other), Taiwan Province of China, the United States, and the rest of the world.[8] We use a five-sector aggregation for the simulations, focusing on textiles, clothing, food, manufacturing, and services, and a five-factor general equilibrium model. The detailed results of these simulations are reported in Ananthakrishnan and Jain-Chandra (2005).

References

Ananthakrishnan, Prasad, and Sonali Jain-Chandra, 2005, "The Impact on India of Trade Liberalization in the Textiles and Clothing Sector," IMF Working Paper No. 05/214 (Washington: International Monetary Fund).

Andriamananjara, Soamiely, Judith Dean, and Dean Spinanger, 2004, "Trading Textiles and Apparel: Developing Countries in 2005," paper presented at the GTAP Conference (Washington).

Cerra, Valerie, Sandra A. Rivera, and Sweta Chaman Saxena, 2005, "Crouching Tiger, Hidden Dragon: What Are the Consequences of China's WTO Entry for India's Trade?" IMF Working Paper No. 05/101 (Washington: International Monetary Fund).

Chadha, Rajesh, Devender Pratap, Saurabh Bandyopadhyay, Praveen Sachdeva, and Bindu Kurien, 2000, "The Impact of Changing Global Trade Policies on India," (New Delhi: National Council of Applied Economic Research).

Diao, Xinshen, and Agapi Somwaru, 2001, "Impact of the MFA Phase-Out on the World Economy: An Intertemporal Global General Equilibrium Analysis," TMD Discussion Paper No. 79 (Washington: International Food Policy Research Institute).

---

[8]In this chapter, we present the results for India and China.

Elbehri, Aziz, Thomas Hertel, and Will Martin, 2003, "Estimating the Impact of WTO and Domestic Reforms on the Indian Cotton and Textile Sectors: A General-Equilibrium Approach," *Review of Development Economics*, Vol. 7, No. 3, pp. 343–59.

European Commission, 2005, *Sectoral Issues, Textile Sector Statistics*, available via the Internet at www.ec.europa.eu/comm/trade/issues/sectoral/industry/textile/stats. htm.

Goldman Sachs, 2004, "Textile, Apparel and Footwear, 2005 Quota Elimination Survey Results" (September).

Government of India, 2005, *Union Budget 2005–06* (New Delhi).

Hummels, David, 2001, "Time as a Trade Barrier" (unpublished; West Lafayette, Indiana: Purdue University).

Kathuria, Sanjay, Will Martin, and Anjali Bhardwaj, 2001, "Implications for South Asian Countries of Abolishing the Multifiber Agreement," World Bank Policy Research Working Paper No. 2721 (Washington: World Bank).

Manole, Vlad, 2005, "Winner or Loser? Effects of Quota Abolition in World Markets for Textile and Apparel," World Bank DECRG (unpublished; Washington: World Bank).

Ministry of Textiles, *Annual Report*, various years (New Delhi).

Nordas, H.K., 2004, "The Global Textile and Clothing Industry Post the Agreement on Textile and Clothing," WTO Discussion Paper No. 5 (Geneva: World Trade Organization).

Reserve Bank of India, 2004, *Report on Currency and Finance, 2002–03* (Mumbai).

United States Department of Commerce, Office of Textiles and Apparel, various data, available via the Internet at www.otexa.ita.doc.gov/.

United States International Trade Commission, 2004, *Textiles and Apparel: Assessment of the Competitiveness of Certain Foreign Suppliers to the U.S. Market*, USITC Publication 3671 (January).

———, various data, available via the Internet at www.usitc.gov/.

World Bank, 2004, *Trade Policies in South Asia: An Overview*, Report No. 29949 (Washington).

World Trade Organization, 2002, 2003, and 2004, *International Trade Statistics* (Geneva).